Jorge L

Architectural Patterns for Parallel Programming

Jorge Luis Ortega-Arjona

Architectural Patterns for Parallel Programming

Models for Performance Estimation

VDM Verlag Dr. Müller

Impressum/Imprint (nur für Deutschland/ only for Germany)
Bibliografische Information der Deutschen Nationalbibliothek: Die Deutsche Nationalbibliothek
verzeichnet diese Publikation in der Deutschen Nationalbibliografie; detaillierte bibliografische
Daten sind im Internet über http://dnb.d-nb.de abrufbar.
Alle in diesem Buch genannten Marken und Produktnamen unterliegen warenzeichen-, marken-
oder patentrechtlichem Schutz bzw. sind Warenzeichen oder eingetragene Warenzeichen der
jeweiligen Inhaber. Die Wiedergabe von Marken, Produktnamen, Gebrauchsnamen,
Handelsnamen, Warenbezeichnungen u.s.w. in diesem Werk berechtigt auch ohne besondere
Kennzeichnung nicht zu der Annahme, dass solche Namen im Sinne der Warenzeichen- und
Markenschutzgesetzgebung als frei zu betrachten wären und daher von jedermann benutzt
werden dürften.

Coverbild: www.purestockx.com

Verlag: VDM Verlag Dr. Müller Aktiengesellschaft & Co. KG
Dudweiler Landstr. 99, 66123 Saarbrücken, Deutschland
Telefon +49 681 9100-698, Telefax +49 681 9100-988, Email: info@vdm-verlag.de
Zugl.: London, University College London, 2007

Herstellung in Deutschland:
Schaltungsdienst Lange o.H.G., Berlin
Books on Demand GmbH, Norderstedt
Reha GmbH, Saarbrücken
Amazon Distribution GmbH, Leipzig
ISBN: 978-3-639-17324-6

Imprint (only for USA, GB)
Bibliographic information published by the Deutsche Nationalbibliothek: The Deutsche
Nationalbibliothek lists this publication in the Deutsche Nationalbibliografie; detailed
bibliographic data are available in the Internet at http://dnb.d-nb.de.
Any brand names and product names mentioned in this book are subject to trademark, brand or
patent protection and are trademarks or registered trademarks of their respective holders. The use
of brand names, product names, common names, trade names, product descriptions etc. even
without a particular marking in this works is in no way to be construed to mean that such names
may be regarded as unrestricted in respect of trademark and brand protection legislation and
could thus be used by anyone.

Cover image: www.purestockx.com

Publisher:
VDM Verlag Dr. Müller Aktiengesellschaft & Co. KG
Dudweiler Landstr. 99, 66123 Saarbrücken, Germany
Phone +49 681 9100-698, Fax +49 681 9100-988, Email: info@vdm-publishing.com
London, University College London, 2007

Printed in the U.S.A.
Printed in the U.K. by (see last page)
ISBN: 978-3-639-17324-6

Contents

List of Figures

List of Tables

Chapter 1

Introduction

"Une oevrue qui serait le pur produit d'une combintorie préexistante n'existe pas pour l'historie de la littérature... Aussi l'oeuvre d'art (ou de science) comporte-t-elle toujours un élement transformateur, une innovation du système. L'abscence de différence égale l'inexistence"

"A work that is the pure product of a preexisting combination does not exist for the history of literature... Thus, the work of art (or science) behaves always as a transformer element, an innovation of the system. The absence of difference equals the inexistence"

Todorov

1.1 The Context

Parallel processing is defined as the division of work among multiple processors that operate simultaneously with a common objective. The expected result is, commonly, a faster completion of the objective in comparison with single processor execution. Its main advantage is the ability to handle tasks of a scale that would not be realistic nor cost-effective for other systems. However, it is generally recognised that designing software for parallel computers is hard (Carriero & Gelernter, 1988; Chandy & Taylor, 1992; Darlington &To, 1992). Parallel computers have become a platform for high-performance applications, but remain a challenging environment in which to achieve good performance. One reason for this is the difficulty of estimating the execution time of a parallel application.

Software design is a critical feature in parallel programming because the process is significantly more complex than for programming sequential programs on single processor computers. Examples can be found in the history of parallel software design, where scientific code (such as numerical analysis, fluid dynamics, etc.) has been hand-crafted for specific machines and problems, at immense expense (Andrews, 1991; Brinch-

Hansen, 1977; Foster, 1994; Culler *et al.*, 1997; Pancake & Bergmark, 1990; Skillicorn & Talia, 1996).

Parallel Software Design begins when a particular need for high-performance is identified, and a software designer is asked to start the design of a parallel software program. Usually, hardware and software resources are known and given: a parallel program must be designed, using a specific programming language, for a particular parallel hardware. The problem to solve is normally already described in terms of a data set and an algorithm that performs operations on it. This algorithm can be a sequential algorithm, or better, an already parallelised algorithm. Generally, performance as execution time is the feature of interest to contend with (Pancake & Bergmark, 1990; Pancake, 1996).

Parallel programming relies on the coordination of computing resources, so that they simultaneously work towards a common objective. Achieving this requires extra effort from the software designer, because of the increased complexity involved. Furthermore, as parallel programming is considered a means to improve performance, the software designer has to consider sophisticated and cost-effective practices and techniques for performance measurement and analysis. Most programming problems have several parallel solutions, and therefore parallel software design cannot easily be reduced to recipes. At best, the designer has some parallel organisation structures, and would like to decide which one to use as the basis of the parallel system to be built. Commonly, the selection is carried out based only on the information available at this stage and the intuition of the designer. However, as the cost of the parallel design is high, complementing the information available with quantifiable information would be an important advantage.

1.2 The Problem

Performance is considered as the main driving factor for most of the history of parallel programming. Even though performance is not considered as the only goal of Parallel Software Design, it is important to recognise that the primary objective of using parallel systems is performance (Pancake & Bergmark, 1990; Pancake, 1996).

"Performance refers to the responsiveness of the system — the time required to respond to stimuli (events) or the number of events processed in some interval of time" (Smith &Williams, 1993). Performance is an architectural quality attribute, since it is a function of the amount of interaction between the components of a program. This is especially relevant if the components execute on different computing elements, such as

in parallel or distributed systems. Furthermore, it is still true if all components execute on the same processor (Bass *et al.*, 1998).

In particular, it is of great interest and advantage to obtain performance information during the design stages and before implementation, since this enables the software developer to more reliably select the parallel organisation structure of computations and communications between components. If attention is given to performance estimation during the design phases by working through parallel design alternatives while attempting to meet overall performance objectives, problems and risks during parallel software development can be mitigated.

However, performance is an important aspect generally neglected during design stages in general software development. Usually, traditional software design methods follow a "fix-it-later" approach towards performance, concentrating on software correctness, and deferring performance until the later phases of software development (Smith &Williams, 1993). Typically, methods in Parallel Software Design have adopted the "fix-it-later" approach from traditional software design methods. In these methods, parallel software is analysed for correctness during design phases, but performance issues are deferred to be corrected later. If performance requirements are not met, the software is "tuned" to correct them, or additional hardware is used.

The "fix-it-later" approach is clearly undesirable, in particular for parallel systems. For example, if severe performance problems are discovered late in the development, extensive changes to the whole software and system architecture may be required to deal with them. Furthermore, as these changes are made late in the development process, they can increase development cost, deployment delay, or adversely affect other desirable qualities of a design, such as understandability, maintainability or reusability.

An alternative might be to design for performance from the beginning, by selecting from several parallel organisation structures, using simulations, the one which best performs for the parallel system being built. The simulations can be executed to calculate the performance estimation for each particular parallel organisation structure. Early performance estimation, based on parallel software architecture and simulations, allows the selection of the appropriate architecture before the implementation, using a quantitative criteria.

1.3 The Hypothesis

The main objective of this research can be expressed as the confirmation of the following hypothesis:

"Given a problem to be solved and a set of parallel hardware and software resources for deployment, it is possible to obtain a reasonable estimate of the performance characteristics of a parallel program during the initial stages of parallel software design in order to identify the architectural pattern that will produce the best performance for the program."

Initially, we must establish what "*a reasonable estimate of the performance characteristic of a parallel program*" means. We propose the following two assumptions:

1. *Reproducibility Assumption.* Each execution of a parallel program on a platform yields an execution time. Nevertheless, it is very unlikely that two or more executions of the same parallel program would yield exactly the same execution times. It is well known that the variations in the execution of a real parallel program are due to the non-determinism in its execution environment, which typically arise from sharing computer resources among several programs (Foster, 1994; Culler *et al.*, 1997). Hence, for the purposes of the present thesis, the performance characteristics of a parallel program is presented as an average execution time. This way, our objective would not be to predict a unique execution time, but more likely to estimate an average execution time that is representative of all the possible execution times of the parallel program on the platform. If the execution environment for the parallel program can be held constant, the average execution time can be used to characterise the execution of the parallel program on a given platform.

2. *Fidelity Assumption.* The estimates are accurate approximations, not exact predictions, of the performance characteristic of the execution time of the real parallel program. Thus, the estimated average execution time should be as close as possible to the actual average that can be statistically obtained from all the measured execution times.

We define what is meant by a *reasonable estimate* as follows: An *estimate* is *reasonable* if it can reproduce the performance characteristics of a real parallel program under the *reproducibility* and *fidelity* assumptions. Thus, reasonable estimates can be produced and used for architectural design decisions and for assessing the probable performance characteristic of a parallel program.

1.4 The Approach

An architectural design approach is proposed, providing a method to support perform-ance estimation at the early stages of parallel software design. The main goal is to pro-vide a quantitative criterion for evaluating design alternatives. In this research work, we propose the Architectural Performance Modelling Method as a way of selecting from design alternatives by estimating their performance.

By considering a parallel program as an instance of a software architecture, it can be described in terms of interacting *software components*. Such components can be classi-fied depending on their particular role as:

- components representing or associated with the hardware and software environment (or simply *platform components*);
- components representing the fundamental organisation for coordination and commu-nication (or simply *coordination components*); and
- components providing particular processing functionalities (or simply *processing components*).

The method proposes that the performance of a parallel program can be estimated from the execution times that all individual components require to carry out their coordi-nating or processing activities. Performance is understood, modelled and analysed from an architectural point of view by using "*scale-models*". The objective is to keep these scale-models as simple as possible, while providing acceptable accuracy. This is achieved by considering that processing and communication are activities sharply sepa-rated among coordination and processing components. Even though this may not be always the case, our objective in this research work is to prove that such a supposition does not introduce a considerable error for performance estimation. So, our scale-models can effectively be used to estimate the performance of parallel programs with different coordination organisation, and hence, to select the best performing coordination for the problem at hand.

The scale-model proposed here is the Architectural Performance Model (APM). This model is based on Architectural Patterns for Parallel Programming (descriptions of coor-dination organisations commonly used in parallel programming) and a generic Compo-nent Simulation (a simulation of a component's processing behaviour). An APM can be used to simulate parallel systems, ranging from a complete parallel program to a partially implemented program design. This simulation of a parallel system, using the available hardware and software, makes it possible to calculate an estimate of its performance.

1.5 Contributions

The main goal of this thesis is the development of an Architectural Performance Modelling Method for identifying the best performing coordination, based on the performance estimation of the parallel programs. This covers the following main contributions:

1. The development of the Architectural Performance Modelling Method, allowing parallel program developers to estimate the performance of a parallel program based on information from a particular architectural pattern (Chapter 4), and use this information for comparing purposes between architectural patterns.

2. The Architectural Patterns for Parallel Programming, which describe the coordination at the architectural level of parallel software programs, and their initial selection criteria (Chapter 5).

3. The construction of a Component Simulation that represent the processing time behaviour of the processing components of a parallel software program (Chapter 6).

1.6 Thesis Structure

The thesis is structured as follows:

- **Chapter 2. Background.** This chapter provides an introduction to Parallel Programming, explaining the general nature and characteristics of parallel programs, the factors that influence their development, and the main models of parallel programming used for their design. It also presents an introduction to Software Architecture, describing some standard notions of several concepts in the architecture-oriented research, and some relations between software architecture and performance modelling. Finally, a description of architectural software design is presented, introducing a vocabulary for the present research work, that is used and applied in the following chapters for describing concepts within Parallel Software Design.

- **Chapter 3. Related Work.** This chapter introduces a review of the relevant related work in Software Performance Modelling, as approaches that combine Software Architecture and Performance Modelling, and approaches to performance estimation of parallel and distributed systems. The related work is organised as follows: first, an introduction to Software Performance Modelling is presented, describing some basic notions within this research area. Next, the main approaches that attempt to relate Software Architecture and Performance Modelling are briefly described, paying attention to their main characteristics. The following section describes the main research work in the area of performance modelling of parallel and distributed programming, describing their main features. Finally, descriptions of the Archetypes/ eText project, the Algorithmic Skeletons, and the Structural Modeling are presented as architectural approaches to parallel software design with similar objectives than the Architectural Performance Modelling Method.

- **Chapter 4. Architectural Performance Modelling Method.** This chapter presents the Architectural Performance Modelling Method as a method for estimating the performance of a parallel application, by obtaining and analysing the information and response time of its coordination components at the architectural level.

- **Chapter 5. Architectural Patterns for Parallel Programming.** This chapter introduces the concept of architectural pattern, its relation with performance, and the Architectural Patterns for Parallel Programming. These last ones describe the *coordination* layer of an overall parallel software architecture, and whose initial selection constitutes the first main step of the Architectural Performance Modelling Method. The architectural patterns commonly used in parallel programming introduced here are *Pipes and Filters, Parallel Hierarchies, Communicating Sequential Elements, Manager-Workers,* and *Shared Resource.*

- **Chapter 6. Architectural Performance Model Construction.** The Architectural Performance Modelling Method relies on two types of simulations and a model to estimate the performance of early parallel software plans: the Coordination Simulation, the Component Simulation, and the Architectural Performance Model. The Coordination Simulation is constructed as a runnable instance of an architectural pattern. A Coordination Simulation can execute for typical workload scenarios, which specify the coordination operations to be performed in response to predefined events. Also, this chapter presents the Component Simulation, as a simulation of the processing behaviour and performance of a single active object, using the Active Object Pattern and elements of Queuing Theory. Finally, the Architectural Performance Model is constructed from gathering both simulations, so the effect of the platform, the coordination, and the processing are taken into account for the calculation of performance estimates.

- **Chapter 7. Performance Simulation and Calculation.** This chapter presents the actual performance simulation, executing the Coordination Simulation and the Architectural Performance Model, and the calculation of performance estimates using the data taken from the simulations.

- **Chapter 8. Evaluation of the Method.** In order to test the validity of this method for performance estimation, and its utility for parallel architecture selection, a set of experiments are proposed for: *(a)* testing the modelling method, and *(b)* using the method for comparing three architectural patterns for solving three different problems.

- **Chapter 9. Conclusion.** This chapter presents a review of the research in the form of a critical summary of the research work is presented, restating the hypothesis and contributions of the thesis. A future work section is presented, summarising the next steps to follow into the research of software architecture, and its application to parallel programming.

Chapter 2

Background

"Tous les autres arts obéissaient et se mettaient en discipline sous l'architecture"
"All the other arts were obedient and submitted to the discipline of architecture"

Victor Hugo

The objective of this chapter is to provide *(a)* an introduction to Parallel Programming, explaining the general nature and characteristics of parallel programs, the factors that influence their development, and the models of parallel programming; *(b)* an introduction to Software Architecture, describing some standard notions of several concepts in the architecture-oriented research, and some relations between software architecture and performance modelling; and *(c)* a description of architectural software design, introducing a vocabulary for the present research work, that is used and applied in the following chapters for describing concepts within Parallel Software Design.

2.1 An Introduction to Parallel Programming

Parallel programming is based on the division of a processing task among multiple processors that operate simultaneously. A parallel program is, then, *the specification of a set of processes executing simultaneously, and communicating among themselves in order to achieve a common objective.* The expected result is to perform such processing in a faster way compared to its execution on a single-processor system. Its main advantage is its ability to handle tasks of a scale that would not be realistic or cost-effective for other systems. Nevertheless, it is generally recognised that parallel programming is a difficult activity. In theory, parallel programming is simply to apply multiple processors to a single problem. However, in practice, parallel programming tends to be difficult and costly, since it requires a greater effort from the programmer, who has to consider new forms for understanding and programming in a parallel execution environment. Usually, traditional techniques used in single processor systems for reviewing and correcting defects and for improving the performance are not directly applicable or portable to parallel programming. Moreover, it is necessary to consider that the parallel execution environment is inherently unstable and unpredictable (or simply, *non-deterministic*). Such an execution environment could be a network of workstations, a grid of personal computers, or a high-performance parallel processing system. It is common that, after months of programming a parallel program, it is found that it yields incorrect results, or executes slower that its sequential counterpart.

Generally, performance has been considered the driving factor for most of the history of parallel programming. Performance refers to the response capability of a parallel system, this is, the time required to respond to stimuli (events) or the number of events processed in some interval of time (Smith, 1990). Ultimately, performance is the reason for using parallel systems (Pancake & Bergmark, 1990; Pancake, 1996).

2.1.1 Directions in Parallel Programming

"If one is good, then 10 or 1,000 should be better" (Bond, 1987). Ideas like this originated parallel programming. Even though such a statement is not necessarily true, it proposes a primary attraction towards parallelism. It is a fact that those who have contributed in the development of computing have accepted parallelism as a novel way to solve programming problems.

Several competitive methods were proposed for organising parallel programming, but there was very little evidence as to which design was superior, nor there was sufficient knowledge on which to make a careful evaluation. Flynn (Flynn, 1966) helped initiate an organised study of high-speed computer architecture by showing that parallel programming falls naturally into four classes. Within this classification system, it is possible to make some non-trivial observations about the utility of a computer system and its relative cost-effectiveness on specific types of problems. Flynn proposed that in dealing with parallel computer systems and programming, it is quite natural to classify computers in terms of parallelism within the instruction stream and parallelism within the data stream (Flynn, 1966). In this context, by *instruction stream* we mean the sequence of instructions that are executed in a processing unit. By *data stream* we mean the sequence of operands that are manipulated by the processor. Flynn observed that the methods for achieving a parallel operation depended on replicating the instruction stream and the data stream. This gives rise to four types of computers: the single instruction single data (SISD), which is a sequential computer; the single instruction multiple data (SIMD), which is a vectorial processor that operated one instruction on a data vector; multiple instruction single data (MISD), which is considered as an unrealistic mode for parallel computers; and the multiple instruction multiple data (MIMD), which is composed of various processors, each of which is a complete computer. Only SIMD and MIMD are considered to be realistic approaches to parallel programming.

Parallel programming properly emerged during the late 1960's and 1970's, attempting to model how parallel processes could be expressed in programming terms, and to improve performance of computer systems. The following sections present and describe some of the most influential contributions to parallel programming, which have served as base for the research nowadays.

"Co-operating Sequential Processes", by E.W. Dijkstra

In 1968, E.W. Dijkstra presents his paper "Co-operating Sequential Processes" (Dijkstra, 1968), in which he develops an initial proposal for the treatment of parallelism in a programming language, beginning with elements of sequential programming, and finally proposing new elements of programming using a notation similar to the ALGOL60 programming language.

In this paper, Dijkstra adds some new concepts to sequential programming, in order to extend it into a *concurrent programming*. He defines elements such as *co-routines* or concurrent processes (using the reserved words `parbegin...parend`, which are interpreted as the parallel execution of processes within a program), *mutual exclusion, event synchronisation, critical section*, and the definition of a new data type called *semaphores*. Besides, Dijkstra makes emphasis in a new problem which generates as a result of trying to execute parallel processes, referring to it as *deadly embrace* or *deadlock.*

The central idea in this paper is based on the data exchange among independent and sequential processes which non-deterministically execute at different speeds, through *shared variables*. These variables are modified using indivisible operations of inspection and assignment. In this paper, Dijkstra's objectives are "code clarity and safety of shared information" (Dijkstra, 1968).

The importance of Dijkstra's work relays on the proposal of a base on which support the concepts of parallel and distributed programming. This work is particularly referenced as the background of many other researches by Habermann, Peterson, Hoare, Brinch-Hansen, and others that have proposed new techniques to solve the problems of mutual exclusion and synchronisation around the concept of semaphore.

"Communicating Sequential Processes", by C.A.R. Hoare

Hoare's work has been fundamental for the development of parallel programming during the last years. His main contribution has been the definition of a language for the formal specification of parallel algorithms, known as CSP (Communicating Sequential Processes). This language is defined in the paper with the same name (Hoare, 1978).

In this paper, Hoare starts performing an analysis of the basic structures used in programming: assignment, sequence, repetition, and selection. He comments new structures for expressing parallelism, communication, and control of non-determinism between processes within a multiprocessor architecture.

Hoare exposes the main characteristics for a parallel language, expressing the following proposals (Hoare, 1978):

- Use the concept of *guarded commands*, proposed by Dijkstra, as a mechanism for controlling non-determinism.
- Consider a parallel command based on Dijkstra's `parbegin...parend`, which specifies the parallel execution of commands or processes that compose them. It is considered that all processes initiate simultaneously, and the parallel command finalises only when all its constituent processes finalise.
- Use of simple forms of input and output for communication between processes.
- Communication between processes is established only when a process invokes another process as its output, and the last process invokes the first process as its input. In such a case, the output value is copied from the sending process as an input value to the receiving process. There is no temporal storage or buffering during communication, this is, the two processes that invoke input and output operations suspend their execution until sending or receiving data. The delay is invisible for both processes (but it is not for the execution of the program as a whole).
- The input commands can appear as guards. A guarded command in an input executes only when the associated process to such an input executes an output command. If several input guards are in such a situation, only one is arbitrarily selected and executed, and the others have no effect.

- It is proposed the use of an element of pattern correspondence to discriminate the input structure. Such an element is used to inhibit the input of messages that do not present the specified pattern.

These characteristics largely define the behaviour of programs in CSP. Consequently, CSP is a static language which can be used in a conventional machine with single storage or in a fixed network of processors connected through input/output channels. Also (and due to the previous point) the language does not allow recursion as other programming languages do. Finally, the language is restricted to the necessary bare minimum in order to obtain a more flexible implementation of applications.

Even though this paper by Hoare is a milestone for the development of parallel programming, it has the disadvantage of not proposing a proof method that assists the construction and test of correct programs. In fact, such a method is exposed later in detail by Hoare himself, in a book about the same theme (Hoare, 1985).

"Distributed Processes: A Concurrent Programming Concept",
by P. Brinch-Hansen

Also in 1978, and with the development of network communication among computers, Brinch-Hansen writes a paper in which he proposes another kind of parallelism (Brinch-Hansen, 1978). Brinch-Hansen's proposal for parallel programming is based on the intercommunication of uni-processor systems via a network system. His work introduces the concept of *distributed system* as a form of concurrent programming. It focuses on real-time programming that, in his opinion, has the following characteristics (Brinch-Hansen, 1978):

1. Real-time programming interacts with an environment in which simultaneous events happen at a great speed.

2. A real-time program must respond to a series of non-deterministic inputs from the environment, that is, it is not possible to predict the order in which the inputs arrive, but the program should be prepared to respond within a limit of time.

3. A real-time program controls a computer with a fixed configuration of processors and peripherals, performing in most of the cases a fixed number of concurrent tasks in its environment.

4. A real-time program never ends, but continues serving its environment as long as the computer keeps working.

From these characteristics, and based on the programming language Concurrent Pascal proposed by himself, Brinch-Hansen analyses the properties of a new programming language for real-time applications. These properties are (Brinch-Hansen, 1978):

- A real-time program consists of a fixed number of concurrent processes that start simultaneously. Each process has its own variables; however, there are no common variables among processes.

- A process can generate a call for common procedures defined in another process. This is the only form of communication between processes.

- Processes synchronise through non-deterministic instructions known as *guarded commands*.

- Processes can be used as programming modules of a multiprocess system with shared or distributed memory.

- To satisfy the real-time programming requirements, each processor of the system is dedicated to a single process.

These properties have originated what is known as *remote procedure call* (RPC), which is the base of distributed programming today; for instance, it forms the basis of distributed communication in CORBA (OMG, 1998) and Java's Remote Method Invocation (Hartley, 1998; Smith, 2000). The paper continues with the description of a distributed language based on Concurrent Pascal, examples of some implementations, and some ideas around the implementation of the language. Finally, as a conclusion, Brinch-Hansen mentions that the properties of distributed programming are very similar to Hoare's CSP. The importance of this paper by Brinch-Hansen relays not only on the definition and use of RPCs, but also on the considerations made for real-time programming.

Based on the concepts, properties and characteristics proposed by Dijkstra, Hoare, and Brinch-Hansen, other authors have taken the task to develop further such ideas in formal terms and different languages for concurrent, parallel and distributed programming (Hoare, 1985; Andrews, 1991; Lynch, 1996; Hartley, 1998; Andrews, 2000). In the area of Software Engineering, some authors have developed different methods for parallel programming (Foster, 1994; Culler, 1997).

2.1.2 Factors that influence the Performance of a Parallel Program

Parallel programming is complex activity, aiming for developing specifications of parallel processes which execute simultaneously and non-deterministically. Commonly, parallel programming is developed in order to obtain performance gains about execution time. Nevertheless, the performance obtained when applying parallel programming is affected by *the hardware platform, the programming language,* and *the problem to solve* (Pancake, 1996). The following sections briefly describe some important features of these factors.

The Hardware Platform

Generally, a parallel computer is considered as any hardware collection of processing elements connected through some type of communication network (notice that a "processing element" is composed by a processor and its associated memory as hardware devices). Nowadays, such parallel computers range among prices and sizes, from a group of workstations connected through a LAN, to a high-performance (and cost) computer involving hundreds or thousands of processors, which are connected through a high-speed network. Clearly, the performance of any parallel application is restricted by the speed, capacity and interfaces of each processing element.

Programming a parallel computer depends on the way in which the memory of the hardware platform is "organised" or "divided" among the processors. There are two commonly used organisations of memory: *shared memory* and *distributed memory.* Depending on which organisation is used for a parallel computer, different mechanisms for process communication are selected for programming.

- *Shared Memory.* A shared memory multiprocessor system allows access from any processor of the system to any location within a common memory, through an inter-connection network. In most cases, such network is completely hardware controlled, independent from the activity of the programmer, who only perceives a shared, central, and continuous memory. Each memory location or address in unique and identical for any processor of the system.

  Communication between processes in a shared memory system can be carried out normally by reading or writing *shared variables.* When a processor reads from or writes on a specific memory address, the network proceeds automatically by selecting the appropriate memory block. In order to guarantee data integrity, programming mechanisms have been proposed to support communication between processes, providing planning, synchronisation, and coordination between communicating processes. Common programming mechanisms for a shared memory computer are *semaphores* (Dijkstra, 1968), and *monitors* (Hoare, 1974).

• *Distributed Memory*. A distributed memory multiprocessor system allows that each processor directly accesses only its own memory, communicating with the memory of other processors through explicit I/O operations, and through a interconnection network. This network is composed of a set of connections between processors or *nodes*, based on a specific *topology*. During the execution of a parallel program, the network may remain the same (*static*) or change (*dynamic*) in accordance with the program needs.

Communication between processes in a distributed memory system is performed through *message passing*, which implies the explicit I/O operations of sending and receiving messages. Each processor "recognises" the difference between its local memory and the memory of other processors, so it is able to freely read and write data from its local memory. Nevertheless, when a processor requires to read or write data from another processor's memory, it should do it through request, explicitly by a message passing operation.

Message passing is defined as a communication model for distributed memory systems. The characteristics of such a communication model are *(a)* point to point, *(b)* unidirectional, and *(c)* non-buffered (Hoare, 1978). The actual programming mechanisms used for message passing are *input/ output operations* (Hoare, 1978; Hoare, 1985), *channels* (Pountain & May, 1987), and *remote procedure calls* (Brinch-Hansen, 1978).

The Programming Language

The programming language obviously affects the effort required to parallelise an application. Moreover, extreme variation in compiler capabilities and run-time support environments means that the language also constrains the performance to attain. The type of programming libraries that can be used into a program is often a key indicator of both effort and performance that can be achieved using a particular programming language.

In general, a parallel language can be considered as such mainly by its capacity to express basic characteristics of parallelism, sequencing, communication, and control of non-determinism between processes (Hoare, 1978).

- *Parallelism.* A parallel language should be able to describe the parallel execution of processes, using an instruction for parallel composition. This instruction is required since the sequential programming languages normally do not have a programming construction defined to express parallelism. The need for such an instruction has been notorious since the beginning of parallel programming (Dijkstra, 1968; Hoare, 1978). Dijkstra (1968) proposes an extension to ALGOL60, using a structure based on the delimiters `parbegin...parend`. Processes declared between these delimiters are executed simultaneously. This is known as a *parallel composition*.

  Dijkstra's considerations have given as a result what constitutes in various parallel languages as the *parallel instruction*, which represents the simultaneous activation of disjoint processes, with an independent execution speed among themselves. The parallel instruction successfully finishes only when all the processes it generated successfully finalise.

  There are various derivations of the parallel instruction depending on the language. Parallel instructions, for example, are the instructions `cobegin...coend` of Concurrent Pascal (Brinch-Hansen, 1978), the construction `P1||P2||...||PN` of CSP (Hoare, 1978; Hoare, 1985), and the instruction `PAR` of the Occam programming language (Pountain & May, 1987). These instructions represent what is considered as inter-process parallelism. There are other examples of mechanisms which allow to represent intra-process parallelism, as it is the case with Java threads (Smith, 2000), and tasks in Ada (Burns & Wellings, 1997).

- *Sequencing.* The expression of sequential instructions is present as the basic feature of most sequential programming languages. However, in a parallel programming language, it is necessary to explicitly represent a sequential composition (or *sequential instruction*), in order to contrast its action with the parallel composition.

  The *sequential instruction* express a set of disjoint processes that activate in sequence as they appear within the instruction (Hoare, 1978). It successfully finalises if all and each process in the sequence finalise; on the contrary, it is interrupted, and its execution fails.

  In general, several programming languages explicitly express the sequential instruction through the inclusion of the symbol ";" between the instructions of the sequence. Languages such as ALGOL60, Pascal, C, and others present such an expression, which has been also considered by several parallel languages. Examples are the construction P1;P2;...;PN in Concurrent Pascal (Brinch-Hansen, 1978) and in CSP (Hoare, 1978; Hoare, 1985). Other parallel languages, such as Occam, explicitly introduce the SEQ instruction (Pountain & May, 1987).

• *Communication and synchronisation.* A parallel language has to provide expressions for communication and synchronisation of processes. There are several mechanisms for communication and synchronisation between parallel processes. Normally, their use depends of the organisation of memory used: shared memory or distributed memory. A parallel language for a shared memory system requires to express communication through *shared variables* by primitives for read or write (or simply assign) such variables. The synchronisation of such actions is based on the use of mechanism such as semaphores (Dijkstra, 1968) or monitors (Hoare, 1974). A parallel language for a distributed memory system expresses communication through *message passing* by primitives for send and receive messages (Hoare, 1978; Brinch-Hansen, 1978).

In particular for message passing in distributed memory systems, the synchronisation is based on blocking the processes during communication, considering the following characteristics (Hoare, 1978): *(a)* the send instruction in the sending process specifies a expression whose evaluation is assigned to a variable in the receiving process; *(b)* the receive instruction in the receiving process specifies a variable which is assigned to the result of the expression in the sending process; *(c)* the data type of the variable in the receiving process and the result of the expression evaluation in the sending process should have the same data type; *(d)* the send or receive instruction in a process remains blocked until its counterpart in another process is successfully executed, which establishes communication; *(e)* once the communication is completed, both processes continue their independent execution; and *(f)* in case that a parallel program finalises, and a process within such a program has not successfully carried out a send or receive instruction, the whole program fails.

Examples of send and receive instructions are respectively P1!expression (send) and P2?variable (receive) in CSP (Hoare, 1978; Hoare, 1985), and C!expression (send in P1) and C?variable (receive in P2), which uses a channel C in Occam (Pountain & May, 1987). Additional examples for shared variables include the `synchronized` keyword in Java (Smith, 2000), and entry calls in Ada (Burns & Wellings, 1997).

- *Non-determinism.* A parallel language has to provide expressions for controlling non-determinism. Non-determinism is a characteristic of concurrent and parallel programming in which the order (or track) of simultaneous operations performed by a set of parallel processes (each one executing at different speed) is arbitrary. If such operations are, for example, send or receive operations, the characteristic of non-determinism establishes that the order of how those send and receive operations cannot be known beforehand during programming. Each execution of the program produces a (probabilistic) different order of instruction performed through time. Nevertheless, the simultaneous sequential processes involved in the parallel program are expected to still execute their operations in the order defined for each one of them.

Even though non-determinism is generally considered as a consequence of parallel execution, in several cases it is not convenient to allow a completely random parallel execution. Many times, it is necessary to verify several conditions, for instance, to receive a message. So, non-determinism is normally controlled using a boolean expression, known as *guard*, that conditions the execution of some particular instructions. The set of guards and instructions are known as *guarded command*, and it is the base of another kind of instructions used for dealing with non determinism: the *alternative instruction* (Hoare, 1978).

In an alternative instruction, all guards are simultaneously evaluated, executing only the guarded command associated with the successful guard, this is, the boolean expression which resulted true. In case that more than one guard is evaluated as true, the instruction arbitrarily selects a guarded command associated with one of the successful guards. The alternative instruction is executed, expecting that at least one guard is verified. If no guard is verified, the instruction fails.

Examples of alternative instructions are the instruction $[C1 \rightarrow P1 \ [] \ \ldots \ [] \ CN \rightarrow PN]$ in CSP (Hoare, 1978; Hoare, 1985), and the `ALT` instruction of Occam (Pountain & May, 1987). Another example is the select statement in Ada (Burns & Wellings, 1997).

The Problem to Solve

The division of the problem to solve, expressed as an algorithm and/or a set of data, is a key for the success or failure of a parallel program. In particular, the patterns for data access and the algorithm order indicate the way in which processing has to be carried out, an in turn, it is related with performance. Furthermore, if partitioning of an algorithm and/or data is the base for parallel execution, then parallel programming is strongly affected by the order and dependence among instructions (as elementary parts of the algorithm) and/or datum (as basic part of the data), independently of the nature of the actual problem to solve. This is due to the "orthogonal dimension" that characterises concurrent execution (Wegner, 1987).

Even though some simple, well-structured problems have been successfully solved by means of improvements in the area of compilers design (for example, the automatic parallelisation in Fortran, as developed by Burke et al. (1988), Kuck et al. (1998), and many other authors), other problems have remained as a challenge for obtaining an efficient parallel solution.

Based on this idea, Parallel Software Design has been developed during the last few years, providing a way to organise software that contains relatively independent parts and at the same time to efficiently make use of multiple processors. The goal is to solve a given problem faster or equivalently to solve a larger problem in the same amount of time. Although there are many parallel programming applications, such applications employ only a small number of "programming structures" as solutions. Many approaches have been presented up to date: *outlines of the program* (Chandy & Taylor, 1992), *programming paradigms* (Kleiman *et al.*, 1996), *parallel algorithms* (Hartley, 1998), *architectural patterns for parallel programming* (Ortega-Arjona & Roberts, 1998a), *high-level design strategies* (Lewis & Berg, 2000), and *paradigms for process interaction* (Andrews, 2000).

2.1.3 Models for Parallel Programming

A question that now arises is *how do we select a programming structure in order to build a parallel program?* On a large spectrum of approaches, three basic models for parallelism deserve special mention: *functional parallelism, data parallelism*, and *activity parallelism*. These models are conceived from the partitioning policy of data and/or algorithm (see Section 2.1.2), establishing three different forms to think about parallelism, and design parallel programs. Moreover, they also represent different ways of analysing parallelism.

Each one of the models of parallelism can be envisioned in terms of a characteristic of a parallel programming: the program's algorithm, the program's data, or both. So, the three models are described as follows:

1. **Functional parallelism.** Functional parallelism (also known as *task parallelism* or *specialist parallelism*) focuses on the decomposition of the algorithm (Carriero & Gelernter, 1988; Chandy & Taylor, 1992; Foster, 1994; Pancake 1996). The objective is to divide the algorithm into disjoint tasks, which are able to be executed simultaneously. Once divided into disjoint tasks, the data requirements of each task (input data and output data) should be examined. If the data requirements for each task is also disjoint, then the division is completed. Nevertheless, if the data requirements overlap significantly, considerably communication is necessary in order to avoid replication of data.

   In functional parallelism all tasks start simultaneously, but initially most tasks will have to wait until data is available for them. Different tasks may carry out different operations, and all these are organised so they accomplish the algorithm as a whole. Once under way, different tasks operate on different pieces of data. The main idea behind functional parallelism is to allow the execution of tasks, by overlapping and proceeding simultaneously. Also, each task is normally assigned to perform one specified kind of work or operation, and they all work in parallel up to the natural restrictions order and precedence imposed by the problem (Carriero & Gelernter, 1988; Pancake 1996).

2. **Domain parallelism.** Domain parallelism (also known as *data parallelism* or *result parallelism*) is based on decomposing the data associated with the problem (Carriero & Gelernter, 1988; Chandy & Taylor, 1992; Foster, 1994; Pancake 1996). If possible, the data is divided into smaller pieces of approximately equal size. Now, the algorithm is divided, typically by associating each task with the data it operates on. This division yields a number of tasks, each comprising some data and a set of operations on that data. An operation may require data from several tasks, so communication is required to move data between tasks.

   In domain parallelism all tasks start simultaneously. Separate tasks are set to operate on different data at the same time. They all proceed in parallel, up to the point until the work on a piece of data cannot proceed until another is finished. In sum, each task is assigned to produce one piece of the result, and they all work in parallel up to the natural restrictions of order and precedence imposed by the problem (Carriero & Gelernter, 1988; Pancake 1996).

3. **Activity Parallelism.** Activity parallelism (also known as *agenda parallelism*) requires partitioning both, the data and the algorithm (Carriero & Gelernter, 1988; Pancake 1996). A number of independent tasks are set to operate on the data. Different pieces of data are operated on by different tasks. Each task can be considered as a "worker", capable of grabbing some data, performing part of the algorithm on it, and returning a result. When it has finished, it grabs another piece of data. Tasks have no particular identity. They all do whatever needs doing.

In activity parallelism, all tasks also start simultaneously, grabbing pieces of data and operating on them. As there is no special commitment to any part of the data, tasks are able to operate in disorder. However, occasionally there can be a sequence of actions. Tasks have to coordinate their operation on a piece of data. Also, from the activity of each task, they have to assemble a single final result. In sum, each task is assigned to pick a piece of data, operate on it, produce a result, an repeat until the whole data has been operated. They all work in parallel up to the natural restrictions of order and precedence imposed by the problem (Carriero & Gelernter, 1988; Pancake 1996).

The boundaries between these three models can sometimes be fuzzy, and often, their elements are mixed in order to deal with a particular problem. This means that a functional parallelism approach may use activity parallelism, for example, assigning a team of workers to some special operation. It is, nonetheless, an essential issue to point out that these three models represent three clearly separate ways of thinking about the problem (Carriero & Gelernter, 1988). Later, in Sections 5.2.7 and 5.3, these models of parallelism are re-taken when classifying and selecting the Architectural Patterns for Parallel Programming, as architectural descriptions of solutions commonly used in parallel programming.

2.1.4 Performance Measures in Parallel Programming

Performance measurement is a crucial issue in parallel programming. Commonly, for the users of parallel programming, the whole point is to develop parallel programs that run fast. Once a parallel application is up and running, it is necessary to explore and know how well it is doing, and how to do better. Normally, if the parallel program does not run faster as more processors are made available, at least to a point, it is considered a failure (Carriero & Gelernter, 1988; Freeman & Phillips, 1992).

Execution Time

The most common and used measure of parallel systems performance is the execution time, this is, the time that elapses since a parallel program starts executing until it finishes. In fact, this is the most important feature to be considered about the performance of a parallel program. As a parallel program is intended to decrease the execution time, execution time is in itself a measure that reflects the global performance of a parallel system.

The execution time of a parallel program can be subdivided into a sequential part and a parallel part (as it is described below by Amdahl's Law), or in a *processing time* and a *communication time*. Considering this subdivision, a trivial parallel application is that which does not require communication among its processors. Thus, execution time in such a parallel application tends to be linear. However, most parallel applications are not trivial, since communication among processors is unavoidable in most cases. In fact, the execution time of a parallel program depends on a balance between processing time and communication time. An optimal point can be looked for, in which the amount of processing carried out by each processor does not conflict with the communication time required for exchanging messages.

For the actual purposes of this thesis, execution time (in fact, its average over a set of measurements) is considered as the main measure of the performance that a parallel program is able to achieve (see Section 1.3).

Speed-up and Efficiency

Other common and usual measures of parallel performance are *speed-up* and *efficiency*, which are generally derived from measuring the execution time. Hence, speed-up and efficiency are defined from execution times by mathematical expressions. Let T_p be the execution time for a parallel program on p processors, thus:

- S_p, the *speed-up ratio on p processors*, is given by (Freeman & Phillips, 1992):

$$S_p = \frac{T_0}{T_p}$$

where T_0 is the time for the fastest sequential algorithm on a single processor.

It should be noted that this definition of speed-up ratio compares a parallel program with the fastest sequential algorithm for a given problem. Hence, it attempts to measure the benefit to be gained by moving the application from a sequential computer with one processor to a parallel computer with p identical processors. Even if the same algorithm is employed, it is normally expected that the time taken by the parallel implementation executing on a single processor (T_1) to exceed the time taken by the sequential implementation on the same processor (T_0) because of the overheads associated with running parallel processes.

- $\bar{S}_p$, the *algorithmic speed-up ration on p processors*, is given by (Freeman & Phillips, 1992):

$$\bar{S}_p = \frac{T_1}{T_p}$$

This expression represents the speed-up to be gained by the parallelisation of a given program. It thus directly measures the effects of synchronisation and communication delays on the performance of a parallel program. This definition of speed-up ratio is basically the one used throughout this thesis.

Ideally, it would be desirable that $\bar{S}_p$ to grow linearly with p. Unfortunately, even for a "good" parallel program, at best it is expected that speed-up initially grow at a close to linear rate, and then eventually to decline as more processors are used, and hence, synchronisation overheads and communication delays start to dominate the execution.

- E_p, the *efficiency on p processors*, given by (Freeman & Phillips, 1992):

$$E_p = \frac{\bar{S}_p}{p} \times 100$$

Notice that the efficiency of a parallel program is obtained as a percentage, and that in an ideal situation it is hoped to get 100% efficiency for all p. In practice, however, efficiency decreases as the number of processors p increases.

It should be mentioned that, as defined here, both speed-up and efficiency are obtained in terms of the number of processor employed, rather than the number of processes. Nevertheless, speed-up and efficiency are considered by many authors as the driving forces behind the development of a parallel program.

Amdahl's Law

From the definitions provided for speed-up and efficiency, it can be observed that the ideal situation for a parallel program is one in which *(a)* the speed-up ratio increases linearly with p, with slope 1, and *(b)* giving an efficiency of 100% for all p. Such a situation rarely occurs in practice, partly because of the need to synchronise parallel processes. Moreover, there is a further consideration which arises from the inescapable fact that there are likely to be portions of a parallel program which are inherently sequential. This observation is embodied in *Amdahl's Law*: Suppose that r is the fraction of a program which is parallelisable and that $s = 1 - r$ is the remaining inherently sequential fraction of such a program. Then, on p processors, the algorithmic speed-up ratio $\bar{S}_p$ satisfies that (Freeman & Phillips, 1992):

$$\bar{S}_p \le \frac{1}{s + r/p}$$

Amdahl's Law appears to have serious consequences as far as parallelisation of algorithms is concerned, since it imposes an upper bound on the speed-up ratio. For example, if only 50% of an algorithm can be parallelised, then as the number of processors increase ($v \to \infty$), the speed-up ratio has to accomplish that $\bar{S}_p \le 2$. This means that for this particular algorithm, the speed-up ratio is limited to 2, regardless the number of processors used.

2.1.5 Summary of Parallel Programming

A parallel program executing on a parallel (or distributed) hardware specifies a message passing system of communicating sequential processes. This is the entity which we attempt to model its performance. It is normally used to solve problems of a scale that would not be realistic nor cost effective to be solved using sequential systems. Moreover, it is noticeable that the hardware platform, the programming language, and the order and dependence between instructions and/or data impose a limit to the performance that each sequential process within the parallel program can achieve. The sequential processes execute non-deterministically, probabilistically generating different interactions for each parallel program execution. This situation makes it difficult to track parallel execution using analytical models, so simulation models are proposed to represent a parallel program in execution. Nevertheless, the cost of simulating a parallel program execution tends to be extremely high in terms of time. A feasible solution proposed here is to use a parallel simulation of the parallel program.

2.2 An Introduction to Software Architecture

Although there are a great deal of definitions to the term software architecture, a distillation of commonly used ideas is that software architecture is the overall description of a software system in terms of components and interfaces. In its strict sense, *"a software architecture is a description of the subsystems and components of a software system, and the relations between them"* (Buschmann et al., 1996). An architecture thus attempts to define the internal *structure —"the way in which something is constructed or organised"* (Oxford dictionary)— of the resulting software. Nevertheless, concrete definitions of the expression *Software Architecture* by recognised authorities are but few, and those few tend to be periphrastic. In order to have a better understanding of how such an expression could be defined, it will be convenient to consider what software designers mean when they speak of a software system.

Many products may be regarded as an integration or assembly of parts. The parts are independent, following the cohesion heuristic, that is to say that their properties can be defined without reference to other parts (Parnas, 1972). A software product made up in this way of a collection of separable parts is called a *software system.* The parts of which it is built are usually called *software components* (Broy et al., 1998).

The components of a software system are the simplest parts that are to be considered as distinct units. Just how simple these parts are is a quite arbitrary choice. Often, the software components, so called, are themselves made up of still simpler sub-components. However, in a given analysis or description of a software system, it is usually convenient to limit the resolution to a certain level of complexity, and the parts so revealed are simply thought of as components. This does not, of course, preclude the possibility of sometimes referring to sub-systems, that is, an assembly of software components forming less than the complete software system.

The simpler the components are chosen to be, the simpler will be their design and implementation (in general), but, of course, the more there will be of them. Thus, the choice of the components is often an attempt to strike a balance between analytical problems arising from over-complex descriptions of individual components, and others arising from the sheer number of components to be handled.

However, there may be other bases of choice. Quite often, the software designer chooses software components from a list of *available* units (the meaning of "available" here will be considered below), in which case what is to be treated as a component is, in effect, fixed. Thus, for example, it has for some years been quite possible to design a software system or application using ready-made parts. The design of the software system is based on the properties of the available components and how these are assembled together, in many cases without the need for any non-standard part. Thus a complete software system may be constructed as a simple assembly-job of software components, following a pre-defined relationship, configuration or pattern, using only the simplest tools, and perhaps without coding at all.

Software components are described here as "available", but this term merits some further consideration. What is meant by available is either that the software component can be had at once, say from a commercial provider, or that there is a reasonably high probability that it can be implemented by modification or development of other existing components. In the latter case, software products are being considered within the category of things known to be feasible and makeable, either by virtue of being within the range of current technology, or so little beyond it that the prospect of successful development is good. Thus, available software component in this sense can be thought as having a high probability of being available in pre-implemented form at the time when the software system is assembled. From this point of view, whether they are actually in existence at the time when software design is carried out or whether it is merely known that they could be produced is of secondary importance.

Whenever the number of software systems of fairly similar kind to be produced (or the number of types of components in a given system) is large enough to permit component production on an extensive scale, the balance of advantage tends to swing strongly in the direction of software system construction as an assembly of pre-implemented components. Thus, the design problem resolves itself into selecting the right components from those available and inter-connecting or assembling them in the right relationship, configuration or pattern.

Therefore, Software Architecture is defined here simply as *the discipline or study of designing software systems, as the result of an "assembly-job" of software components.* Although the emphasis is commonly on existing standard components, the use of available components specially made for the software system is not excluded.

The essential basis of Software Architecture, so understood, is a concern with the assembly of components, whose properties are largely given. Hence, a software architect (who acts as a translator between the client's problem domain concepts and the programmer's solution domain concepts) is concerned with the problems of deriving the overall software system properties from those of the components, and with questions of compatibility between components with the software system as a whole. The software architect is not, however, concerned with the detailed design of elements, but is satisfied to treat them as having certain established specifiable properties. To sum up, the software architect's attitude to the software system may be either analytical or synthetic, but regarding all its components under a purely phenomenological light.

2.2.1 Directions in Software Architecture

It is not very clear from a study of literature who started the use of the term *software architecture*. Certain it is, however, that the remarkable book "The Mythical Man-Month", by Fred Brooks Jr. (Brooks, 1975) made the expression *system architecture* meaningful to a large public.

More specifically, within the software literature, the paper "Foundations for the Study of Software Architecture" by Perry and Wolf (1992) used the term for describing the design of software systems at the organisation level. Since then, the *architectural approach, the overall view of software*, or simply, Software Architecture, has become something *sine qua non* of modernism in certain fields of software design.

Software Architecture has received considerable attention. A special issue of the IEEE Software magazine (IEEE, 1995) has been devoted to "The Artistry of Software Architecture". This issue contains several articles on Software Architecture, emphasising the importance of mixing requirements and implementation-driven approaches to producing quality software systems.

During the mid-90's, however, Software Architecture started to emerge as a broader discipline involved with the studying software structure in a more generic way (Shaw & Garlan, 1996). This gave rise to a number of interesting notions involved with the design of software at different levels of abstraction. Some of these notions can be useful during the architectural design, as well as during the detailed design of a specific software system. But they can also be useful for designing generic systems, leading to the design of families of systems or product lines. Interestingly, most of these notions can be seen as attempts to describe, and thus reuse, generic design knowledge. Nowadays, at least several books cover the subject. Much of the current work in Software Architecture primarily addresses the product, known as architectural structure, and its description through views rather than the process to generating it. The published studies cover topics such as classifying architectures, mapping architectural styles and software patterns to particularly appropriate applications, and the use of software frameworks to assemble multiple related software systems, known as families. In the terminology, work on architectural styles and software patterns is attempting to classify the high level forms of software and their application to particular software problems.

Architectural views

Different high-level facets of a software design can be and should be described and documented. These facets are often called *views*: *"a view represents a partial aspect of a software architecture that shows specific properties of a software system"* (Buschmann et al., 1996).

A view describes a system with respect to some set of attributes or concerns. The set of views chosen to describe a software system is variable. An adequate set of views should be complete (cover all aspects of the software system), and mostly orthogonal (capture different pieces of information). Different views pertain to different issues associated with the design of software, for example, the logical view (satisfying the functional requirements), the process view (concurrency issues), the physical view (distribution issues), and the development view (how the design is broken down into implementation units) (Kruchten, 1995). Other authors use different terminology, e.g., behavioural, functional, structural, and data modelling views.

The key idea is that a software design is a multifaceted artifact produced by the design process and generally composed of relatively independent and orthogonal views

(Finkelstein et al., 1993; Kruchten, 1995; Bass et al., 1998; Buschmann et al., 1996; Booch et al., 1999; Budgen, 1994; IEEE, 1998).

Architectural Styles

An architectural style is *"a set of constraints on an architecture (that) define a set or family architectures that satisfies them"* (Bass et al., 1998). An architectural style can thus be seen as a meta-model that can provide the high-level organization of a software system. At the most general level, a style is defined by its components, connectors, and constraints. The components are the things from which the software systems is composed. The connectors are the interfaces by which the components interact. A style sets the type of components and connectors which make up the system. The constraints are the requirements which define system behaviour. In the current usage, the architecture is the definition in terms of the form, which does not explicitly incorporate the constraints. To understand the constraints, it is necessary to look at additional views.

A number of major styles have been identified by various authors. Some of the styles proposed include pipes and filters, object-oriented, event-based, layered, and blackboard (Shaw & Garlan, 1996). A pipe and filters architecture contains filters as components that potentially operate incrementally and concurrently on a stream of data, and pipes allow the flow of such a stream between filters. An object-oriented architecture is built from components that encapsulate both data and function, and which exchange messages. An event-based architecture has as its fundamental structure a loop which receives events, interprets the event in the context of the system state, and takes actions based on the combination of event and state. Layered architectures make emphasis on horizontal partitioning of the system with explicit message passing and function calling between layers. Each layer is responsible of providing a well-defined interface to the layer above. A blackboard architecture is built from a set of concurrent components which interact by reading and writing asynchronously to a common area.

These styles can (tentatively) be organised as follows (Bass, et al., 1998; Bosch, 2000; Booch et al., 1999; Pfleeger, 1998):

- General structure (e.g., layers, pipes and filters, blackboard);
- Distributed systems (e.g., client-server, three-tiers, broker);
- Interactive systems (e.g., Model-View-Controller, Presentation-Abstraction-Control);
- Adaptable systems (e.g., micro-kernel, reflection);

- Other styles (e.g., batch, interpreters, process-control, rule-based).

Each style carries its advantages and disadvantages. Each style encompasses descriptions of implementations from a software implementor's point of view. They are not descriptions from the user's point of view, or even from the point of view of the hardware implementor. A coherent style, at least of the types currently described, gives a level of conceptual integrity that assists the builder, but may not help the designer or the user. Having a coherent implementation style may help in construction, but it is not likely to yield dramatic improvements in productivity or quality because it does not promise to cut the size of what must be implemented.

Software Patterns and Pattern Languages

The progression from "inspired" Software Architecture to formal software design methods is through long experience. Long experience in software development by its practitioners eventually yields tested software patterns of function and form. Software Patterns and Pattern Languages or Systems are a formalisation of this progression in the software development and evolution.

Design matures in a domain as designers identify reusable components and repeating patterns of connection. They recognise recurring patterns of form and their relationship to patterns in problems. In mature domains, patterns in both problem and solution develop rigorous expression. For instance, a formalisation of patterns in building architecture is due to C. Alexander (Alexander et al., 1977; Alexander, 1979). Working within civil architecture and urban design, Alexander developed an approach to synthesis based on the composition of formalised patterns.

Succinctly, a pattern is *"a common solution to a common problem in a given context"* (Alexander et al., 1977; Alexander, 1979). A Software Pattern is a recurring structure within software design. It consists of both a problem or functional objective for a software system, and a solution or form of the software system.

In general, patterns are described in narrative form. A template for defining a pattern is (Buschmann et al., 1996):

1. A brief name which describes what the pattern accomplishes.
2. A concise problem statement.
3. A description of the problem including the motivation for the pattern and the issues in resolving the problem (called "forces").

4. A solution, preferably stated in the form of an instruction.

5. A discussion of how good or bad the pattern solves the problem, and how it relates to other patterns.

Some categorisation of software patterns classify them as *architectural*, *design*, and *idioms*. Architectural patterns describe the high-level organisation of software systems. Design patterns can be used to describe details at a lower, more local level. Idioms describe local solutions based on the characteristics of a particular programming language (Buschmann et al., 1996). Another popular classification scheme presents design patterns as *structural, behavioral,* and *creational* (Gamma et al., 1994).

A Pattern Language or System is a set of patterns complete enough for design within a domain. It is a method for composing patterns to synthetise solutions to diverse objectives (Buschmann et al., 1996). In the Alexandrian method, the architect consults sets of patterns and chooses from them those patterns which evoke the elements desired in the project (Alexander, et al., 1977). The same approach is intended in software development. Software Patterns become the building blocks for synthesis, or suggest important elements that should be presented in the software system. Each software pattern suggests instructions for solution structure, or contain a solution fragment. The fragments and instructions are merged to yield a system design.

Families of programs and Frameworks

The progression in software is through the construction and standardisation of components embodying behaviours closer and closer to problem domains. Instead of programming in what was considered a "high-level language", the designer can now build a software system from components close to the problem domain. The programming language is still used, but primarily to knit together pre-build components. Programming libraries have been in common use for many years. The libraries shipped with commercial software development environments are often very large and contain extensive class or object libraries, for example.

One possible approach to allow the reuse of software designs and components is to design families of systems —also known as software product lines— which can be done by identifying the commonalities among members of such families and by using reusable and customisable components to account for the variabilities among the various members of the family (Bass et al., 1998; Bosch, 2000; Pressman, 1997).

Whenever a family of related systems is built, a set of accepted design abstractions appears and forms the basis for a specialised design discipline. If the family becomes important enough, the design discipline will attract enough research attention to build scientific foundations. At the same time, the set of design abstractions will be recognised as "architectures" for the family (Shaw & Garlan, 1996).

In the field of Object-Oriented Programming, a key related notion is that of framework (Buschmann et al., 1996; Bosch, 2000; Booch et al., 1999): a framework is *"a partially complete software subsystem which can be extended by appropriately instantiating some specific plug-ins (also known as hot spots)"*.

2.2.2 Software Architecture and Performance

Many software systems are driven by quantitatively stated performance objectives. These software systems may also contain complex behaviour or other attributes, but its performance objectives are of most importance to the client. For these software systems, it is common to take a performance-centred approach to specification, decomposition, and synthesis. Real-time systems must perform their behaviours within a specified time-line. Absolute deadlines produce "hard real-time systems". More flexible deadlines produce "soft real-time systems". The question of whether or not a given software architecture will meet a set of deadlines has been extensively studied (Stankovic et al., 1995; Kopetz, 1997; Sanz & Zalewski, 2003). To integrate these considerations within Software Architecture requires integration of timing to the descriptions of architectural structures based on styles and patterns. In particular, two interesting approaches have attempted to deal with performance issues in software from a design perspective: ROOM and the UML Performance Profile. Both are briefly discussed as follows.

Real-time Object-Oriented Modeling — the ROOM method

ROOM stands for Real-time Object Oriented Modelling, and was developed some years ago by Bran Selic and others (Selic *et al.*, 1994). Since then, it has received quite some attention from the (real-time) software area. Although initially intended for designing and building telecommunication systems, the ROOM method can also be used for the design of other types of embedded systems.

ROOM designs contain primarily actors, ports, bindings and state machines (Selic *et al.*, 1994):

- An *actor* is an autonomous piece of code that plays a specific role in the system. The main distinction between an actor and an object is the fact that an actor behaves autonomously. An advantage of this is that the encapsulation goes a step further: objects only offer data encapsulation while actors offers data and thread encapsulation. Thread encapsulation means that two different threads cannot alter the internal state of the object at the same time. This ensures that the data is always left in a consistent state.

- A *port* is an opening on the encapsulation shell of the actor through which it can send and receive messages. A port has also a specification (protocol) associated with it.

- A *binding* is a connection between two ports. Actors can exchange messages via bindings. It is only possible to create a binding between ports that have the same protocol.

- A *state machine* describes the internal workings of an actor. This state machine describes how the actor will respond to (external) messages and the states it will be in.

The ROOM method has some new and interesting ideas: *(a)* it introduces thread encapsulation that hides the internal thread mechanisms; *(b)* it offers and alternative way of connecting software components by means of bindings; *(c)* the idea of port protocols is an advantage since it enforces a designer to only connect compatible ports; and *(d)* to conclude, it offers the ability to generate code (by putting code into transitions of the state machines) and model execution.

ROOM however lacks a consistent way to annotate time in designs. In general, ROOM has no support for the annotation of non-functional constraints, like memory and bandwidth constraints.

UML Performance Profile

During the last few years, the UML Performance Profile has been proposed as a framework defined by the Object Management Group (OMG, 2001)[2]. The objective of such a performance profile is to enable the construction of models that can be used for quantitative predictions regarding these characteristics.

The original first document was issued in march 1999, and it was followed by the first "Response to RFP" submission in august 2000. The last revised submission was

---

2. Notice that the development of the UML Performance Profile in 2001 is latter than the submission of the present thesis. Nevertheless, even though many of the ideas presented in the UML Performance Profile are common to those proposed in this thesis, it only defines notational conventions; it is not a complete method.

issued in june 2001 (OMG, 2001). The later includes some additional aspects not covered by the formers, among which is a section dealing with performance analysis.

The proposed performance profile extends the UML metamodel with stereotypes, tagged values and constraints, which make possible to attach performance annotations (such as resource demands and visit ratios) to a UML model. The performance profile provides facilities for (OMG, 2001):

- capturing performance requirements within the design context,
- associating performance-related QoS characteristics with selected elements of the UML model,
- specifying execution parameters which can be used by modelling tools to compute predicted performance characteristics, and
- presenting performance results computed by modelling tools or found by measurement.

The profile describes a domain model which identifies basic abstractions used in performance analysis. Scenarios define response paths through the system, and can have QoS requirements such as response time. Each scenario is executed by a job class, called here workload, which can be closed or open, and has the usual characteristics (number of clients or arrival rate, for example). Scenarios are composed of scenario steps that can be joined in sequence, loops, branches, fork/joins, etc. A scenario step may be an elementary operation at the lowest level of granularity, or may be a complex sub-scenario composed of many basic steps. Each step has a mean number of repetitions, a host execution demand, other demand to resources, and its own QoS characteristics. Resources is another basic abstraction, and can be active or passive, each with its own attributes.

The performance profile maps classes representing the basic abstractions to a stereotype that can be applied to a number of UML model elements, and each class attribute to a tagged value. For example, the basic abstraction PStep is mapped to the stereotype <<PAstep>> that can be applied to the following UML model elements: Message and Stimulus (when the scenario is represented by an interaction diagram) or Action-State and SubactivityState (when the scenario is represented by an activity diagram).

In order to conduct quantitative performance analysis of an annotated UML model, the performance profile establishes that it is necessary *(a)* to translate it into a performance model, *(b)* use an existing performance analysis tool for solving the performance model, and *(c)* import the performance analysis results back in the UML model.

The UML Performance Profile cannot be considered as a complete guide to performance modelling, but as a framework. It establishes the steps to follow in order to develop performance models and performance analysis. Most of the approaches to performance modelling based on information described in terms of UML diagrams (or other similar diagrammatic representation) follow closely these steps, providing and developing different types of performance models from software descriptions, solving (in the case of analytical models) or executing (in the case of simulation models) them, and using their results as feedback for the original description of the software system.

As it can be observed in the cases of ROOM and the UML Performance Profile, timing considerations require integration of scheduling and scheduling analysis to Software Architecture. In spite of the extensive study, this is still at least partly an art. Theoretical results yield scheduling and performance bounds, and some associated scheduling rules, but can do so only for relatively simple systems. When system functions execute interchangeably on parallel processors, run times are random, and events requiring reaction occur non-deterministically, there are no deducible, provably optimal solutions.

2.3 Architectural Software Design

Even though software has being successfully used in standardising and automating other industries, paradoxically it is having trouble achieving a similar success on its own field. The increase in productivity and quality has been lower in software development compared to other industries, like building construction or electronics. By analysing how we develop software, it is possible to find out some things that contribute to this situation.

Usually, software programs produced by software designers and developers can be accessed only through the source code or as a executable system. At source code level, programmers can only see programming language constructs —functions, classes, and so on— whose sizes are quite small relative to the global size of most software systems. Therefore, it is very difficult to notice any larger scale structures by inspecting a software system at the level of its code. This lack of visibility of the larger scale structures in software systems is a major cause of the apparent complexity commonly associated with software systems (Rechtin & Maier, 1997).

Industries, such as building construction, have an advantage over the software industry due to their ability to manage the complexity of their products and the process of developing them (Rechtin & Maier, 1997; Bennett, 1997). However, what does building construction have that software development lacks? From our point of view, there are three common design elements in building construction that would be very useful to have in software development. Briefly, these elements are: a base of design experience and techniques, a tangible representation of the product structure, and measurements and evaluations to determine if desired attributes are found in the final product.

- **A Base of Design Experience and Techniques.** New building designs start out as ideas. When a new building design is proposed, it is often initially examined with informal design studies to reveal feasibility problems and to determine the economic potential of the new building. In general, building architects and engineers have handbooks to provide established design experience and techniques. Design experience and techniques range from simple diagram representations to formal, mathematical simulations of the product design (Rechtin & Maier, 1997).

- **A Tangible Representation of the Building Structure**. In building construction, an architect represents a project with diagrams such as drawings or plans of a building. These diagrams describe a form as the static structure of the complete building as a whole. From these diagrams, the architect describes how the occupants will carry on doing their jobs within the building structure. However, these diagrams do not explicitly expose the structural steel, the mechanical or electrical views of the building. The architect has to provide room in the structure for all those things, and for all the uses and functionalities that the building will accommodate (Bennett, 1997).

- **Measurements and Evaluations.** During building construction, to achieve the interconnection of a newly designed components with other standard or designed components, it is necessary to have a measurement system that allows a comparison between the actual construction parts and those specified in the design. In general, we need *(a)* a way to measure the property of interest, and *(b)* an evaluation guideline for the range of measured values that are acceptable (Tichy, 1998).

These three design features of building construction constitute what we define as the architectural design elements of building architecture. In the following sections, we present some approaches that actually attempt to work out similar features for software development.

2.3.1 Design Experience and Techniques — Software Patterns

Mature industrial and engineering disciplines work with handbooks of design experience and techniques that describe successful solutions to known problems. Most designers do not create their designs from scratch, but reuse standard design solutions with successful track records contained in such handbooks. The extra performance available by starting a design from scratch typically is not worth the cost (Buschmann *et al.*, 1996).

Software design problems should be addressed by good practice experiences and proven techniques. Several approaches have focused on capturing and systemising successful experience and techniques used in previous software developments. In particular, Software Patterns is one of the most important efforts, aiming for the creation of a handbook of good design and programming practices for software development (see Section 2.2.1). Patterns were originally developed for building architecture (Alexander *et al.*, 1977; Alexander, 1979), and adopted later for software construction (Gamma *et al.*, 1994; Buschmann *et al.*, 1996; Gabriel, 1996). Their use is spreading in the software community to the benefit of those undertaking design and implementation tasks.

Software Patterns are an attempt to describe successful solutions to common software problems. Their long term goal is to gather design experience and techniques for software development. Even though there is still a long way to reach that goal, Software Patterns have proven to be useful helping people to reuse successful software practices. They not only teach useful techniques, but also help people to better communicate their experience, and reason about what they do and why they do it.

Defining what is a software pattern is not an easy task. It involves several philosophical and practical considerations. Inside the Pattern Community, it is generally accepted that a pattern is *"a recurring solution to a standard problem"* (Coplien, 1994; Gabriel, 1996). In a wider sense, a pattern is *"a way to capture and systemize proven practice in any discipline"* (Alexander *et al.*, 1977; Alexander, 1979). In the particular case of the software industry, a software pattern can be considered as *"any reusable software design abstraction or identifiable piece of software, that may be exploited in several contexts"* (Gamma *et al.*, 1994; Buschmann *et al.*, 1996).

For our purposes, a software pattern is *a function-form relation that occurs in a context, where the function is described in problem domain terms as a group of unresolved trade-offs or forces, and the form is a structure described in solution domain terms that achieves a good and acceptable equilibrium among those forces.* This definition of a software pattern follows from our intention to relate them to an architectural design for software.

2.3.2 A Tangible Architectural Description of Software

A tangible architectural description for software systems consists of components, connectors, and a boundary of the system. The components are made tangible, enclosed in implementation containers. Every level of implementation container has a contain relationship with one another, so that the software subsystems have the same relationships with each other (see Section 2.2.2). Based on the concept of the Layers of Change (Brand, 1994), components can be classified and grouped into "layers" of design and implementation, depending on their change rate (the speed in which different components tend to evolve during the lifetime of a software system) (Ortega & Roberts, 1999a; Ortega & Roberts, 1999b). This generic architectural description of software provides a basis for designing emergent properties of the software system. Emergent properties include changeability, maintainability and any others that depend on the whole system for their expression.

For our actual purposes, a three layered architectural description model seems to be sufficient to analyse the characteristics of a parallel program. The intention is to keep this

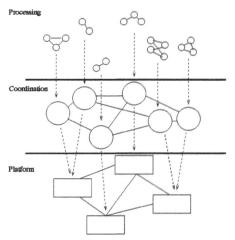

Figure 2.1 An architectural description of Software

model as simple as possible. Some components are clearly related to elements of hardware, and some are clearly software components. Therefore, an architectural description is composed of the following layers (Figure 2.1):

- **Platform.** This represents the connection to elements of the hardware architecture of the system.
- **Coordination.** This represents the fixed and stable subsystems that comprise the system, and the form in which they are connected by communication components.
- **Processing.** This represents the software elements designed for and explicitly allocated to the subsystems focusing on data and behaviour, that make up the software architecture.

The objective of classifying the components of a software system into layers is merely to deal with complexity during design and implementation, by arranging them in a hierarchy of "contains" relationships between components. In this sense, the term *components* refers to pieces of software, put together into a "container", representing code processed by a processor (see Section 2.2). Thus, the software subsystems of the Coordination layer are contained in each hardware subsystem of the Platform layer, and the software elements of the Processing layer have, similarly, a "contained-in" relationship with the Coordination layer subsystems. The distinction between layers is based on recognising what is "fixed" and what is "transient", that is, on what must be put in the system, or installed, in order to run it (Ortega & Roberts, 1999a; Ortega & Roberts, 1999b). During architectural software development, fixed layers like Platform and Coordination are considered at the beginning because they define the basic functionality of the software system as a whole. Transient layers, such as the Processing layer, are considered later, defining the detailed behaviour of each piece of software. However, this is not to say that the transient components of the software systems are not important or that they do not have to be considered during architectural design. They do. They are just not part of the fixed layers.

2.3.3 Measurement and Evaluation for Software Design

The main reason for adopting an architectural design approach for software in the first place is to obtain software quality. *"Software quality is the degree to which software possesses a desired combination of attributes"* (Barbacci *et al.*, 1995; Barbacci *et al.*, 1997; Bass *et al.*, 1998). Software quality must be built-in by design and considered from the beginning. In our approach, defining an architectural description of software is the earliest point of a software system design, in which we can start measuring and evaluating to obtain a good idea how well the software system will meet its requirements.

The Need of Measurement and Evaluation

Repeatability is the most important issue for any design development. It ensures that good results can be reproduced. If a software system has certain qualities, it is very important to be able to reproduce these in other software systems. However, this requires the ability to measure those qualities, evaluating them to confirm their presence or absence in a design.

Software quality means that software systems possess some relevant attributes, like low cost, reliability, rapid development, safety, and so on (Barbacci *et al.*, 1995; Barbacci *et al.*, 1997). To determine whether a particular software development method or technique allows the inclusion or improvement of a particular quality attribute of interest present in a software system, we need a way to measure it. Merely stating that a software system possesses such an attribute conveys no real information. Instead, applying measurements for that quality attribute of interest, we can state if such a method or technique results in a software system that achieves our expectations more or less effectively (Tichy, 1998). Depending on the quality attribute of interest, relating it to a measurement scale is fairly straightforward. If the attribute of interest is "performance", then execution time would be our measurement (Tichy, 1998; Zelkowitz & Wallace, 1998).

Evaluating Software Alternatives

In order to evaluate alternative software architectures as potential solutions to a problem, they should be measured on their ability to satisfy the requirements that emerge from the system as a whole (Bass *et al.*, 1998). The architectural description presented in Section 2.3.2 can help with this, because it represents the tangible physical structure of the entire system. Software architectures are considered different if at the level of at least one of their layers they are different. Different software architectures can be compared and evaluated on their ability to satisfy the requirements of the software system. For this, it is necessary to have explicit goals for each layer of the architectural description, and evaluate each layer against goals for that layer. Thus, the requirements should be stated as specific instances of change that the system should support.

Significantly, there are several run-time attributes of a software system that do not manifest themselves until all of the subsystems that make up the software system are working together. These attributes include reliability, performance, throughput, and availability. Software architectures should be evaluated against the specific levels of each of those run-time properties (Abowd *et al.*, 1997; Barbacci *et al.*, 1997; Bass *et al.*, 1998). However, that is easier said than done. The process of evaluating a system for reliability and performance is a large task, often involving large simulations or trials on working systems (see Chapter 3).

2.4 Summary

In this chapter we present an introduction to parallel programming, describing it and presenting a general overall of its origins, the factors that influence it, and the main models used for parallel programming.

The origins of parallel programming are described as the main research contributions by Flynn, Dijkstra, Hoare, Brinch-Hansen, and many others, which have resulted on concepts of notions that represent the basics of parallel systems development.

Parallel programming is normally considered as a mean for getting higher performance, in terms of processing speed. There are three factors of parallel programming that influence the performance that can be achieved by a parallel program: the hardware platform, the programming language, and the very problem to parallelise. This last one is influenced by the order and dependence between instructions and data, which directly affect the possibility of simultaneous execution.

Functional parallelism, domain parallelism, and activity parallelism are presented here as three model for parallel programming, used as a base for developing parallel programs.

Also in this chapter, an introduction to software architecture is presented, describing its main standard research notions. Notice, however, that as a discipline, software architecture lacks of a comprehensive study of performance modelling, particularly in the context of parallel programs. Two approaches within software architecture are presented, which attempt to relate it with performance modelling.

Finally, we introduce a vocabulary of architectural design based on software architecture standard notions, and particularly for the purposes of this thesis, presenting its key elements. These elements are a base of design experience and techniques, a tangible architectural description, and considerations for measurements and evaluation. In the following chapters, we use the interpretation of these elements applied to software design to propose and investigate the initial stages of parallel software design.

Chapter 3

Related Work

"Verständige Leute kannst du irren sehn In Sachen, näemlich, die sie nicht verstehn"
"Understanding people you may see erring in those things, to wit, which they do not understand"

Goethe

This chapter presents a review of the relevant related work in Software Performance Modelling, as *(a)* approaches that combine Software Architecture and Performance Modelling, *(b)* approaches to performance estimation of parallel and distributed systems, and *(c)* other similar approaches in Parallel Software Design to the Architectural Performance Modelling Method. Nevertheless, it is important to mention that the present PhD work was originally developed between september 1997 and august 1999. So, this chapter considers the relevant related work that was published or was started before 1999, by the time of this PhD submission. Other related work developed later, from 1999 until 2003, is also presented here in order to show how such more recent approaches have developed similar ideas as those originally proposed in 1999 by the present PhD thesis.

The related work is organised as follows: first, an introduction to Software Performance Modelling is presented, describing some basic notions within this research area; next, the main approaches that attempt to relate Software Architecture and Performance Modelling are briefly described, paying attention to their main characteristics; next, the following section describes the main research work in the area of performance modelling of parallel and distributed programming, describing their main features, and; finally, a description is presented about the most relevant architectural design approaches related to the problem of describing, programming and estimating the performance behaviour of a parallel and distributed systems based on information about their coordination structure.

3.1 Software Performance Modelling

Performance analysis of software systems is commonly carried out by measurement or by modelling techniques. In general, direct measurement of an actual implementation provides an accurate assessment of the performance of a software system. This is relatively simple and straightforward to do, but requires to build a system implementation *before* the measurement can take place. Implementing a complex system is usually a time-consuming, error-prone, and expensive task; mastering this complexity is the goal of all the software development processes which have been proposed in the literature.

Software performance modelling is challenging, since it is difficult to derive meaningful performance information from specifications, models, or static analysis of code. The reason is that software performance is heavily dependent on the hardware platform on which the software executes, and also, on the usage pattern the software is subject to. Moreover, software performance modelling cannot be carried out on one component at a time, as critical issues may arise only when different components interact. In general, software performance modelling can be obtained by analytical or simulation techniques (Rechtin & Maier, 1997).

3.1.1 Analytical Techniques

Most of the research in the area of software performance modelling is based on developing analytical models. Many performance models have been proposed in the literature; these models include queuing models (also known as Queuing Networks or QN) (Kleinrock, 1975), Petri Nets (Petri, 1962) and Stochastic Process Algebra (Hermanns *et al.*, 1995). At the moment, there is no clear consensus on which analytical model should be preferred in practice. The general understanding is that different models are suitable for different domains.

The vast majority of the software performance modelling approaches proposed so far (whether analytical or even simulations) base its estimations on a certain type of analytical models. This is motivated by the fact that those models are well studied and understood. Also, they can sometimes be solved analytically, providing performance results which are exact, and optionally, can be expressed parameterically with respect to one or more unknown variables. This, however, has a price.

Analytical models can usually built only by imposing some structural restrictions on the original system architecture, depending on the specific modelling formalism used;

the reason is that analytical models have often a limited expressiveness. While it is sometimes possible to simplify the model of the system in order to make it analytically tractable, there are many cases in which the significant aspects of the system cannot be effectively represented into the analytical model.

Moreover, the analytical models which can be solved exactly can be derived only by imposing some limitations on the software architecture from which they are derived. Generally, they can be efficiently computed only for special classes of systems, with constraints about their topology. Also, analytical performance models are often structurally very different from the software architecture from which they are derived. This makes very difficult to report performance results from the model to the original software architecture. This is very limiting, as software performance evaluation is supposed to provide the modeller with feedback about possible performance problems. Finally, many approximate techniques used to analyse the performance results of analytical models do not provide any error consideration of their results, meaning that it is impossible to quantify whether the obtained performance value is an adequate approximation or not.

3.1.2 Simulation Techniques

Simulation is a powerful modelling technique that allows general system models that can represent arbitrarily complex situations, which can be too difficult or even impossible to represent by analytical models. Simulation models can be arbitrarily detailed, in that, informally, they impose no restrictions on what they can model. The modeller has the maximum degree of freedom in selecting the aspects of the system to model, and at which level of detail. This freedom comes at some cost: the drawback of simulation is that very complex models may require a lot of time and computational resources in order to be executed. The results also require sophisticated statistical techniques in order to be correctly understood. While it is true that any given system can be represented at an arbitrarily high level of detail by a simulation model, the modeller often ignores the exact inner working of the system being simulated. This is certainly the case with Software Architecture, since components are defined at a high level of abstraction, and many details are postponed until the implementation phase (see Section 2.2). However, while the software architect may ignore the inner details of the system being designed, he could have more or less detailed knowledge of part of the architecture (for example, if some pieces are taken from an existing, already implemented system). Whenever additional information is available, it should be used to obtain better and more realistic performance estimates.

In general, a simulation modelling follows the process shown in Figure 3.1. The starting point is an architectural description of the software system to be simulated. Such a description is a set of structural and behavioural representations (commonly, descriptions containing UML diagrams). This information is used to derive a simulation performance model. The model is a simulation program, which eventually is executed. Simulation results are a set of performance measures that can be used to take decisions about the software architecture, or to provide a feedback at the original architectural description. Normally, the feedback should give hints to the software designer about how the problem can be solved, and possibly pinpoint performance problems on the software architecture. This cycle can be iterated until a software architecture with satisfactory performance is obtained.

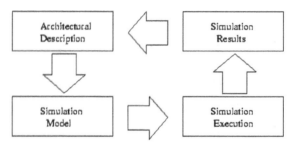

Figure 3.1 The simulation performance modelling process.

3.2 Approaches to Software Architecture and Performance Modelling

There is a growing interest in quantitative analysis of software systems, which is important for software design, and it has been recognised that performance analysis should be integrated in the software development life cycle from early stages (Smith 1990; WOSP 2000; WOSP 2002). Since software architectures describe the structure of software systems at a high level of abstraction, they have been devised as the appropriate design level to perform quantitative analysis (Bass, *et al.*, 1998). To this aim, several approaches have been recently proposed to integrate or combine performance analysis and software architecture specification. Various types of performance models and different specifications have been considered. Some approaches refer to the entire software life cycle, whereas others refer to a certain software stage, usually design specification.

In this section, we consider some approaches that derive performance models from a software architecture specification. We present a review of such different approaches, focusing on their proposed method and type of performance model. The feedback to the software designer of the results of the software performance analysis is another important issue to be considered, i.e., how easily can the designer interpret the quantitative results obtained by the performance evaluation at the software architecture design level. Several approaches refer to a software specification based on the Unified Modeling Language (UML) (Booch *et al.*, 1999), which is becoming the standard notation for the specification of software systems. It provides several kinds of diagrams, which allow the description of different aspects and properties of systems, like static and behavioural aspects, interaction among system components and physical implementation details.

Each approach is based on a certain type of analytical performance model. These models include queuing networks (QN), and their extensions, such as Extended Queuing Networks (EQN), Layered Queuing Networks (LQN), and Augmented Queuing Networks (AQN); Petri Nets (PN), and their variations, namely Stochastic Timed Petri Nets (STPN) and General Stochastic Petri Nets (GSPN); and Stochastic Process Algebras (SPA), particularly their derivation as Stochastically Timed Process Algebra (STPA).

Many of the proposed methods are based on the Software Performance Engineering (SPE) methodology introduced by C.U. Smith (Smith, 1990). This methodology has been the first comprehensive approach to the integration of performance analysis into the software development process, from the earliest stages of design. The SPE methodology is based on two models: the *software execution model* (based on execution graphs (EG) and represents the software execution behaviour) and the *system execution model* (based on queuing network models and represents the computer system platform, including hardware and software components). The analysis of the software execution model gives information concerning the resource requirements of the software system. The obtained results, together with information about the hardware devices, are input parameters of the system execution model, which represents the model of the whole software/hardware system.

More recently, Pooley (2000) outlined a road-map that shows how software performance can be integrated within the Software Engineering process. Performance engineering is described as an experimental approach to predicting the likely performance of systems. It can involve building and monitoring the system under the workloads of interest, or using models to represent the system. Modelling has many advantages over building/monitoring, which makes it used in most of the work of interest to software performance engineering. The challenge is to bring the areas of Software Architecture and Performance Modelling analysis together, which can be achieved by embedding performance analysis techniques into design methods and tools.

3.2.1 General Methods

Some approaches propose general methods for deriving performance models from software architecture specifications. These methods refer to different architectural specifications and performance models, and they consider the combination of different tools and environments for system performance evaluation.

- Williams and Smith (Williams & Smith, 1998) apply the SPE methodology to evaluate the performance characteristics of a software architecture. The emphasis is in the construction and analysis of the software execution model, which is considered the target model of the specified software architecture, and it is obtained from sequence diagrams. The class and deployment diagrams contribute to complete the description of the software architecture, but they are not involved in the transformation process. The SPE process requires additional information that includes software resource requirements for processing steps and computer configuration data.

- Menascè and Gomaa (Menascé & Gomaa, 1998) present a method to derive QN performance models from software architecture specification. It has been developed and used by the authors in a design of client/server applications. The method is based on CLISSPE (CLIent-Server Software Performance Evaluation), a language for the software performance engineering of client/server applications (Menascé, 1997). Although the method does not explicitly use UML, the functional requirements of the system are specified in terms of use cases, and the system model is specified by the analogous of a class diagram. The use cases, together with the client/server software architecture specification and the mapping associating software components to hardware devices, are used to develop a CLISSPE program specification. The CLISSPE system provides a compiler that generates a corresponding QN model. By considering specific scenarios, it is possible to define the QN parameters and apply the appropriate solution methods, such as the Layered Queuing Models (LQN) (Rolia & Sevcik, 1995; Woodside *et al.*, 1995), to obtain performance results.

- Balsamo, Inverardi and Mangano (Balsamo, *et al.*, 1998) provide a method for the automatic derivation of a queuing network model from a software architecture specification, described using the CHAM formalism (CHemical Abstract Machine). Informally, the CHAM specification of a software architecture (Inverardi & Wolf, 1995) is given by a set of *molecules* which represent the static components of the architecture, a set of *reaction rules* which describe the dynamic evolution of the system through reaction steps, and an initial *solution* which describes the initial static configuration of the system. This work presents an algorithm to derive a QN model from the CHAM specification of a software architecture. It is based on the analysis of the Labelled Transition System (LTS) (Ghezzi, *et al.*, 1991; Kemppainen, *et al.*, 1992; Rabinovich, 1992; Valmari, 1992) that represents the dynamic behaviour of the CHAM architecture, and that can be automatically derived from the CHAM specification. Although, the algorithm does not completely define the QN model, whose parameters, such as service time distributions and customer's arrival processes, have to be specified by the designer. The solution of the QN model is derived by analytical methods or possibly by symbolic evaluation. Parameter instantiation identify potential implementation scenarios and the performance results allow to provide insights on how to carry on the development process in order to satisfy given performance criteria.

- Cortellessa and Mirandola (Cortellesa & Mirandola, 2000) propose a method making a joint use of information from different UML diagrams to generate a performance model of the specified system. This work attempts to provide an automatic translation from UML diagrams into a queuing network based performance model. The goal is to complement the UML notation with a method that encompasses the performance validation task (which includes model generation and validation) as an integrated activity within the development process. The paper refers to the SPE methodology, and specifies the software architecture by using deployment, sequence and use case diagrams. The target performance model is composed of two parts: the Software Model (SM) based on Execution Graphs (EG); and the Machinery Model (MM), based on Extended Queuing Network (EQN) models. By combining SM and MM, a complete (parameterised) EQN based performance model is obtained, which is then solved using some known techniques.

This approach is a more formal extension of the approach by Williams and Smith (Williams & Smith, 1998), and consists of the following steps:

1. Complement the use of use case diagrams (UCD) by assigning a probability to every edge that links a type of user to a use case, so that such probability applies to the execution of the corresponding set of sequence diagrams. Use case diagram are used, then, for deriving the user profile and software scenarios. This leads to the definition of the workload of the performance model.

2. For each use case in the UCD, process the corresponding set of sequence diagrams to obtain the *meta*-EG (execution graph). The algorithm incrementally builds the EG by processing in turn all the sequence diagrams and building, for each one, the part of the EG it contributes to. It considers only sequence diagrams without *no-reply* and *asynchronous* interactions.

3. Use the deployment diagram both to obtain the EQN model of the hardware platform and to appropriately tailor the *meta*-EG, so obtaining an EG-instance that defines the workload of the EQN. Also, the deployment diagram is used to identify the hardware/software relationships that improve the accuracy of the performance model. In this step, the basic idea is to enrich the deployment diagram that shows the topology of the platform and the type of sites, with the information needed to build the EQN, such as the internal structure and parameters of devices. Moreover, the EG-instance defines the type of communication and the size of data exchanged. However, the paper does not present the details of the EQN construction from the deployment diagram.

4. Assign numerical parameters, defined by the designer, to the EG-instance.

5. Combine EG-instance and EQN model to solve the obtained performance model by using the SPE approach.

Note that a key point of the method is adding the information concerning performance evaluation to the considered UML diagrams, and to obtain the EQN model. In this paper, the method is not yet implemented as a tool, and to achieve this, the authors consider that there are two further steps to take: *(a)* choosing an appropriate syntax to represent the UML diagrams involved (and perhaps some supporting data structures), and *(b)* studying the underlying syntax of the existing SPE tools in order to ease the translation from UML notation to performance modelling representation.

- The approach by Aquilani, Balsamo and Inverardi (Aquilani *et al.*, 2000) concerns the derivation of QN models from Labelled Transition Systems (LTS) (Ghezzi, *et al.*, 1991; Kemppainen, *et al.*, 1992; Rabinovich, 1992; Valmari, 1992) describing the dynamic behaviour of software architectures. Starting from a LTS description of a software architecture makes it possible to abstract from any particular software architecture specification language. The approach assumes that LTSs are the only knowledge on the system that they can use. This means, in particular, that it does not use any information concerning the system implementation or deployment. This approach considers a finite state representation independent of a specific architectural description language, and modelling more complex interaction patterns and synchronisation constraints that can be represented by EQNs. Such EQNs model the software concurrent execution and component interaction at the software architecture design level.

- Bernardo, Ciancarini and Donatiello (Bernardo *et al.*, 2000) propose an architectural description language based on Stochastically Timed Process Algebras. This approach provides an integration of a formal specification language and performance models. The aim is to describe and analyse both functional and performance properties of software architectures in a formal framework. The approach proposes the adoption of an architectural description language called AEMPA, giving its syntax with a graphical and contextual notation, and its semantics in terms of EMPA specifications, which is a Stochastically Timed Process Algebra (Bernardo, 2000). The authors illustrate various functional and non-functional properties, including performance evaluation which is based on the generation of underlying Markov chains that are numerically solved. To this aim, the authors propose the use of TwoTowers (Bernardo, 2000), a software tool for systems modelling and analysis of functional and performance properties that support the system EMPA description.

- Cortellesa and Mirandola (Cortellesa & Mirandola, 2002) present an approach for translating UML sequence diagrams, use case diagrams, and deployment diagrams into a performance model based on EQN, using an intermediate transformation into Execution Graphs. System performance evaluation is presented as an incremental process integrated in the software development life cycle, by using information of different kinds of UML diagrams from the early stages of the development process. The level of detail of the model is extended as the software development proceeds. This allows incremental building of a performance model of the system, which can be used to improve or modify the software architecture. The UML diagrams are annotated with quantitative informations, which are necessary to set the parameters of the model. Actors are annotated with the frequency they may appear in the system. Associations between actors and use cases are annotated with the probabilities that each actor executes each use case. Sequence diagrams are annotated with timing information attached to events, and messages sent among objects are tagged with their sizes. Deployment diagrams represent various kinds of resources, and they are annotated with suitable parameters such as bandwidth for network links, or speed of computational resources. Finally, the three types of UML diagrams (use case, sequence, and deployment) are used together to build a EQN model.

- Gu and Petriu (Gu & Petriu, 2002) derive performance models based on LQN models from a description of software architecture. They use UML activity diagrams, annotated as defined in the UML Performance Profile (OMG, 2001). Diagrams and annotations are saved in XML files in the XML Metadata Interchange format (XMI), and then translated in LQN models through Extensible Stylesheet Language Transformation (XSLT).

- Lindermann, Thümmler, Klemm, Lohmann, and Waldhorst (Lindermann, *et al.*, 2002) develop an algorithm for deriving performance models based on Generalized Semi-Markov Processes from UML state and activity diagrams. These diagrams are annotated with exponentially distributed or deterministic delays applied to events, and timed events trigger a state transition. Annotations are based on an extension of the UML Performance Profile (OMG, 2001).

The Architectural Performance Modelling Method presented in this thesis is similar in spirit to these general methods, in the sense that it describes a method to develop performance models (based on two types of sub-models) for performance estimation. Nevertheless, these general methods to performance estimation are based on too general descriptions of the software architectures, making them difficult to apply to a parallel programming application. As it is shown later, the Architectural Performance Modelling Method bases its estimations on models created from common architectural patterns used in parallel programming, simplifying both the process of model creation and the process of parallel application development.

3.2.2 Methods based on Architectural Patterns

Architectural Patterns identify frequently used architectural solutions, and commonly are used to describe software architectures. Each pattern is described by its structure (what are the components and their responsibilities) and its behaviour (how the components interact). Some approaches consider software specification of architectural patterns, and derive their corresponding performance models. Normally, they use UML specification. The main idea is to identify a direct correspondence between a pattern and its performance model, which can be immediately derived.

- Petriu and Wang (Petriu & Wang, 1999; Petriu, 2000) consider a significant set of architectural patterns (pipe and filters, client/server, broker, layers, critical section and master-slave) specified by UML collaboration diagrams, that are combined class and sequence diagrams, showing explicitly the collaborating objects. The approach shows the corresponding performance models based on LQN models. Moreover, they propose a systematic approach to building performance models of complex software architectures based on combinations of the considered patterns. The approach follows the SPE methodology, and generates the software and system execution models by applying graph transformation techniques. Software architectures are specified using UML collaboration, deployment and use case diagrams. The sequence diagram part of the collaboration is used to obtain the execution model (which is represented as a UML activity diagram); the class part is used to obtain the system execution model (which is represented as a LQN model). Use case diagrams provide information on the workloads, and deployment diagrams allow for the allocation of software components to hardware sites.

- Gomaa and Menascè (Gomaa & Menascè, 2000) investigate the design and performance modelling of component interaction patterns for client/server systems. Such patterns define and encapsulate the way client and server components of software architecture communicate with each other via connectors. The idea is to start with UML design models of component interconnection patterns, using class diagrams (to model their static aspects) and collaboration diagrams (to depict the dynamic interactions between component and connector objects, that is, instances of the classes in the class diagrams). Such models are then provided with additional performance annotations, and translated into an XML notation, in order to capture both the architecture and performance parameters in one notation. The performance models of the considered patterns are EQN and their definition, based on previous work of the authors, depends on the type of communication. The EQN model solution is obtained by Markov chain analysis or approximate analytical methods.

- Petriu and Shen (Petriu & Shen, 2002) develop performance models based on LQN models from a description of software architecture based on architectural patterns. They use UML activity diagrams, annotated as defined in the UML Performance Profile (OMG, 2001). The approach is based on Graph Grammar-based derivation, which is implemented using an automated graph transformation through the PROGRESS tool. The objective is to achieve a UML to LQN transformation through the UML Performance Profile, but the paper presents no performance analysis results.

These approaches are perhaps the most similar to the Architectural Performance Modelling Method, since they all use architectural patterns as a base for model creation, their models are based on queuing models, and they use a method approach based on the SPE methodology. Nevertheless, these approaches were originally developed for dealing with architectural patterns provided by the general programming literature, and not with architectural patterns describing parallel systems. Hence, they do not cover common software architectures for parallel programming. Moreover, their models are developed for executing on a sequential computer system, which normally do not take into consideration important issues during parallel execution —such as the effect of non-determinism over the execution time— which tend to increase simulation costs. The Architectural Performance Modelling Method deals with this issues by *(a)* using Architectural Pattern for Parallel Programming (Ortega-Arjona & Roberts, 1998a) as common architectural pattern specifically developed for parallel programming, and *(b)* developing parallel models that execute on the real parallel system, which takes into consideration a real parallel execution environment and, at the same time, decreases simulation costs.

3.2.3 Simulation Methods

Some approaches to software performance estimation are based on simulation methods that consider simulation packages to define the model, and whose structure and input parameters are derived from the information obtained from UML diagrams.

- The approach proposed by Arief and Speirs (Arief & Speirs, 1999a; Arief & Speirs, 1999b; Arief & Spiers, 2000; Arief, 2001) develop an automatic tool for deriving simulation models from UML diagrams, as a simulation framework. The UML diagrams describe the classes and behaviour of a particular software architecture. The approach consists of transforming such UML diagrams into a simulation model described as an XML document. The XML notation used to describe the simulation model has been called SimML (Simulation Modeling Language). This model is then translated into a simulation program, which can be executed, and provides performance results. What makes this approach particularly interesting is that the simulation model is decoupled from its implementation. This makes it possible to implement the simulation model using different languages. A proposed UML tool allows the used to draw class and sequence diagrams, and to specify the information needed for the automatic generation of the process oriented simulation model. The authors develop two different back-ends for translating the SimML model into simulation programs written in C++Sim and JavaSim.

- The approach by De Miguel, Lambolais, Hannouz, Betgè-Brezetz, and Piekarec (De Miguel, *et al.*, 2000) proposes extensions of UML diagrams to express temporal requirements and resource usage, and their automatic evaluation. The interest of this work is on the specification of architecture and requirements of real-time systems, which pays special attention to timeliness, performance and schedulability. The extension is based on the use of stereotypes, tagged values, and stereotyped constraints. These standard UML extension techniques are used for specifying a UML profile where they collectively specialise and tailor UML for specific domain process. Constraints represent specific semantics of modelling elements with linguistic notations, stereotypes define new meta-model constructors, and tagged values identify new parameters or information associated with the modelling elements. UML diagrams are used as input for the automatic generation of scheduling and simulation models. Software architectures are specified using the extended UML diagrams without restrictions of the type of diagrams to be used. The diagrams commonly employed include the class, collaboration and activity diagrams. Then, these UML diagrams are used as input for the automatic generation of the corresponding simulation models in OPNET. There are two tools used: Analysis Model Generator (AMG), which implicitly defines a middleware model that affects the scheduling analysis; and Simulation Model Generator (SMG), which allows an automatic generation of OPNET model. They also define a middleware model for scheduling analysis.

The simulation model is defined by instantiating with the application information the generic models that represent the various UML metaclasses. The approach generates submodels for each application element and combines them into a unique simulation model of the UML application. The approach provides also a feedback mechanism: after the model has been analysed and simulated, some results are included in the tagged values. This constitutes a relevant feature, which ease the software architecture design in obtaining feedback from the performance evaluation results.

The proposed performance evaluation sequence is as follows:

1. Construction of the architectural model of the system to be analysed. This is done by a UML CASE tool. UML elements are annotated with stereotypes, tagged values, and stereotyped constraints in order to provide parameters to the simulation step. An XMI representation of the UML model is exported and used in the next phases.

2. Configuration of the simulation. Given that the UML model might contain different alternative scenarios and alternative behavioural specifications for the same elements, during this phase it is possible to choose which scenarios and which behaviours to execute.

3. Configuration of the simulation parameters. These parameters are essentially statistics to collect, which filter to apply to simulation results, and the length of the simulation period.

4. Generation of the OPNET simulation model.

5. Execution of the OPNET simulation model.

Simulation results are finally displayed using OPNET facilities, and may provide hints to reconfigure the UML architecture or used as a criteria for architecture selection.

- Henning and Eckhardt (Henning & Eckhardt, 2001) and Henning, Hentschel, and Tyack (Henning *et al.*, 2003b) describe a UML-based simulation framework for early performance assessment of software/hardware systems described as UML sequence and deployment diagrams. The framework follows a design-evaluation-feedback cycle. The simulation cycle starts with a collection of UML diagrams, from which a subset is extracted and compiled into an XML document describing the simulation experiment. The UML deployment diagrams are used to describe the physical environment on which the software system executes. Also, the UML collaboration diagrams are used to model the workload applied to the system and the internal behaviour of the application being modelled. A converter module generates code for the network and behaviour components of the simulator. The simulator itself is based on the discrete event simulation package OMNet++. It contains core modules and specific SPE extensions (i.e., an scheduler and a workflow execution engine) as well as pre-modelled components. The statistics of performance observations collected during the execution of the simulator can be fed back into the original UML model as tagged values. The same approach is used in Henning *et al.* (2003a) for the automatic generation of small components emulating the behaviour of a real one.

Even though the approaches described above are similar to the Architectural Performance Modelling Method —since they are based on simulation models developed from the information extracted from UML diagrams—, they have the disadvantage of being dependent of a particular simulation language, which commonly does not consider several parallel issues (such as simultaneous execution of software components or communication and synchronisation between them). Including such issues as part of the simulation model and language would increase simulation costs, and at the same time, make them considerably more complex to be used and understood. In contrast, the Architectural Performance Modelling Method presented here develops simple simulation models —which are based on queuing structures that are easy to program in most programming languages. Moreover, these simulation models are developed to be expressly executed on a parallel environment.

3.2.4 Applications and Case Studies

Some approaches present the generation of performance models from a software specification through an application example or a case study. They consider UML specification and different types of performance models.

- Smith and Williams (Smith & Williams, 1997) present an example to illustrate the derivation of a performance model from an object-oriented design model, and propose the use of the SPEED tool, that supports the SPE methodology, to evaluate object-oriented systems. Starting from a set of scenarios described by Message Sequence Charts (MSC), execution graphs (EG) are derived that define the software execution model, and then, by the modeller specification of computer resource requirements, a system execution model is defined. The model is analysed by approximate analytical methods or by simulation integrated in the SPEED tool. This work is related to the Williams & Smith (1998) approach.

- Pooley and King (Pooley & King, 1999) describe some preliminary ideas on how to derive a queuing network model from UML specification of a system. Their goal is to integrate the performance estimation with the system design process. They suggest that successful efforts towards this goal most likely come from projects that attempt to build performance analysis directly into accepted design method such as UML. They describe how the various kinds of UML diagrams can be used for performance evaluation purposes. Use case diagrams are used to specify the workloads and the various classes of requests of the system being modelled, by identifying actors in use case diagrams with workloads applied to the system. Implementation diagrams (deployment diagrams) are used to define contention and to quantify the available system resources, by mapping on a queuing network model representing the computational resources (service centres in the QN) and communication links (queues in the QN). The idea is to define a correspondence between combined deployment and component diagrams and queuing network models, by mapping components and links to service centres. Sequence diagrams can be used as traces to drive a simulation program. Finally, they suggest modelling of UML state diagrams using Markovian models. To demonstrate their approach, a queuing network model is derived from a UML description of an ATM system. The approach adds textual notations to UML diagrams to include useful information for performance evaluation (i.e., time labels in sequence diagrams). Such annotations are used to produce more complete models of software systems. It should be noted that their approach, in general, can be applied regardless the particular performance model derived.

In this paper, the UML sequence diagram are initially thought to have the potential to generate and display useful information relating the performance. In the end, it is decided that the sequence diagrams are more suited to being a display format rather than a detailed behavioural specification format. It is mentioned that the sequence diagrams have been used as traces of events generated from a simple discrete event simulator. The work have also found a mapping from the deployment diagram to queuing models, and have built a simulation library around collaborations with state machines. The challenge lies in setting the foundation for an integrated performance engineering approach on the whole UML notation. The use of collaboration diagrams with embedded state machines seems promising, as well as its extension to incorporate collaborations within deployment diagrams.

- King and Pooley (King & Pooley, 1999) describe how UML designs can be transformed systematically into Petri nets, showing how to generate Stochastic Timed Petri Net (STPN) models from the UML specification of systems with an example. They consider use case diagrams and combined diagrams consisting of a collaboration diagram with state diagrams (i.e., statecharts) of all the collaborating objects embedded in them. The idea is to translate each state diagram that represents an object of the collaboration diagram into a Petri Net: states and transitions in the state diagram are represented by places and transitions in the Petri Net, respectively. The obtained Petri Nets can be combined to obtain a unique STPN model that represents the whole system, specifically a Generalized Stochastic Petri Net (GSPN) (Ajmone *et al.*, 1986; Marsan, *et al.*, 1995). The merging of nets is only explained via the running example, i.e. the paper does not include a general merging procedure. The GSPN can be analysed by specific tools such as the SPNP package. Further explorations of systematic mappings from UML is undertaken by developing a graphical front-end. The possibility of employing LQN (on top of Petri Nets) as the targets of UML transformation is also considered.

- Pooley (Pooley, 1999) describes how to derive Stochastic Process Algebra models from UML specifications. More precisely, the starting point is like in King & Pooley (1999): the specification of a system via a combined diagram consisting of a collaboration diagram with state diagrams (i.e., statecharts) of all the collaborating objects embedded within them. The idea is to produce a Stochastic Process Algebra description of each object of the collaboration diagram, and to combine them into a unique model. This paper shows how this can be done on a real although simple example. It presents also an attempt to generate a continuous-time Markov chain directly from the combined UML diagram of the running example. The key observation here is that, at any time, each object of the collaboration diagram must be in one and only one of its internal states. The combination of the object current states is called "marking". The idea is to derive all possible markings by following through the interactions: this allows building the corresponding state transition diagram and, then, the underlying Markov chain.

- King and Pooley (King & Pooley, 2000) propose a method for deriving performance models based on Generalized Stochastic Petri Nets (GSPN) (Ajmone *et al.*, 1986;

Marsan, *et al.*, 1995) from UML collaboration and statechart diagrams. They propose the use of a combination of UML diagrams (state diagrams embedded into collaboration diagrams) to express the global state of a system.

- Bernardi, Donatelli, and Merseguer (Bernardi *et al.*, 2002) derive a GSPN model from UML state and sequence diagrams. They define two levels of modelling: a class level and an instance level. The class level is represented by state diagrams, and it is used to describe the behaviour of single entities of a system. The instance level uses sequence diagrams to show patterns of interaction among objects (instances of classes). The GSPN model is then created merging together the information provided by the diagrams of the two kinds of levels.

- Petriu and Woodside (Petriu & Woodside, 2002) describe the UCM2LQN converter as a tool that automates the conversion of a Use Case Maps (UCM) scenario models into LQN performance models. A UCM is a collection of elements that describe one or more scenarios throughout a system. A scenario is represented by a path, shown as a line from a start point to an end point, and traversed by a token from start to end. Paths can be overlaid on components which represent functional or logical entities. Responsibilities on the path represent functions to be accomplished.

The performance modelling of this approach assumes that computational workload is associated with responsibilities, or is an overhead implied by crossings between components. Responsibilities are annotated by service demands (number of processor or disk operations, or calls to other services) and data store operations.

The tool is based on a Scenario to Performance Model Transformation Algorithm (SPT), doing the following:

1. Identify when the path crosses component boundaries;
2. Determine the type of messages sent or received when crossing component boundaries;
3. Capture the path structure and the correct sequence of path elements;
4. Create the LQN objects that correspond directly to UCM elements; and
5. Handle fork, joins, and loops.

The UCM2LQN converter connects high-level design in the form of UCMs with performance analysis using LQNs.

- Xiuping, McMullan, and Woodside (Xiuping *et al.*, 2003) propose an approach for performance prediction based on Component-based Software Engineering (CBSE) to develop *performance submodels* for components, and combine their action through a *system assembly model*. The idea is to obtain and specify performance information of already developed components, and use such an information to create the performance submodels. These submodels are developed using a queuing model (specifically, LQN), whose parameters characterise the workload when it is executed on a "standard" platform. These parameters include processor demands on a nominal architecture, service request parameters between elements of the component, and service request rates to stub services. However, it is not clear how such parameters are chosen.

In order to get a performance model of the system, submodel are assembled together to form a high level assembly model, derived from the software architecture of the system. This model is also based on LQN models, representing slot components and "glue" for integrating them.

Thus, a system performance model is created from the component assembly model and the component submodels, using a tool called *component assembler.* This tool generates the task instances and their parameters, based on the information from the assembly model through an automated process. Hence, this approach presents a tool and a method to automatically generate performance for component-based systems. Its main advantages are *(a)* its parameterisation reflects the software component performance attributes under different environments, *(b)* component submodels are reusable, just as components themselves, and *(c)* interface and stubs are defined in the component submodel, and can be used for calibration tests.

The Architectural Performance Modelling Method is similar to these approaches in the sense that it uses UML diagrams and descriptions (provided by the architectural pattern descriptions) to develop simulation models based on queuing models an Markov chains. Nevertheless, as these approaches refer to a particular application or case study, their description seems to be difficult to be used in a more general form. Furthermore, these approaches do not develop applications or case studies for parallel programming. On the other hand, as the Architectural Performance Modelling Method is based on the concept of architectural pattern, it does provide a certain generality to be used in more than a single parallel application or case study.

3.3 Approaches to Performance Estimation of Parallel and Distributed Systems

Quantitative analysis of performance estimation has been recognised to be useful for parallel and distributed software design. Specifically, it is generally accepted that performance analysis should be integrated in the development life cycle of parallel software from early stages. To this aim, several approaches have been recently proposed to integrate or combine performance analysis and software architecture specification to parallel and distributed programming. In this section, we present a brief description of some approaches, focusing on the proposed methods and the type of performance model, the implementation, and how easily the obtained performance results can provide feedback to the software designer. The different approaches have been proposed considering the use of analytical and simulation approaches.

3.3.1 Analytical Approaches

The analytical approaches consider the use of a set of parameters combined by means of a mathematical rule, allowing the prediction of a performance attribute (see Section 3.1.1). So, the analytical approaches to parallel and distributed performance analysis are as follows:

- Architectural Modelling Box (AMB) (Jonkers *et al.*, 1998) is a modelling and design language that provides a unified basis for the design process as well as functional an quantitative analysis of distributed systems. The aim of this language is to bring together system designers and performance modellers by introducing a design language that includes quantitative properties of the system. AMB is formed by a graphical language that models systems, their behaviour, as well as other relevant data. In general, AMB models consists of two parts: the resource or entity model, that describes the static aspects of the system (i.e. its components, their physical properties, and the way they can interact), and the behaviour model, that describes the dynamic aspects (i.e. the process or actions performed by the system, in terms of related activities). Specifications written in the AMB design language can then be automatically translated into models for performance analysis (such as graph models, timed Petri nets, or hybrid models) or for functional analysis.

- Kähkipuro (Kähkipuro, 1999) presents a framework for creating, using, and maintaining performance models of object-oriented distributed systems. The architecture of this performance modelling framework consists of four main element:

1. The method of decomposition (MOD) that provides the foundation of the framework by defining an algorithm for finding an approximate solution for performance models

2. UML based performance modelling techniques, which provide the means for modelling complex information systems by using abstraction for separating application level issues from the use of technical resources.

3. The Performance Modelling Methodology, which provides a link to the Software Engineering process by indicating how the proposed UML modelling techniques can be used at different stages of system development to produce useful performance models for the system.

4. The Object-Oriented Performance Modelling and Analysis Tool (OAT), whose purpose is to automate some tasks required by the framework, such as: *(a)* transformation of UML-based performance models into a format solvable by the MOD algorithm; *(b)* implementation of the MOD algorithm to produce an approximate solution for the performance model; and *(c)* conversion of the solution into a set of relevant performance metrics that are used in the performance modelling methodology.

This approach makes use of four performance model representations, each one with its own notation. The mappings between them are defined by the framework architecture:

1. *UML representation.* A description of the system with UML diagrams.

2. *PML representation.* An accurate textual notation for representing performance related items in the UML diagrams. The purpose is filtering out the UML information that has no significance for performance modelling.

3. *AQN representation.* A description of the system in an augmented queuing networks (AQN) format that may contain simultaneous resource possessions and allows the MOD algorithm to solve the model.

4. *QN representation.* A description of separable queuing networks with mutual dependencies that correlate them to the same overall system.

The UML notations employed in this work are class diagrams (for deriving the resource or queues), as well as collaboration and sequence diagrams (which are used in conjunction with one or more workload specifications to describe the behaviour of the application and the infrastructure of the system). It is mentioned that the state and activity diagrams could also be used for expressing the performance related information conveniently.

- Hoeben (Hoeben, 2000) describes how UML diagrams can be used for performance evaluation of distributed systems, discussing some rules that can be used to express or add information useful to derive performance evaluation from the various UML diagrams. The approach uses UML class and component diagrams to represent information used for modelling the system dynamics. Sequence and collaboration diagrams are used to model the behaviour of the distributed system, and deployment diagrams represent processors and network connections. This work proposes some UML extensions based on the use of stereotypes and tagged values, and some rules to propagate user requests specified by UML models to define the performance model. These rules allow performance evaluation of UML models at various levels of abstraction, and a prototype performance model tool is derived from the combination of diagrams to automatically create performance estimates based on QN models. This prototype tool is the used to calculate the system's response time and utilisation. However, the author provides just some hints on how to obtain a QN model from the UML model of a system, and not a complete tool description.

The UML use case diagrams are used for capturing the tasks that the system has to complete (i.e., its workload), and the tool calculates response times for each of these tasks. The interaction diagram (i.e. the sequence and collaboration diagrams) provide the translation of user tasks to hardware resources. In order to avoid the diagrams becoming too big, multiple interaction diagrams are used to get the entire decomposition, where each diagram represents the behaviour of a single method. The class and component diagrams are not of great importance for performance estimation, but they are used to model information that is later used to understand the dynamics of the system. The deployment diagram convey the properties of the processors and network connections, which are useful in performance estimation. More information needed for performance estimation can be supplied using the standard extension mechanisms, i.e. tagged values and stereotypes, but this only shows that there needs to be a more robust way for incorporating performance related information into UML design.

- Andolfi, Aquilani, Balsamo and Inverardi (Andolfi *et al.*, 2000) propose an approach to automatically generate queuing network models from software architecture specifications described by means of Message Sequence Charts (MSC), that correspond to sequence diagrams in UML terminology. The idea is to analyse MSCs in terms of the trace languages (sequences of events) they generate, in order to single out the real degree of parallelism among components and their dynamic dependencies. The authors present an algorithm to perform this step. This approach is built on the previous work by Balsamo *et al.* (1998) to overcome the drawback of the high computational complexity due to possible state space explosion of the finite state model of the CHAM description.

- Gomaa and Menascè (Gomaa & Menascè, 2001) use UML diagrams to represent the interconnection pattern of a distributed software architecture. Class diagrams are used to illustrate the static view of a system, while collaboration diagrams show the dynamic behaviour. Collaboration diagrams are extended with new elements showing the interconnections and communication ports, and they are added with performance annotations written in XML. Such annotations refer to routing probability between objects, average message processing time, average message size, and average arrival rate of requests. Then they derive a performance model based on QN.

- Kähkipuro (Kähkipuro, 2001) proposes a framework on UML notation for describing performance models of component-based distributed systems. The performance model is based on Augmented Queuing Networks (AQN). The approach works as follows: UML diagrams are first converted into a textual notation called Performance Modeling Language (PML). The PML model is translated into an AQN, which is then solved with approximate techniques. The results obtained from the AQN model are subsequently propagated to the PML model, and finally, to the software architecture model.

These approaches for estimating the performance of parallel and distributed systems are based on analytical models, and they attempt to take into consideration as many aspects of parallel and distributed programming as they can, providing a certain level of accuracy. Nevertheless, as it has been discussed before (see Sections 2.1.2 and 3.1.2), the execution of a parallel program involves several non-deterministic issues that are difficult to take into consideration using analytical models. Hence, in order to deal with the complexity of parallel execution, they work with simple models, and provide an improvement on the accuracy of estimates. Several other methods use simulation models instead of analytical models. This is the case of the Architectural Performance Modelling Method.

3.3.2 Simulation Approaches

There are several simulation approaches that have been developed to estimate the performance of parallel and distributed systems. Some relevant approaches are listed as follows:

- DisCo (Distributed-Co-operation) (Jarvinen & Kurki-Sunio, 1991) is a formal specification method for reactive systems which incorporates a specification language, a method for using the language for building specifications, and a simulation tool supporting the method. It focuses on the collective behaviour of objects, i.e. how they cooperate with each other, as well as supporting an object-oriented approach. DisCo is based on the joint action approach which concentrates on the interaction between different components instead of the components themselves. This increases the level of abstraction, i.e. the bias towards particular hardware and software architecture is minimised.

  The DisCo language supports modularisation (due to its object-oriented paradigm) and incremental specification (which means that the level of the specification's details can be gradually increased until the desired level is met). A DisCo specification consists of a set of layers, which are composed of classes and actions. New layers can be constructed by composing two or more separate layers, or refining existing layers by superposition. The DisCo tool provides a way to validate a specification by using animated simulations. Animation makes specifications more understandable, and promotes communication between the people involved. The DisCo tool also supports graphical representation of execution scenarios, using Message Sequence Charts (MSC).

- Rapide (Luckham, 1996) is a computer language for defining and executing simulation models of distributed system architectures. It introduces an *interface connection architecture*, which means that every communication between modules is explicitly defined by connections between interfaces. In Rapide, an architecture consists of a set of *specification modules* (interfaces), a set of *connection rules* (for defining the communication between interfaces), and a set of *formal constraints* which determines whether a pattern of communication is legal or not. A *component* consists of a *module* and an *interface*. A module either encapsulates an executable prototype of the component, or it describes the hierarchical structure of the component (when a component is composed of other components). An interface defines what a module requires-from or provides-to other modules, and connections are defined between the features in interfaces.

The Rapide language is accompanied by a set of tools which help in the specification, design and testing of software modules and architectures. In general, the Rapide language is composed of five sub-languages:

1. *The Type Language* describes the interface components. It supports object-oriented and abstract data type styles of defining interfaces, as well as multiple interface inheritance.

2. *The Pattern Language* provides a general language for defining event-based reactive constructs or dynamic architectures.

3. *The Executable Language* is used for writing executable modules which are defined by a set of processes that observe and react to events.

4. *The Architecture Language* models the interface connection architecture and defines dataflow and synchronisation between modules.

5. *The Constraint Language* provides features for specifying formal constraints on the behaviour of components and architectures.

Rapide is very extensive, and provides a simulation tool using an event-based execution model, named POSET (Partially Ordered Set Of Events). Nevertheless, Rapide only supports purely behavioural simulation, and thus, does not adequately support performance estimation.

• Botti and Capra (Botti & Capra, 1996) propose an approach to model and evaluate concurrent applications based on Generalised Stochastic Petri Nets (GSPN). An interesting idea is that this approach considers experimental simulation over their target parallel architecture, and uses this information for performance prediction. The paper discusses experienced performance metrics and parameter assignment criteria, and characterise an application in terms of its performance and to support its mapping over a parallel platform.

The approach describes a methodology based on the Multi Micro Language (MML) and its related environment (MME). In an example, they describe the target hardware, composed of two processing units, based on a DEC LSI11 and a Motorola MC68010.

Both are connected with a serial link. The modelling by GSPNs consider the use of stochastic parameters, which are measured and retrieved to produce latter simulation models for performance prediction over the target parallel platform.

- Howell (Howell, 1996) proposes *Reverse Profiling*, which is a technique that applies an MPI performance model for a hardware platform to a user's program to generate an estimate of the run time on that platform. The performance model is automatically generated by running an "MPI characterisation" routine on the target parallel platform, rather than being crafted from in-depth knowledge of such a platform. It also includes a method for evaluating performance by computing delays using the profiling interface of MPI. Rather than use profiling to extract timing data from a run of the program, Reverse Profiling inserts estimated times.

The performance model consists of separate equations for each MPI function giving the average, minimum and maximum times for a given parallel platform and message size. Running this produces a LaTEX document, which is a "datasheet" for estimating the performance. The equations given in the model may be used for analytical performance predictions of a program to experiment with alternative designs at an early stage. Nevertheless, this approach is considered between analytical and simulation techniques, since it uses both for performance estimation. Based on the analytical model, simulation is introduced at the process level. Because it does not involve full simulation, each process keeps track of its own simulation time, and updates it whenever a function is called. This means that a normal trace can be generated. A model of any parallel machine may be used, and any MPI implementation can be used as the development environment.

- El-Sayed, Cameron, and Woodside (El-Sayed *et al.*, 1998) develop a process for automatic performance model-building for distributed systems, which starts from a design expressed in SDL processes and a set of scenarios, and produces a performance model. Initially, the process uses the SDL model, which is executed for the set of scenarios, recording traces from each scenario, and the performance model structure and data is extracted from the traces. The performance model is constructed using LQN models.

In order to build submodel from traces, five steps are followed:

1. Convert a trace into an *angio trace* (Hrischuk, *et al.*, 1995).

2. Identify the types of messages in the trace.

3.Identify the different services provided by each process.

4.Find the precedence relationship between activities in each service.

5.Map the software architecture model into an LQN model.

The performance models produced in this work reflect by construction the structure of the software or system design in SDL, combined with the coverage of scenarios. If some part of the design is not activated by the scenarios, then it will not be in the model.

- Autofocus (Huber *et al.*, 1998) is a tool prototype for the formally based development of reactive systems, mainly in the area of distributed systems. It supports system development by offering integrated, comprehensive, and mainly graphical description techniques for specifying different views and abstraction levels of the system. There are four different description techniques provided to cover the different views on the system:

    1.*System Structure Diagrams* (SSD) describe the static aspects of distributed systems by viewing them as a network of interconnected components with an ability to exchange messages over their communication channels.

    2.*Data Type Definitions* (DTD) represent the types of data processed by a distributed system in a textual notation.

    3.*State Transition Diagrams* (STD) describe the dynamic aspects, i.e. the behaviour of a distributed system and its components.

    4.*Extended Event Traces* (EET) provide an extra behavioural view of a distributed system (on top of STDs) through exemplary runs from a component-based view.

Autofocus supports component-oriented development of systems, where a component represents a structural part of the system, possibly described by different views using the description techniques above, which allow different levels of system granularity to be specified. Autofocus uses a prototyping and simulation approach for observing and validating the properties of a system being developed. To support this approach, Autofocus provides a tool component called "SimCenter" that facilitates: *(a)* the generation of executable prototypes; *(b)* the execution of these prototypes in a simulation environment; *(c)* the visualisation of executions using the same description techniques as used for designing the system; and *(d)* an optional connection between the simulation environment and third-party front-ends such as multimedia visualisation tools or external hardware systems. Both Autofocus and SimCenter are written entirely in the

Java programming language.

- The Performance Modelling for ATM based Applications and Services (PERMA-BASE) project (Akenhurst & Waters, 1999a; Akenhurst *et al.*, 1999; Utton *et al.*, 1999; Waters *et al.*, 2001) was carried out by British Telecom and the University of Kent at Canterbury. This project deals with the automatic generation of performance models from software systems specified in UML. The aim of this project is to provide performance feedback as part of the object-oriented design process for distributed systems, through an automatic generation of a performance model directly from the system design model. This project tries to address the lack of use of physical environment (hardware) specification in distributed system designs. The software system is described in terms of the following specifications or model views:

  1. *Workload specification.* A description of the workloads (human operators or other systems) that drives the system; this includes classes of components considered as external to the system.

  2. *Application specification.* A description of the behaviour of the software system, specifying the class of components that constitute the software or logical behaviour of the system, i.e. the system logic components (software, firmware or hardware logic).

  3. *Execution environment specification.* A description of the physical environment, identifying classes of components that are physical components providing resources used by the application during system operation (e.g. processors, networks, and other resources that the system operates over).

  4. *System scenario specification.* A specification of a particular system instance, describing the configuration of the system (which components are present, and how they are connected). This specification defines the instances of declared components (of the three above) and the connections between them, which form a specific system architecture or configuration.

UML is used to specify the workloads, the application behaviour and the execution environment. The descriptions above are combined into a Composite Model Data Structure (CMDS) of the entire system. The CMDS is then translated into a performance model (a discrete event simulation), whose execution provides feedback that is reported back to the CMDS.

This project tried to use, and adapt if necessary, the UML notations for the representation of the four domain specification areas. For example, the Execution Environment Specification can be described using the class diagram, while the System Scenario view can be represented using the deployment diagram.

As a follow on from the PERMABASE project, Akenhurst and Waters (Akenhurst & Waters, 1999b) propose a list of UML deficiencies with respect to performance modelling.

- Ortega-Arjona and Roberts (Ortega-Arjona & Roberts, 1999c) propose an approach to performance estimation of a parallel software architecture based on Architectural Performance Models. These models encompass the design knowledge of architectural patterns for parallel programming, a component simulator, and a performance analysis for estimating the performance of a parallel application. The basic idea is to estimate the contribution to performance from the Software Structure, described by an architectural pattern. The component simulator generates probabilistic processing times of sequential components, using a queuing model based on Markovian chains. The workloads are set specifically for a particular use case, which represents the normal operation of the parallel program as defined by its architectural pattern. Finally, the performance analysis of the results produces estimates that represent average execution times of the parallel system, depending on the use case.

In order to decrease the cost of simulating a parallel environment (hardware and software), this approach proposes to take advantage of such an environment to carry out its own simulation. This fact simplifies the use of more complex models for describing parallel system and parallel software architectures.

- Ayles, Field, and Magee (Ayles *et al.*, 2003) propose a stochastic extension to the Finite State Process (FSP) notation, as part of the Labelled Transition System Analyser (LTSA) tool, adding probabilistic choice and arbitrary time delays modelled by clocks. The analysis of this extension is carried out using discrete-event simulation. The result of this extension is a Stochastic Finite State Process (SFSP), which defines scripts as a collection of constant definitions, named processes, performance measures, and named process compositions. For simulation, the SFSP processes are translated into stochastic timed automata, which essentially are stochastic extensions of the original labelled transition system. The simulation explicitly traverses the state space of the automata using distribution sampling to resolve probabilistic choice and non-determinism, and to set clocks.

- Gemund (Gemund, 2003) presents an hybrid approach combining analytical modelling with a performance simulation language called PAMELA (PerformAnce ModElling LAnguage). The approach aims to minimise prediction cost, while providing an accuracy sufficient to enable code and mapping decisions.

PAMELA allows a symbolic analysis that enables its models as symbolic performance models, which trade accuracy for the lowest possible solution cost. The PAMELA performance modelling process is based on the construction of program and machine models, for which a PAMELA model is constructed (manually or generated). Once expressed in the language, the both models are gathered and compiled into a symbolic performance model.

The paper presents a group of modelling examples to demonstrate the approach to modelling parallel programs and machines. These examples consider pipelining, branching, vectorisation, and others. The predictions are validated by their comparison with actual measurements on the parallel system, reporting the prediction errors. These range from 10% to 77%, and the author claims that the latter are due to trivial modelling inaccuracies rather than inherent inaccuracy of the PAMELA approach.

The approaches based on simulation methods for estimating the performance of parallel and distributed systems seem to be the most similar to the Architectural Performance Modelling Method. Most of them develop methods to create simulation models based on a description of the parallel or distributed system to model. Nevertheless, only the approach by Ortega-Arjona and Roberts (Ortega-Arjona & Roberts, 1999c) is based on architectural patterns for parallel programming, as common software structures used to organise the simultaneous execution of software components, and as a criteria for selecting different organisations of parallel programs. The rest of the approaches pay a lot of attention to several issues regarding simulation modelling and parallel execution, but they do not consider a software design base (like architectural patterns) to be reused in other design situations.

3.4 Architectural Design Approaches for Parallel Software

Parallel programming is based on the division of work among multiple processors that execute simultaneously, cooperating with a common objective. However, because most highly complex programming problems can be partitioned in different ways, Parallel Software Design results to be a difficult task, meaning that a single problem programming may have several parallel solutions. Over the last few years, this fact has resulted on a growing interest in Parallel Software Design. Particularly, some research efforts have been carried out to investigate paradigms and techniques to support and evolve the design of parallel software, based on an structural or architectural design approaches. The objective of using these architectural design approaches is to minimise the range of partitioning options, selecting common coordination structures used previously in experienced parallel software programs. Research efforts on architectural design for parallel and distributed systems have been proposed capturing and expressing the basic organisation, elements, experience, methodology and formalism in parallel and distributed programming, and trying to develop methods for performance estimation.

In this section, we describe three of these architectural design approaches that we consider are the most significant and similar to our Architectural Performance Modelling Method (based on Architectural Patterns), by identifying and capturing general Parallel Software Design experience. These approaches are the Archetypes/eText project (Chandy, 1994), the Algorithmic Skeletons (Cole, 1989), and Structural Modeling (Schopf, 1997). We consider them as the most significant because they provide similar features, like a description of common configurations used as coordination in Parallel Software Design, a development strategy, a performance modelling for estimating the execution time of resulting parallel systems, and a classification for selecting coordination structures.

It is important to mention that in this section we only aim to describe each one of these approaches around these features. Nevertheless, these descriptions will be revisited in chapter 8, comparing and analysing commonalities and differences with our research work.

3.4.1 The Archetypes/eText Project

Archetypes were conceived by K. Mani Chandy, as a central part of the Archetypes/ eText project in the California Institute of Technology. Briefly, this project proposes a system of parallel software construction, intended to provide a systematic process for teaching parallel programming constructs, and for capturing designer's rationale and experiences in various parallel machines, algorithms and problems (Rifkin, 1993).

Archetypes — Definition and Description

Even though refinements to the definition have been made, most of them are just variations of the original definition proposed by Chandy (Chandy, 1994):

> *"An archetype is (a) a method of problem-solving, (b) a program design strategy associated with the method, and (c) a collection of exemplar problems to which the method could be applied, and a collection providing reference implementations in different languages and runtime systems and on different architectures of each examplar problem"*

The original program design strategy associated with an archetypes has several parts. These parts are expected to capture information about the structure, experience and techniques for the development of applications based on an specific archetype (Chandy, 1994):

1. The structural description of a class of programs, including their common control and data-flow structures. Consider for example, the graphic representation of the control and dataflow structures for the One-deep Divide-and-Conquer Archetype, showed respectively in Figures 3.2 and 3.3.
2. Methods for parallelising sequential code from specifications.
3. Rationale about the correctness and performance of archetype programs.
4. Suggestions for test suites and debugging, based on the structural description and from experience of similar applications.
5. Suggestions for performance tuning, based on models and experience, on different target computer architectures.
6. Detailed documentation and suggestions for an specific application.
7. Descriptions of other archetypes used by this archetype.

Archetypes offer a software construction guidance method at three different levels: Archetypes, Applications, and Programs (Rifkin, 1993):

- *Archetypes level.* The Archetypes level is the highest in the method. It presents a catalogue containing archetypes as general patterns for problem-solving. Each one represents a strategy that has been used as a solution for a particular problem using parallel programming. Therefore, many problems can be solved choosing and applying an appropriate archetype. Examples of archetypes are Divide-and-Conquer, Matrix Operations, Mesh Computation, Dynamic Programming, Spectral Methods, etc. The catalogue of archetypes is presented in a narrative form that describes each archetype.

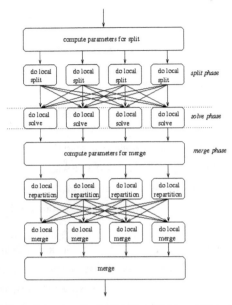

Figure 3.2 Control structure for the One-deep Divide and Conquer Archetype (Chandy, 1994; Rifkin, 1993).

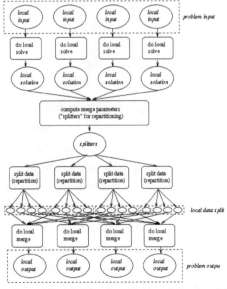

Figure 3.3 Data-flow structure in One-deep Divide and Conquer Archetype (Chandy, 1994; Rifkin, 1993).

Each description is intended to unify all examples into a common algorithmic framework, capturing information and experience about the way it solves the problem.

* *Applications level.* At this level, an archetype is refined to show how it can be used in a specific application. However, no implementation detail is addressed. The description of an application is properly intended to explain which problems can and cannot be solved by the archetype, using again the narrative form.

* *Programs level.* Finally, at the Programs level of refinement, programs and source code are presented as particular examples of applications, using a particular programming language for a specific parallel or sequential machine. This level tries to capture and provide the experience obtained during the implementation of such programs. The narrative form is again used to describe both programs and source code.

Narrative description

As mentioned above, a uniform narrative form is used in the description of components (Archetypes, Applications and Programs). This form contains the following elements (Rifkin, 1993):

* *Documentation.* An introduction or explanatory text that describes a given component, discusses its methodology approach, gives clues to recognise the problem and provides a reference list of other related components.

* *Algorithm.* A formal statement of the problem addressed by a component is provided, containing a description of the steps to develop a solution of the stated problem.

* *Correctness abstraction.* A correctness argument/proof discussion is presented, where verification issues are confronted and discussed. This point should provide a systematic correctness outline, including proof obligations for components, safety and progress considerations, invariants and termination verification strategies.

* *Efficiency abstraction.* A performance analysis covering points like efficiency analysis overview, parallel issues such as granularity, mapping and communication, comparisons between task-parallel and data-parallel approaches, and so on. This analysis usually includes examples of implementations using a particular language and a target machine at the Applications and Programs levels.

* *Debugging Tips/ Test Suite Design.* Techniques are provided to help debugging common errors and capture design and implementation experience. Some creative pseudo-code strategies are provided to develop a test suite for each component.

This five-element way of describing Archetypes, Applications and Programs was designed to introduce the reader to an archetypal language that uniformly guides the entire design process from conceptual requirements to code (Rifkin, 1993). The Archetypes/eText project goal is to develop a library of parallel program archetypes that can reduce the effort required to create correct and efficient parallel programs, using particular languages and machines (Chandy, 1994).

Parallel Program Development Strategy

Attending to their description, archetypes are used in the context of a parallel program development strategy. This general strategy is briefly described as follows (Massingill & Chandy, 1997):

1. A sequential algorithm or problem description is proposed.

2. An archetype is identified as an appropriate solution.

3. An initial archetype-based version of the algorithm is developed by structuring the original algorithm to fit the archetype. As this initial archetype-based version of the algorithm can be executed sequentially, giving the same results as parallel execution, it is possible to correct and debug the sequential program using familiar tools and techniques.

4. The initial archetype-based version is transformed into an equivalent algorithm suitable for efficient execution on the target architecture, using transformations that preserve semantics and hence correctness.

5. Implement the efficient archetype-based version of the algorithm using a language or library suitable for the target architecture.

Performance Models

Originally, the archetypes approach considers performance as an optimization of the sequential execution time. Performance concerns are introduced late in the program development strategy, in a "fix-it-later" approach.

Archetypes address performance issues through simple performance models, describing methods for determining granularity and for mapping processes to processors. The objective of these performance models is mainly to simplify the process of performance analysis by exploiting commonalities in programs. In general, archetype performance models are expressed in the form of equations. For example, an attempt of performance analysis using equations is presented by Rifkin & Massingill (1998), aiming for refinement of existing parallel applications. They propose a performance model in two steps:

1. *Analysis.* The program is analysed, producing an equation that involves some benchmarked values. This is achieved by decomposing the program into a set of sub-programs, and expressing their running times in terms of the benchmark values. The finer the decomposition grain makes the model equation more predictive of the program behaviour.

2. *Instantiation.* A number representing a prediction of the program's expected running time is produced from the equation with the appropriate benchmarked values. Benchmarked values are simply substituted into the equations developed during the previous step.

Structured Induction

Structured induction is the base for this decomposition approach and equation production to performance modelling. it allows the expected running time of a parallel program to be computed from the expected running times of its components. For example, a program s is decomposed into two sequential programs, s_1 and s_2 (Rifkin & Massingill, 1998):

$$S = S_1;S_2$$

The running time $\mathfrak{R}(S)$ of program S can be modelled as:

$$\mathfrak{R}(S) = \mathfrak{R}(S_1) + \mathfrak{R}(S_2)$$

Since s_1 and s_2 consist of a single computation or communication, $\mathfrak{R}(s_1)$ and $\mathfrak{R}(s_2)$ can be modelled as the maximum expected running times of that computation or communication on all of the processors. As a result for the expected running time, we have:

$$\mathfrak{R}(S) = max\mathfrak{R}_p(S_1) + max\mathfrak{R}_p(S_2) \qquad \forall p$$

Archetypes Summary

Archetypes are abstractions that capture the common features of a class of problems, relating them with a parallelisation strategy to produce a pattern of data-flow and communication. Archetypes describe and model coordination structures, aiming and looking for structural solutions in parallelism. They present a development strategy considering three levels of software construction —Archetypes, Application and Programs—, being Archetypes at the high-level organisation of components. About performance modelling, the Archetype approach provides performance models and analysis in the form of simple equations, exploiting commonalities found in parallel programs. Finally, Archetypes provide a clear classification scheme to organise their structural configurations. More recently, archetypes are considered by their own authors to be a particular kind of design patterns in the Software Patterns sense, "restricted" for the modeling of the computation and communication structure of a parallel program (Rifkin & Massingill, 1996; Massingill & Chandy, 1997).

3.4.2 Algorithmic Skeletons

Algorithmic Skeletons have been proposed as a functional programming approach and methodology for parallel programming. In general, Algorithmic Skeletons are used in the form of implementation templates (Cole, 1989).

Skeletons — Definition and Description

Some definitions of Algorithmic Skeletons are:

- *"Algorithmic forms that abstract the useful computational structures from applications"* (Darlington & To, 1993).
- *"An algorithmic form common to a range of programming applications, as polymorphic higher-order functions that represent common parallelisation patterns"* (Darlington *et al.*, 1993).
- *"High-level, parallel programming language constructs encapsulating the expression of parallelism, communication, synchronisation and embedding, and having an associated cost complexity"* (Campbell, 1996).
- *"Generic patterns of parallel computation which can be parameterised by a small number of sequential functions or procedures (called here customising functions)"* (Deldarie et al., 1995)

From these definitions, it can be noticed that, essentially, skeletons are useful patterns of parallel computation and interaction that can be packaged up as constructs, that is, programming elements having structure but lacking detail. These constructs can be parameterised by other pieces of code, possibly referencing or not explicit parallelism.

Skeletons can be represented using an informal graphical description (Campbell,

1996), but more commonly, they make use of a functional language, like Haskel (Dar-lington & To, 1993; Darlington *et al.*, 1993). Consider for example the representation of the FARM skeleton in Figure 3.4.

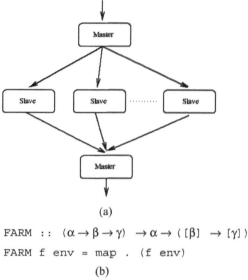

(a)

$$\text{FARM} \ :: \ (\alpha \rightarrow \beta \rightarrow \gamma) \ \rightarrow \alpha \rightarrow (\ [\beta] \ \rightarrow [\gamma] \ )$$

FARM f env = map . (f env)

(b)

Figure 3.4 Representation of the FARM skeleton: (a) graphical, and (b) expressed in Haskel (Darlington & To, 1993; Darlington *et al.*, 1993).

When used as building blocks in a functional language, skeletons are represented by an interface or *meaning*, and by an implementation or *behaviour* for a set of computa-tional problems. The declarative meaning of a skeleton can be established by its func-tional language definition, which is independent of any particular implementation. The specific behaviour of a skeleton depends on the particular parallel machine on which the skeleton is implementable. All aspects of parallelism in a program derive from the behaviour of the skeletons contained in the program on the machine in question. Func-tions used by or contained in skeletons are executed sequentially (Darlington & To, 1993; Darlington *et al.*, 1993).

Implementations of skeletons for parallel systems provide several advantages (Dar-lington & To, 1993):

• Programming complexity is reduced by allowing the programmer to first address the correctness or meaning of the program, and then to tackle the behaviour to ensure effi-ciency.

- Take previous experience to quickly and efficiently produce specialised implementations on particular machines, without low level programming concerns.
- Performance can be predicted through the use of performance models attached to each skeleton.
- Portability is provided by various implementations on different machines.

Examples of skeletons are Divide and Conquer, Iterative Combination, Cluster, Task Queue, Pipe, Farm, Geometric, Client-Server, etc. (Campbell, 1996; Darlington & To, 1993; Darlington *et al.*, 1993; Marr & Cole, 1993, Cole, 1989).

Skeletons Development Process — Program Transformation

Program transformation is used in the development process of skeleton programs at all levels. At high-level, program transformation can be used to transform problem specifications into initial skeleton forms. At middle levels it can be used to convert programs from one skeleton form to another (e.g. for the purposes of portability). At the low-level, program transformation can be used to fine-tune, for example, varying the grain-size used in an application, or configuring the program for a particular machine size. Whenever possible, the skeletons methodology aims to avoid producing a new solution program from scratch by selecting from a limited range of previously experienced possibilities. Together, skeletons and program transformations compose a decision-tree, in which the programmer or developer can navigate to map high-level specifications onto concrete machine architectures (Darlington & To, 1993; Darlington *et al.*, 1993).

Performance Models

Several approaches to performance modeling have been developed for skeletal parallelism. For example, Cole (1989) describes four skeletons, but only the fixed degree divide-and-conquer skeleton is analysed to obtain a predicted execution time which depends on the execution times of customising functions. Also, Deldarie *et al.*, (1995) makes a similar attempt to derive models for the execution time of an overall program. However, this approach differs from Cole's, making explicit the notion of a higher-order function, extending the modelling process to cover scalability, restricting to a specific application area (image processing), and considering machine specific parameters into the computational model.

A more general approach is presented by Darlington *et al.*, (1993), using performance models to predict performance and suggest improvements. They define the performance model of a skeleton as a formula which predicts the execution time and whose variables are problem and machine parameters. For example, the performance model for their divide-and-conquer skeletons, assuming a binary division function, is:

$$T_{sol_G} > T_{div_G} + T_{sol_{G/2}} + T_{comb_{G/2}} + T_{comms}$$

This formula contains T_{sol_x} as the time to solve a problem of size x on one processor, the problem specific parameters T_{div_x} and T_{comb_x} which represent respectively the time to divide and the time to combine problems and solutions of size x, and the machine-specific parameter T_{comms}, as the time to communicate a problem and results between processors.

As each skeleton/machine pair has an associated performance model to predict the performance of a program written using the skeleton on that machine, the formula can be expanded to calculate the total time required to solve a problem of size G on M processors:

$$T_{sol_G} = \sum_{l=1}^{\log M} \left(T_{div_{G/2^{l-1}}} + T_{comb_{G/2^l}} + T_{comms} \right) + T_{sol_{G,M}}$$

We consider this approach to performance modelling as a more general one since it is not dependent on any computational model or machine. A specific implementation of the skeleton requires then that the general performance model must be instantiated for the target machine. A drawback is that it may not always be possible to reliably derive all the machine-specific parameters. While this may currently seem a restriction, the limitation is in fact a reflection of the current diversity of parallel machine models.

Algorithmic Skeletons Summary

The goal of skeletons is to avoid producing a new solution program from scratch, by selecting and instantiating a fixed range of alternatives, presented as a set of general purpose skeletons. As expressed by Darlington & To (1993), the aim is for *"Building parallel applications without programming"*. With skeletons, useful patterns of parallel computations and interactions are packaged together as a construct, and then parameterised with other pieces of code. Such constructs are skeletons in that they have structure, but lack detail, much as the top-most structural model shows the structure of the application with respect to its constituent task implementations, but the details of the tasks themselves are supplied by individual component models. In this sense, skeletons represent a particular form of describing and modelling coordination structure in parallel systems as functional language constructs, encapsulating structural and design information. They provide a simple performance modelling, using formulas or equations based on problem and machine parameter for performance estimation.

3.4.3 Structural Modeling

Structural Modeling is a work on prediction models for high-performance distributed applications, as part of the AppLeS project in the Computer Science and Engineering Department, University of California, San Diego. Originally, Structural Modeling was proposed by Schopf (1997), when applying a structural performance model to predict performance on a cluster of distributed resources.

Structural Modeling — Description

Structural Modeling presents a *structural performance model* to predict the performance of an application on a set of distributed resources. This model is composed by a *structural model*, a *component model* and an *application profile*.

- The structural model represents the top-most level of an application functionality, providing a flexible and adaptable mechanism for predicting its performance. Originally, the structural model is constructed from a developer's description of the application. Often, this description is defined in the form of a graph representation or pseudocode. Figure 3.5 shows an example of both descriptions for the Master-Slave computation.

- A structural model is composed of component models. These component models are recursively defined as arithmetic combinations of input values (benchmarks, latency and bandwidth measurements, CPU performance, operation counts, etc.), according to an application profile.

- An application profile is a form for selecting the input values for the component models, using descriptions of where execution time is spent. In the original description, the application profiles are just estimate percentages for each component (Schopf, 1997). This is a simple and easy way to express an application profile, but mostly, the percentage relations are fixed arbitrary, in accordance with the developer's experience. A second approach proposes the use of interval values, defined as a value and a variation range with a normal probabilistic distribution (Schopf & Berman, 1997). These interval values seem to more closely the range of possible input values. How-

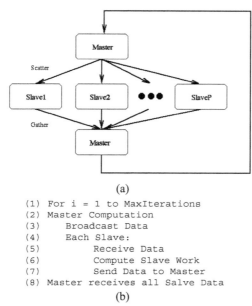

(a)

```
(1) For i = 1 to MaxIterations
(2) Master Computation
(3)     Broadcast Data
(4)     Each Slave:
(5)             Receive Data
(6)             Compute Slave Work
(7)             Send Data to Master
(8) Master receives all Salve Data
```

(b)

Figure 3.5 Description of the structural model for a Master-Slave computation using (a) a graph and (b) pseudocode (Schopf, 1997)

ever, as component models are arithmetic expressions using the values, an arithmetic operation definition is needed to deal with the precision of predictions. Further, in a third approach, stochastic values are introduced to the performance model (Schopf & Berman, 1998). Stochastic values are now the input values associated with a normal probabilistic distribution. This again requires the definition of arithmetic operations for stochastic values.

Structural Modeling Approach

Informally, the Structural Modeling approach follows four steps to build a structural performance model for performance prediction (Schopf, 1997):

- The structure of the application is examined to propose and construct a top-level structural model to represent this structure, based on a developer's description and experience.

- An application profile is proposed, describing where execution time for the application is spent, to determine which components must be modelled to achieve the needed accuracy. Again, this application profile is created based on developer's description and experience.

- The selection and development of component models is performed, guided by available data sources and error allowance.
- The accuracy of the model is analysed to determine a course of action.

Structural Performance Model

The structural performance model is created expressing each model —the structural model and the component model— in the form of equations.

For example, the structural model for the Master-Slave computation presented previously is (Schopf, 1997):

$$ExTime = Master + Scat + max[Slave_i] + Gat$$

where $ExTime$ is the total execution time of the application, $Master$ represents the execution time of the master computation (line 2 of the pseudocode in Figure 3.5), $Scat$ is the execution time to communicate data from master to all slaves (lines 3 and 5), $Slave_i$ is the execution time in the ith slave computation (line 6), and Gat is the time to send data to master from the slaves. Each one of these times is represented by a component model, which at the same time is an equation containing values and parameters of component execution. Consider, for example, the model for the slave computation $Slave_i$. There are two approaches used to model the performance of the slave components: (1) counting the number of operations involved in computing one element, and (2) benchmarking. The performance models for both cases respectively are (Schopf, 1997):

$$Slave_i1 = NumElt_i \times (Op(i, Elt))/(CPU_i)$$
$$Slave_i2 = NumElt_i \times BM(Slave_i)$$

where $NumElt_i$ is the number of data elements computed by a slave on the ith processor, $Op(i, Elt)$ is the number of operations that a slave requires to compute a single element on the ith processor, CPU_i is the time to perform one slave operation on the ith processor, and $BM(Slave_i)$ is the benchmark time for a slave to process a single element on the ith processor.

Finally, we have the three approaches to determine the application profile:

- As estimate percentages, the application profile for a *"congested network with a large amount of data flowing"* (Shopf, 1997) can be expressed as for example:

$Master = 10\%$, $Scat = 40\%$, $max[Slave_i] = 10\%$, $Gat = 40\%$

- As interval values, the application profile values are expressed in the form $x_i \pm v_i$, representing a normal distribution, where x_i is the mean and v_i is the standard deviation (Schopf & Berman, 1997).
- As stochastic values, the assumption is that interval values are now represented in the form $x_i \pm a_i$, again representing normal distributions, where x_i is the mean and a_i is two standard deviations. However, to operate these values, a rule for combining stochastic values is used, based on standard statistical error propagation methods (Schopf & Berman, 1998).

Structural Modeling Summary

Structural Modeling presents a structural performance model to predict the performance of an application executing on a set of distributed resources, describing and modelling their coordination structure. The approach is based on decomposing the application performance in accordance with the structure of the application into interacting component models corresponding to component sub-tasks. Next, using the application profile and available information as guides, equations are selected and used appropriately to model the behaviour of each component, allowing different modeling approaches for different application components as needed. The Structural Modeling goal is precisely to obtain models for distributed performance estimation, defined recursively as arithmetic combinations of input values. In this approach no classification of common structures, selection method, or benefits and liabilities of using different structural descriptions, are considered. Every stage depends strongly on the previous experience of a developer.

3.5 Summary

In this chapter, we have presented a brief introduction to basic concepts on Software Performance Modelling, and references to the most significant research work in the literature on Software Architecture and Performance Modelling, and on performance estimation of parallel and distributed systems, considering those approaches published or started before the present PhD work (1999). In general, each approach is briefly described around its most relevant objectives and characteristics. Notice, however, that during the last few years, references of many other approaches have been published after the submission of this PhD work. Nevertheless, it seems also valid to consider all these approaches as related work to the present thesis, since they present or describe approaches to performance modelling that have similar or common features with the Architectural Performance Modelling Method proposed here.

In this chapter, we have also presented the three most significant pieces of research work in parallel and distributed programming with a similar objective and approach than our Architectural Performance Models. Archetypes, Skeletons and Structural Modeling have been presented according to their definition and/or description of their constituent parts, and their application methodology for parallel or distributed programming. Also, we have described the basics of their modeling for performance prediction or estimation. Finally, a summary is presented for each one of them, describing briefly their major objectives.

Later, in Chapter 8, a comparison with related work is presented, summarising similarities and differences of these approaches with our Architectural Performance Modelling Method.

Chapter 4

Architectural Performance Modelling Method

> "And there, in the middle of the arched concrete cellar, clean as a monastery cell, lay a gigantic copper cylinder resting on cement supports. It was closed on all sides except at the top, where there was a grating bedecked with seals. Inside the machine all was darkness and silence. With a smooth and regular motion the cylinder thrust forth a piston which slowly rotated a fly-wheel. That was all. Only the ventilator in the cellar window kept up a ceaseless rattle."
>
> Karel Capek.

This chapter presents the Architectural Performance Modelling Method as a method for identifying the best performing architectural pattern for a parallel application. This is carried out by estimating and analysing its performance, based on its coordination components at the architectural level.

4.1 Motivation

Architects build scale-models as literal models of buildings, often producing models of considerable artistic quality. These models can be abstract enough to convey the feel and style of a building, or can be precisely detailed to assist in construction planning. Normally, scale-models share their form with the prospective building, but expressed at different space scale. Few competent architects would design a project of any size or consequence without making one or more scale-models, usually during the initial schematic and design development stages. When an architect builds a scale-model of a prospective building, the objective is to provide a "real-life" perspective that portrays how the building would actually look to the human eye. However, scale-models are designed not only to allow clients to understand how the building will look, but also may function as part of behavioural or performance modelling as well (Rechtin & Maier, 1997).

Software architects may also make use of scale-models to demonstrate partial characteristics of a software system. Building a scale-model, whose components consist of functionless stubs, may help to create, guide, or clarify the structure and behaviour of the software system. Commonly, software scale-models also share their form with the prospective software system, but at different time scale. As with building architecture, such a scale-model may be generated during the software development process, in order to take design decisions about which structure to use for the software system during initial stages of its design. Consider, for instance, scale-model simulations that represent the functionality of a software system, but they do not execute any functionality in real time. The results of the simulations can be used as quantitative evidences for supporting a design decision about which structure to use for the software system (Rechtin & Maier, 1997).

Nevertheless, the creation of detailed scale-models is typically expensive and labour intensive. Often, the effort to create such a detailed scale-model for a software system is similar or equivalent to create the software system itself. So, the relative advantage of using scale-models of software systems can be diminished. A possible solution to this problem could be the development of non-detailed scale-models, which only reflect the relevant properties for comparison purposes, and are expressive enough to provide useful information for making design decisions.

4.2 Performance Models

Performance models are scale-models that describe how effectively a system carries out or satisfies some functionality. Performance models are usually quantitative, and the most important ones are those related to system functionality, that is, properties observed from the system as a whole but not individually possessed by any of its subsystems. They are commonly used to evaluate properties like overall sensitivity, accuracy, latency, adaptation time, weight, cost, reliability, and many others. In consequence, to formulate a quantitative performance model, it is necessary to know beforehand an architectural description about the system's behaviour and structure.

The performance of a software system is often expressed as the number of operations per unit of time, or as the amount of time it takes to complete a computation.

Hence, performance is a function of the coordination activities among components and the processing actions within each component of the software system. This is especially true if the components occupy the same processor, but it is still true if the components all execute on distributed computing elements. The amount of interaction among components (by function invocation, process synchronisation or other communication mechanisms) is a performance driver, which makes performance strongly dependant of software architecture (see Section 2.2.2).

Performance models are generally classified according to their internal structure, falling into one of the following categories (Rechtin & Maier, 1997):

- *Analytical models.* Analytical models are described by a set of parameters, which are combined by means of a mathematical rule, allowing the prediction of a performance attribute. In order to meet a required performance target, these performance models are normally presented along with a set of proposed values for the parameters (see Section 3.1.1).

- *Simulation models.* In essence, simulation models are similar to analytical models because the performance attribute of interest is obtained in terms of a set of parameters. However, simulation models are used when the relationship between the set of parameters and the performance attribute of interest is just too complex and difficult to explicitly identify. Therefore, if a mathematical rule that combines the parameters cannot be easily identified or computed, a simulation can be used instead of the mathematical rule of combination (see Section 3.1.2).

The following sections provide background information on the Architectural Performance Modelling Method, as a method for selecting an architectural pattern based on a performance estimation using scale-models. These scale-models are simulation models used to answer questions about the performance of a parallel software system during early stages of software design.

4.3 The Architectural Performance Modelling Method

The Architectural Performance Modelling Method is a simulation modelling process for identifying which architectural pattern presents the best performance, based on estimating the response time of a parallel program, using *(a)* information about the available hardware and software resources, *(b)* the description of the problem to solve, and *(c)* the architectural pattern descriptions, used for designing the potential parallel solutions.

4.3.1 Problem and Assumptions

In order to develop a suitable performance model for any system, it is necessary to take into consideration several issues and concepts surrounding such a system, as well as some basic assumptions to develop the modelling method. In this section, let us describe some issues and concepts about the parallelisation problem, a suitable and generic description of a parallel program (which is the system we attempt to model), and some assumptions taken in order to carry out the performance modelling of a parallel program during execution.

Software Problem *vs* Parallelisation Problem

When developing a parallel solution to a problem, the software developer faces not only the very "software problem", but also the "parallelisation problem". Let us briefly describe both of them in the following paragraphs, in order to notice the basic differences between these two kind of problems, present in parallel software development.

The *software problem* normally arises in any software development, implying the creation of a solution to such a software problem. This solution is commonly described in terms of an algorithm of abstract operations applied to data objects (such as a matrix) with a specific range of values. Most of the developments in programming and software design focus their efforts on solving this software problem.

On the other hand, the *parallelisation problem* is concerned with describing a solution as the simultaneous execution of communicating sequential processes (Dijkstra, 1968; Hoare, 1978; Brinch-Hansen, 1978). The objective is a more efficient execution of the software solution by the simultaneous processing and communication among processes (or *software components*, as defined in Section 2.2), once such a solution has been described in algorithmic terms. Hence, parallel programming only makes sense when the solution to a problem is already known and proposed as an algorithm and the data to be operated on.

Therefore, it is first required to solve the original software problem, whose solution is expressed as an algorithm and data, and only then, solve the parallelisation problem (Sommerville, 1989; Pancake & Bergmark, 1990). This implies the partition of such an algorithm and/or data, attempting to provide a more efficient execution. Thus, parallel programming does not directly deal with the nature of the problem to solve. This problem is actually solved by applying the algorithm to the data. The parallelisation problem is solved by achieving simultaneous execution at the programming level. Hence, there are two problems to be solved during parallel software design: the software problem and the parallelisation problem, which exist in different "design dimensions", as explained by Peter Wegner (Wegner, 1987). This is also pointed out by Ian Sommerville (1989), when introducing parallelism in the software design process as a two-stage activity. Consider, for instance, multiplying two $n \times n$ matrices produces a new $n \times n$ matrix, each of whose n^2 entries is an inner product that can be computed independently of, and thus in parallel with, all other entries (Hoare, 1978; Andrews, 1991; Freeman & Phillips, 1992; Foster, 1994; Kleiman, *et al.*, 1996; Hartley, 1998; Andrews, 2000). For this example, it is required to *(a)* propose an algorithm for developing a numerical solution for the matrix multiplication, and only then, *(b)* consider how to carry out such a numerical solution as a set of parallel processes.

It is important to clarify that the present thesis attempts to aid with solving the parallelisation problem, using architectural descriptions based on architectural patterns, and given that the solution to the software problem has been proposed as an algorithm and data to be parallelised. The solution to the parallelisation problem is not directly affected by the nature of the problem itself, but more precisely, by the order and relation among instructions within the algorithm and/or datum within the data.

Describing Parallel Programs

The objective of the present thesis is to compare design alternatives by developing scale-models to estimate their performance as parallel programs (see Sections 2.1.1 and 2.1.5). However, in order to do such a performance modelling, some characteristics of parallel programs should be taken into consideration in order to describe them in time terms for a performance scale-model development:

- A parallel program only specifies simultaneous processing and communication activities carried out by software components. Nevertheless, software components are prone to remain idle during periods of time, even though this state has not been part of the specification in the parallel program. Idle times result from the non-deterministic parallel environment in which software components are executed. Software components of a parallel program are forced to wait until a particular event occurs (for instance, synchronisation of communication between components or overhead due to the use of common hardware resources). Hence, idle times are a consequence of the components' simultaneous execution at different speeds into a non-deterministic environment (Hoare, 1978; Brinch-Hansen, 1978; see also Section 2.1.1). Any description of the execution of a parallel program must consider idle times for its software components, in order to obtain a realistic time model for the parallel program.

- A parallel program is the specification of a set of sequential software components, processing and communicating among themselves to achieve a common objective. However, due to non-determinism (and the consequent insertion of idle times), the times required for a software component's activities vary from one execution of the program to another (Dijkstra, 1968; Hoare, 1978; Brinch-Hansen, 1978). Hence, times ought to be described more likely as probabilistic values, rather than as deterministic ones. For example, in a message passing parallel program, each time there is a communication between two software components, usually one of them has to wait (idles) for the other, and the time taken for waiting is normally different from one communication to another, and from one execution to another.

- A parallel program finishes only when all the software components it specifies finish (Dijkstra, 1968; Hoare, 1978; see also Sections 2.1.1 and 2.1.2). This may give the impression that all software components have the same execution time, but this is not the case: the software components specified in the parallel program would have to wait until the very last of them achieves its end, and this happens at a particular point of time. Only then, the parallel program finishes. This is described when introducing the parallel composition (Dijkstra, 1968) and the parallel instruction (Hoare, 1978) to express parallelism in a language (see Section 2.1.2). Normally, all software components keep processing, communicating or idling until the whole parallel composition finishes. The only reason that it could fail, is due to deadlock.

Based on these characteristics, the execution of a parallel program is described in time terms, using a *space-time view* as the one shown in Figure 4.1 (Notice that this figure shows only an example of how an execution of a generic parallel program could be seen, and it is used only for illustration purposes).

The space-time view displays the activities of individual (sequential) software components of a software architecture, executing on the parallel platform, like a Gantt chart (Geist *et al.*, 1994). Listed on the left-hand side of the view are identifiers for the software components. Each software component is related to a horizontal bar stretching out in the *Time* direction. During execution, the state of each software component (as a proc-

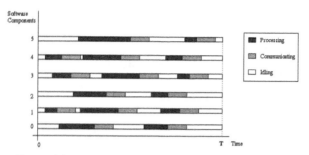

Figure 4.1 Space-Time View description of a parallel program of 6
software components. Each component spends its time processing,
communicating, or idling.

ess of the parallel program) is considered to be *processing*, *communicating*, or *idling*. These states are indicated by the change of colour of the horizontal bar. In a message passing parallel system, let us define such states as follows:

- A software component is defined to be *processing* when it instructs its processor to modify the state of its local memory (Hoare, 1978; Brinch-Hansen, 1978). Hence, such a software component is programmed to modify local data, and its processor time is only devoted for such activity.

- A software component is defined to be *communicating* by message passing when it instructs its processor to modify *(a)* the state of another processor's memory (by a send operation), or *(b)* the state of its own local memory by a request from another processor (by a receive operation) (Hoare, 1978; Brinch-Hansen, 1978). Hence, such a software component is programmed to modify remote or local data, and its processor time is mainly devoted for message passing.

- A software component is considered to be *idling* when it is not in a processing or communicating state, but waiting for an event to occur in order to continue later with a processing or communicating state. Hence, such a software component does not modify neither local nor remote data. Nevertheless, it still consumes processor time.

Moreover, this time description of a parallel program using space-time view includes the basic characteristic that a parallel program only finishes when all its software components have finished processing, communicating or idling. This situation is defined to happen in the space-time view at a time T. However, such a time T is not a fixed value, since processing, communicating, and idling times are probabilistic values, influenced by the non-determinism of the parallel hardware environment. Thus, from a statistical point of view, we refer to such a time as *the average total execution time*. This is the value that our performance modelling method attempts to estimate.

Assumptions to develop a Performance Model of a Parallel Program

The most immediate and important decision to make at the beginning of parallel programming is to decide which coordination (an architectural description, such as the "logical structure" as described by Somerville (1989), or an architectural pattern) may be the most viable for parallelising a problem, using given parallel hardware and software resources. In general, there are many possibilities to parallelise an algorithm or data, and a parallel program developer will not know in advance which of the various alternatives will have the desired runtime behaviour on a given computer platform. There are two possibilities for finding an answer to this question:

1. One can implement the various alternatives. However, the implementation requires a lot of time and is therefore very expensive.

2. One can use a method based on performance estimation, producing non-detailed models of the various alternatives, and trying to find which can be considered as the optimal solution by evaluating the models. This approach is less expensive.

Considering the second approach, we propose a method for comparing design alternatives using performance estimation, which considers the following general and performance assumptions:

General Assumptions

1. A problem, involving a large computation which applies an algorithm on a certain amount of data, is identified to be solved using a parallel program.

2. The parallel program can be described in terms of the Architectural Description of Software (see Section 2.3.2), as Platform, Coordination and Processing components.

3. The Coordination of the parallel program is modelled by more than one architectural pattern.

4. The given inputs are *(a)* the problem statement, *(b)* the amount of data to be operated on, and *(c)* the parallel hardware and software resources available.

5. The execution of the large computation should meet performance requirements within a specific time frame.

6. The performance of the parallel program mainly depends on the time it takes for all its components to carry out coordinating or processing activities. Thus, a performance model for such a parallel program can be represented as a scale-model that reflects such coordinating and processing activities.

7. The coordination components organise the communication between processing components, by issuing requests for processing and providing the data to be operated on. Thus, coordination components spend most of their time coordinating and communicating data between processing components.

8. The processing components carry out the operation on the provided data, and return a result. Processing components, then, spend most of their time processing data.

9. The functionality of platform and coordination components can be represented by a runnable implementation of an architectural pattern, that only represents the coordination among major components on the parallel resources available. The execution of this implementation, using the data of the problem, produces the same pattern of simultaneous communication and idling present in the execution of the *real* parallel program, which uses such an architectural pattern. This is due to both, the runnable implementation and the real parallel program share the same form, expressed in terms of the architectural pattern used. However, no processing or operation on the data is actually performed, due to scaling (see Section 4.1).

10. The functionality of processing components can be simulated by statistical components. When requested for processing, the statistical components provide an approximated value related to the real-time behaviour of processing components. The objective is to obtain time scaling through processing simulation (see Section 4.1).

The general assumptions set up the basic requirements for the application of the Architectural Performance Modelling Method, whereas the performance assumptions are used in the following sections for the calculation of performance estimates and the construction of scale-models.

4.3.2 The Method

The Architectural Performance Modelling Method obtains the best performing architectural pattern for a parallel system, using as input:

1. A statement of the problem to solve, described in terms of an algorithm and the data

on which the algorithm is to be applied. Both, algorithm and data, are the elements of a program which can be partitioned, and used to select an architectural pattern as an initial coordination structure for the solution.

2. A specification of the known parallel platform (hardware and software) to be used. For the actual purposes of the present thesis, the simulation models for all case studies are developed and executed on a cluster of sixteen computers, using the Java Parallel Virtual Machine (JPVM) environment (Ferrari, 1997; Geist, *et al.*, 1994), which represent the available hardware and software resources. Moreover, all simulation models are programmed in the Java programming language (Smith, 2000; Hartley, 1998). Nevertheless, these contextual conditions do not restrict that modelling and simulation as proposed by the method could be developed and executed considering a different hardware and software platform, in order to estimate the performance of a parallel solution on such a platform.

The method uses information about the architectural description of the parallel system and discrete-event simulation for respectively developing a Coordination Simulation and a Component Simulation:

- The Coordination Simulation is an architectural description presented in terms of the behaviour and form of the parallel system as described in the *Structure, Dynamics* and *Implementation* sections of the Architectural Patterns for Parallel Programming (see Chapter 5). This simulation is used to understand the coordination behaviour of a solution based on a particular architectural pattern, allowing to consider and measure performance information of the time it takes only to carry out communication and synchronisation activities among software components.

- The Component Simulation is a discrete-event simulation used at the level of each sequential software component, in order to take into consideration its sequential behaviour as a value representing its processing time. So, such a simulation is developed as a queuing structure, capable of obtaining a probabilistic estimate of the time it would take for a sequential software component to serve a single request of processing, as a proxy of the system-specific processing, but without actually carrying out any functionality. Because the property of interest is performance, this queuing structure needs only to produce a reasonable estimate of the component's execution time rather than allowing one to predict anything dependent on its behaviour. The sequential set of such estimates are gathered together into the Component Simulation Estimates (see Section 4.3.2). In order to produce such estimates, the queuing structure has been selected as a fairly generic component, which can be parameterised to account for system-dependent aspects. It requires two parameters, λ and μ, which respectively represent the average arrival rate of requests to the sequential software component, and the average service rate provided by the sequential component (see Section 6.2.2).

Notice that, at prediction time, the architectural information available in a given architectural description leads to an accurate Coordination Simulation. Nevertheless, for parallel system's estimation purposes, we do not know beforehand the precise processing behaviour of the parallel system's processing software components, and hence, we cannot predict anything dependent on their behaviour. It is possible to obtain a value of λ for each parallel software component, directly measuring it when data is "passed through" the Coordination Simulation. However, and since the Architectural Performance Modelling Method is proposed as a means to get performance information *before* further implementation is available, there is a substantial difficulty to consider a value for μ in order to execute each Component Simulation. Thus, in order to produce a reasonable estimate of a parallel system's performance, a simple approach is proposed so μ is obtained based on its relation with λ and the average queue length Q (see Section 7.1.4). So, both Coordination and Component Simulations can be gathered together into an Architectural Performance Model, which takes into consideration communication and processing activities, and which is able to obtain performance estimates given the constraints considered in the hypothesis (see Section 1.3).

Based on the previous ideas, the Architectural Performance Modelling Method has the following steps:

1. *Architectural Pattern Selection.* One or several architectural patterns, describing coordination organisations of parallel components, are selected as potential solutions to the problem. These architectural patterns and the platform specification are used to define the configurations for the parallel system, fixing the number of components and the number of processors for each pattern.

2. *Architectural Performance Model Construction.* The objective of this step is the construction of the model for the experimental performance simulation.

   2.1. *Coordination Simulation.* Using the specification of the known parallel platform and the information of the selected architectural patterns, a Coordination Simulation is constructed for each one. The Coordination Simulation is an executable instance of each architectural pattern on the specified parallel platform, representing the coordination among components of the parallel system.

2.2. *Component Simulation.* Based also on the platform specification and the information from each architectural pattern, a Component Simulation is constructed. The Component Simulation is an executable simulation of the time behaviour of a single component, representing its processing time.

2.3 *Architectural Performance Model.* The Architectural Performance Model for experimental performance simulation is finally constructed. This model is an executable program that gathers together the Coordination Simulation (representing coordination among components) and the Component Simulations (each one simulating the processing time of each component).

3. *Performance Simulation.* A single performance estimate for a given configuration of the parallel system is obtained by executing the models, as follows:

3.1 *Coordination Simulation Execution.* The Coordination Simulation, representing the coordination among components of the parallel system, is executed a number of times. From each execution, the time required for coordination among components and the arrival rate of requests to each component are measured. Hence, by performing a number of executions of this model, it is possible to statistically obtain an average coordination time and an average arrival rate of requests (λ) to each component.

3.2 *Architectural Performance Model Execution.* The average arrival rate of requests (λ) to each component is used along with information from each architectural pattern to derive the parameters for the Component Simulations. This makes possible the execution of the Architectural Performance Model, which is carried out a number of times in order to statistically obtain a simulated average processing time.

4. *Performance Estimate Calculation.* Finally, the single performance estimate for the given configuration of the parallel system is calculated, by adding the average coordination time and the simulated average processing time (see Section 4.3.2).

The Architectural Performance Modelling Method produces average execution times that quantify the effect of communicating and processing the program's workload.

4.3.3 Calculation of Performance Estimates

A performance model should be able to explain available observations and perhaps estimate future circumstances, while abstracting away unimportant details. However, conventional computer modelling techniques, which typically involve simulations,
introduce too many details to be of practical use to parallel program designers. In this
section, we introduce the fundamentals for the calculation of performance estimates
within the Architectural Performance Modelling, which provide an intermediate level of
detail (Ortega & Roberts, 1999c).

Let $T_{Proc}{}^i$, $T_{Comm}{}^i$, and $T_{Idle}{}^i$ be the time spent processing, communicating, and idling,
respectively, on the *ith* component of a space-time view of a parallel program. Hence, the
average total execution time T (from Figure 4.1) can be defined as the sum of computation, communication, and idle times on an arbitrary component j (Foster, 1994),

$$T = T_{Proc}{}^j + T_{Comm}{}^j + T_{Idle}{}^j$$

or adding these times over all components, and dividing by the number of components N
($N > 0$),

$$T = \frac{1}{N}\left(\sum_{i=0}^{N-1} T_{Proc}{}^i + \sum_{i=0}^{N-1} T_{Comm}{}^i + \sum_{i=0}^{N-1} T_{Idle}{}^i \right)$$

The last definition is often more useful, since it is typically easier to determine the
total execution time of a parallel program in terms of the time spent computing, communicating, and idling of individual components.

Our goal is to estimate the average total execution time based on the General
Assumption 2 (see Section 4.3.1). Thus, it is necessary to develop a mathematical
expression that specifies execution time as a function of the response times of *platform*,
coordination, and *processing* components. The objective is to keep the scale-models as
simple as possible, while providing acceptable accuracy. This is achieved by considering
that processing and communication are activities sharply separated among coordination
and processing components, which is the base for Performance Assumptions 7 and 8.
Even though this may not be always the case, our objective is to prove that such a supposition does not introduce a considerable error for performance estimation. So, our scale-
models can effectively be used to estimate the performance of a parallel program with
the proposed constraints as expressed by the General Assumption 4 (see Section 4.3.1).

Let us consider that the total processing, communicating and idling times are the
result of the contribution of all the components of the parallel software system, which

spend their time processing, communicating or idling. Based on the Architectural Description of Software (see Section 2.3.2), we can classify all components depending on their particular objective in the software architecture, as *platform*, *coordination* or *processing* components. From this classification, the expression for average total execution time can be presented in terms of these groups of components as:

$$T = \frac{1}{N} \left[\sum_{i=0}^{k-1} (T_{Proc} + T_{Comm} + T_{Idle})^i_{platf} + \sum_{i=0}^{m-1} (T_{Proc} + T_{Comm} + T_{Idle})^i_{coord} \right.$$
$$\left. + \sum_{i=0}^{n-1} (T_{Proc} + T_{Comm} + T_{Idle})^i_{proc} \right]$$

where k is the number of platform components, m is the number of coordination components, and n is the number of processing components, such that $N = k + m + n$ and $0 \leq k, m, n \leq N$. Notice that each summatory in the expression for total execution time represents respectively the times that the *platform*, *coordination* and *processing* components take for processing, communicating and idling.

Based on Performance Assumption 6 (see Section 4.3.1) the average total execution time is composed of the times spent on coordinating and processing activities by the parallel program components. Hence, the average total execution time can be analysed by decomposing it into sub-expressions, representing those coordinating and processing activities:

$$T = T_{RealCoord} + T_{RealProc}$$

where $T_{RealCoord}$ and $T_{RealProc}$ represent the *real* times spent for coordinating and processing activities, respectively. The following subsections define such sub-expressions for both times, and apply some simplifications in order to obtain expressions for coordination and processing simulation estimates. These simplifications are based on the already discussed General and Performance Assumptions (see Section 4.3.1).

Obtaining Coordination Simulation Estimates

The execution of the *real* parallel program, using the data of the problem, produces a pattern of simultaneous communication involving platform and coordination components. So, let us define the *real* coordination time ($T_{RealCoord}$) as the time spent due to this behaviour, which can be actually taken as part of the average total execution time expression, and represented by the following expression:

$$T_{RealCoord} = \frac{1}{N}\left[\sum_{j=0}^{k-1} (T_{Proc} + T_{Comm} + T_{Idle})^{i}_{platf} + \sum_{i=0}^{m-1} (T_{Proc} + T_{Comm} + T_{Idle})^{i}_{coord} \right]$$

Since components in the coordination layer spend most of their time coordinating and communicating data between processing components (see Performance Assumption 7), the time taken due to processing in coordination components can be considered approximately zero. Basically, it is expected that this supposition would not introduce a considerable error. So, this can be expressed as:

$$\sum_{i=0}^{m-1} (T_{Proc})_{coord} \approx 0$$

Thus, applying this simplification to the expression for $T_{RealCoord}$, let us define a Coordination Simulation time ($T_{CoordSim}$) as an estimate of the execution time due only to platform and coordination components (see Performance Assumption 9).

$$T_{CoordSim} \approx \frac{1}{N}\left[\sum_{j=0}^{k-1} (T_{Proc} + T_{Comm} + T_{Idle})^{i}_{platf} + \sum_{i=0}^{m-1} (T_{Comm} + T_{Idle})^{i}_{coord} \right]$$

Obtaining Component Simulation Estimates

Subtracting $T_{RealCoord}$ from the total execution time T expression, the remainder represents the time due to processing activities by processing components. So, let us define the *real* processing time ($T_{RealProc}$) as that time spent due to processing activities, represented by the following expression.

$$T_{RealProc} = \frac{1}{N}\left[\sum_{i=0}^{n-1} (T_{Proc} + T_{Comm} + T_{Idle})^{i}_{proc} \right]$$

Since components in the processing layer spend most of their time processing data (see Performance Assumption 8), the time taken due to communicating in processing components is considered approximately zero. Again, the basic supposition for this is that such simplification does not introduce a considerable error. Hence, this can be expressed as follows:

$$\sum_{i=0}^{n-1} (T_{Comm})_{proc} \approx 0$$

Applying this simplification to the expression for $T_{RealProc}$, let us define a Component Simulation time ($T_{CompSim}$), which represents estimates of the execution time due only to processing components (see Performance Assumption 10).

$$T_{CompSim} \approx \frac{1}{N} \left[\sum_{j=0}^{n-1} (T_{Proc} + T_{Idle})^{i}_{proc} \right]$$

Obtaining the Performance Estimates

Both simplifications to coordination simulation times and component simulation times are due to modelling purposes. They provide a sharp cut between what means processing and what means communicating. Furthermore, they end up adding an error to the performance model, but as experimental results show later, these simplifications do not induce major errors to the estimates, which is part of this thesis' main objective. At the end, performance estimates are approximations to the average total execution time of a parallel system. In this sub-section, one approximation of the average total execution time T is defined from the expressions for Coordination Simulation time and Component Simulation time as follows:

$$T \approx T_{CoordSim} + T_{CompSim}$$

Observe that this expression considers and contains the contributions of each one of the groups of components (*platform, coordination,* and *processing*). Thus, the Architectural Performance Modelling Method proposes to obtain estimates of the total execution time from running the Coordination Simulation and Component Simulation.

4.4 Summary

In this chapter, the Architectural Performance Modelling Method is proposed as a method for identifying the best performing architectural pattern of a parallel application, based on performance estimation. The method requires a given problem to be solved using certain parallel hardware and software resources, and the coordination of the parallel program modelled by architectural patterns. A complete parallel system is modelled as a network of interconnected simulation components, setting up a kind of scale-model which is representative of the complete parallel application. This scale-model reflects the coordinating and processing activities carried out within the parallel application, and permits the calculation of performance estimates.

Chapter 5

Architectural Patterns
for Parallel Programming

"How does one invent program structure? I do it by drawing pictures of it from different viewpoints over and over again until a simple and convincing pattern emerges. Perhaps, there are more systematic ways of inventing structure — I don't know. But I do recognize a good program when I find one"

Per Brinch-Hansen

This chapter introduces *(a)* the concept of architectural pattern and its relation with Software Architecture and Software Performance, and *(b)* the Architectural Patterns for Parallel Programming, which describe the *coordination* layer of an overall parallel software architecture, and whose selection constitutes the first main step of the Architectural Performance Modelling Method. The architectural patterns commonly used in parallel programming introduced here are *Pipes and Filters, Parallel Hierarchies, Communicating Sequential Elements, Manager-Workers*, and *Shared Resource*.

5.1 Architectural Patterns

5.1.1 Software Pattern Categories

Software patterns cover various levels of scale and abstraction. They range from software patterns that help in structuring a software system into sub-systems, to software patterns that support the refinement of sub-systems and components, and to software patterns that are used to implementing particular design aspects in a specific programming language. Based on a description such as this, software patterns are commonly grouped into three categories (see Section 2.2.1), each one consisting of software patterns having a similar level of scale or abstraction (Buschmann, *et al.*, 1996):

- Architectural Patterns. *"An architectural pattern expresses a fundamental structural organization schema for software systems. It provides a set of predefined subsystems, specifies their responsibilities, and includes rules and guidelines for organizing the relationship between them".*

- Design Patterns. *"A design pattern provides a scheme for refining the subsystems or components of a software system, or the relationships between them. It describes a commonly-recurring structure of communicating components that solves a general design problem within a particular context".*

- Idioms. *"An idiom is a low-level pattern specific to a programming language. An idiom describes how to implement particular aspects of components or the relation-ships between them using the features of the given language".*

In the present work, we are concerned about architectural patterns as high-level soft-ware patterns used for specifying the software architecture of parallel software systems. In fact, architectural patterns identify frequently used architectural solutions, and they are used as templates to describe concrete software architectures (Shaw, 1995; see Sec-tion 2.2.1).

5.1.2 Definition and Description of Architectural Patterns

Architectural patterns are *fundamental organisational descriptions of common top-level structures observed in a group of software systems* (Ortega-Arjona & Roberts, 1998a). They specify properties and responsibilities of their sub-systems, and the particular form in which they are organised, by expressing the relationships between them.

The selection of an architectural pattern is a fundamental decision during the design of the overall structure of a software system (Buschmann, *et al.*, 1996; Shaw, 1995). As architectural patterns represent a means to capture and express design experience, their use is expected to be beneficial during early stages of the software system life cycle (Shaw, 1995). In fact, the initial attraction to architectural patterns is the promise of min-imising the effects of imminent changes of requirements on the overall system structure.

Architectural patterns are described using the general software pattern description (see Section 2.2.1). Usually, such a description provides for several aspects of the archi-tectural pattern (such as structure, behaviour, implementation, and so on) and include different kinds of diagrams (commonly using UML), which can be used to model different points of view of the organisation of the software system. Moreover, an architectural pattern is considered as a form-function relation between a software structure (what are the sub-systems and components and how they are arranged into a form) and its behaviour (how the sub-systems and components interact to achieve a common function). This description is consistent with the definition of Software Pattern provided in Section 2.3.1.

5.1.3 Architectural Patterns and Software Architecture

Software Architecture has been defined before as *the discipline or study of designing software systems, as the result of an "assembly-job" of software components* (see Section 2.2). In accordance with this definition, Software Architecture allows to analyse and build software systems through assembly or composition of software components. Such a composition, when based on a regular organisation of software components, provides substantial benefits. These include better comprehension of complex software systems, which aids both development and maintenance.

Architectural patterns are descriptions of such regular organisations of software components. Simply put, architectural patterns allow software designers and developers to understand complex software systems in larger conceptual blocks and their relations, thus reducing the cognitive burden. Furthermore, architectural patterns provide several "forms" in which software components can be structured or arranged, so the overall structure of a software system arises. Software Patterns in general convey the very essence of software design, and architectural patterns address one of the critical design pieces of any software system: they generate the overall structure of such a system.

The concept of architectural pattern is similar to the concept of architectural style (see Section 2.2.1): both provide descriptions of solutions as forms in which software components can be arranged as part of a software system. Nevertheless, architectural patterns are more problem-oriented than architectural styles (Buschmann, et al., 1996). Architectural styles describe a family of software systems in terms of their structural organisation, expressing a generic solution from a point of view that is independent of an actual design situation. On the other hand, architectural patterns precisely describe an actual design situation by providing not only a solution as a structural organisation, but also *(a)* a context statement that describes a situation "when" such a solution is applicable, and *(b)* a problem statement that describes the "tension" or "conflict" among the elements of the context, which the solution attempts to "balance". It seems important to clarify that the original concept of architectural style, as originally proposed by Perry & Wolf (1992), considered a *rationale* for describing the various choices made in defining a software architecture, capturing the motivation for the selection of a particular architectural style, and explaining the "underlying philosophical aesthetics" that motivate the architect. Nevertheless, such part was dropped as people started doing research on software architectures.

Architectural patterns also provide a vocabulary that may be used when designing the overall structure of a software system, to talk about such a structure, and feasible implementation techniques. As such, architectural patterns refer to concepts that have formed the basis of previous successful software architectures. Architectural pattern names constitute central terms of design vocabulary and experience in Software Architecture.

5.1.4 Architectural Patterns and Software Performance

The study of Software Architecture needs to go beyond the details of particular functionality, to address those aspects that affect software system performance. Several approaches to the study of software performance have been proposed so far, in order to include it as part of the software design (see Section 2.2.3) or to estimate it from architectural descriptions of software (see Chapter 3). Commonly, these last approaches are based on descriptions such as software architecture specifications (see Section 3.2.1), architectural patterns (see Section 3.2.2), UML diagrams (see Section 3.2.3), and applications and case studies (see Section 3.2.4).

Architectural patterns help the software designer to understand the overall organisation of software through multiple design diagrams or views. However, by themselves, architectural patterns cannot answer a question on how a particular software design will perform. The problem is that it is often necessary to know beforehand whether a software system will deliver its performance requirements or not, or whether one scenario will give a better performance than another.

Particularly, there has been some work done in an attempt to estimate a system's performance before the system is built, considering the software specification of architectural patterns, and deriving their corresponding performance models (see Section 3.2.2).

These approaches identify a direct correspondence between each architectural pattern and its performance model, which can be immediately derived. Nevertheless, these approaches are just some of the work attempting to incorporate software performance estimation and architectural patterns. Such work in the performance estimation area suggests that it is a useful thing to do with regard to architectural patterns. Our approach in tackling this problem for parallel programming is by using a partial simulation to mimic the execution of a real parallel program, hence enabling its performance to be analysed and calculated beforehand. This involves the generation of a simulation program from the architectural pattern specification.

5.2 Architectural Patterns for Parallel Programming

A parallel program is *the specification of a set of processes executing simultaneously, and communicating among themselves in order to achieve a common objective* (see Section 2.1). This definition is obtained from the research work in parallel programming provided by E.W. Dijkstra (1968), C.A.R. Hoare (1978), P. Brinch-Hansen (1978), and many others, who have established the main basis for parallel programming (see Section 2.1.1). The Architectural Pattern for Parallel Programming introduced in this work are proposed keeping this definition in mind.

5.2.1 Parallel Software Design

Practitioners in the area of parallel programming recognise that the performance a parallel program is able to achieve is affected by three main factors: the *hardware platform*, the *programming language*, and the *problem to solve* (see Section 2.1.2). Nevertheless, it is noticeable from a review of literature that most of research in parallel systems and parallel programming has normally been devoted to the first two factors: the hardware platform and the programming language. It is just until late that several authors have focused on parallel programming from the point of view of the problem to solve, proposing the area of Parallel Software Design in order to study how and at what point the organisation of a parallel program affects the development and performance of a parallel system.

As it has been exposed previously in Section 4.3.1, the term "problem to solve" in parallel programming is really composed of two problems: the *software problem* and the *parallelisation problem*. The software problem refers to the actual creation of a programmed solution to a problem, commonly described in terms of an algorithm of abstract operations applied to data objects. This solution, presented as a software program which embodies the algorithm applied on the data, actually *solves* the software problem. On the other hand, the parallelisation problem refers to describe such a solution as the simultaneous execution of communicating sequential processes (Dijkstra, 1968; Hoare, 1978; Brinch-Hansen, 1978). This means that, once a solution to the software problem has been found and described as an algorithm and data, the objective is to get a more efficient execution of such a solution as a parallel program.

Parallel Software Design proposes programming techniques to deal with the parallelisation problem. The research in the area covers several approaches that provide forms to organise software with relatively independent parts which efficiently make use of multiple processors. The goal is to solve the parallelisation problem (thus, solving the software problem faster, or equivalently, to solve a larger software problem in the same amount of time). Nevertheless, designing parallel programs can be frustrating:

- There are lots of issues to consider when parallelising a program. How to choose a solution that is not too hard to program and that offers substantial performance compared to uniprocessor execution?
- The overheads involved in synchronisation among multiple processors may actually reduce the performance of a parallel program. How to anticipate and mitigate this problem?
- Like many performance improvements, parallelising increases the complexity of a program. How to manage such a complexity?

These are tough problems: we do not yet know how to solve an arbitrary problem efficiently on a parallel system of arbitrary size. Hence, Parallel Software Design, at its actual stage of development, does not (cannot) offer universal solutions, but tries to provide some simple ways to get started. By sticking with some common parallel "program structures", it is possible to avoid a lot of errors and aggravation.

Many approaches to Parallel Software Design have been presented up to date, proposing organisational descriptions of top-level structures observed in parallel programming. Some of these descriptions are: Outlines of the Program (Chandy & Taylor, 1992), Programming Paradigms (Kleiman *et al.*, 1996), Parallel Algorithms (Hartley, 1998), Architectural Patterns for Parallel Programming (Ortega-Arjona & Roberts, 1998a), High-level Design Strategies (Lewis & Berg, 2000), and Paradigms for Process Interaction (Andrews, 2000).

All these descriptions provide common overall structures in parallel programming (such as, for example, "master-slave", "pipeline", "workpile", and others) that represent assemblies of parallel software components in the Software Architecture sense (see Sections 2.2 and 2.2.2) that execute and communicate simultaneously. Furthermore, these descriptions support the design of parallel programs since all of them introduce structures (forms) that such assemblies have as part of the descriptions.

It is interesting to notice that all these descriptions present programming structures as "flow" systems (Chandy & Taylor, 1992; Kleiman *et al.*, 1996; Hartley, 1998; Ortega-Arjona & Roberts, 1998a; Lewis & Berg, 2000; Andrews, 2000). Nevertheless, this seems to be consistent with the general description of a parallel process, which is defined to be composed of a group of (sequential) software components that are spatially distributed in order to simultaneously execute and communicate (see Sections 2.1, 4.3.1 and Figure 4.1). This means that, commonly, all approaches tend to arrange their algorithms and/or data into overall structures of parallel programs as flow systems. This, in fact, has several advantages: *(a)* it produces software components not too difficult to program; *(b)* it simplifies communications among such software components, considerably reducing the overheads involved in synchronisation; and *(c)* it helps to understand the overall description (in terms of structure and behaviour) of a parallel program. So, it is the general practice to find overall structures of parallel programs as flow systems.

5.2.2 A Note on Relaxation Algorithms and Parallel Programming

A relaxation algorithm approaches a solution iteratively; in each iteration, a new result is computed from the partial results of previous iterations. There are several examples of relaxation algorithms: the Jacobi algorithm (Kleiman *et al.*, 1996; Hartley, 1998; Andrews, 2000), successive over-relaxation (SOR) algorithm (Andrews, 2000), and others.

A relaxation algorithm in parallel programming can be programmed in two forms: *(a)* as an iteration through time, in which the result of an algorithmic step in time t is used to produce a new result in time $t+1$ (Kleiman *et al.*, 1996). Normally, many overall structures of parallel programs can be proposed to manage this kind of relaxation, where several results are simultaneously computed; and *(b)* as a feedback through space, which introduces cycles in the very structure of a parallel system, normally in the form of communication between spatially distributed software components (Kleiman *et al.*, 1996).

Generally, it is not advisable to introduce cycles as part of the overall structure of parallel programs (Hyde, 1994). There are three main reasons for this:

- Communication cycles in a parallel program structure produce the possibility of a deadlock, so most parallel programmers advise to avoid them always when possible (see Section 2.1.4). It may seem a simplistic solution to deadlock, but it is also widely known that, effectively, parallel programs without cycles cannot deadlock (Kleiman, 1996; Hyde, 1994).

- Usually, communication cycles in the structure of a parallel program require to enforce sequencing among process and communication operations (Kleiman, et al., 1996; Hyde, 1994). Hence, their inclusion diminishes the possibility of simultaneous operations, which is the main base for parallel processing.

- Communication cycles are normally introduced only as part of the structure of a parallel program. Cycles do not generate a complete parallel software architecture by themselves, but only a part of it. Hence, their introduction is made only once the overall structure of a parallel program has been previous proposed at an architectural level, and the use of communication cycles is justified (Kleiman, et al., 1996).

Hence, in the general practice of parallel programming, it is normally not found (or often not even allowed) the use of feedback at the Software Architecture level.

5.2.3 Basics of the Architectural Patterns for Parallel Programming

The most important step in designing a parallel program is to think carefully about its overall structure. There are many descriptions about how to organise a parallel program (Chandy & Taylor, 1992; Kleiman et al., 1996; Hartley, 1998; Ortega-Arjona & Roberts, 1998a; Lewis & Berg, 2000; Andrews, 2000). From all these descriptions, the Architectural Patterns for Parallel Programming stand out (Ortega-Arjona & Roberts, 1998a), since they have the following advantages:

1. The Architectural Patterns for Parallel Programming (as any Software Pattern) provide a description that links a problem statement (in terms of an algorithm and the data to be operated on) with a solution statement (in terms of a organisation structure of communicating software components) (see Sections 2.3.1 and 5.1.2). This is an advantage during the initial stages of parallel software design, since an architectural pattern description aids as a first criterion to decide whether a software structure can be potentially used for a parallel program or not. Other approaches that provide

descriptions of overall structures used in parallel programming focus mainly on only describing such structures, and perhaps some of their important features, but do not provide a way for linking it with the parallelisation problem at hand.

2. The partition of the problem to solve is a key for the success or failure of a parallel program. Hence, the Architectural Patterns for Parallel Programming have been developed and classified based on the kind of partition applied to the algorithm and/or the data present in the problem statement. In particular, the patterns for data access and the algorithm order indicate the way in which processing has to be carried out. Partitioning for parallel processing is strongly affected by the order and dependence among instructions (as elementary parts of the algorithm) and/or data (as basic part of the data), independently of the actual problem to solve (see Sections 2.1.3, 4.3.1, and 5.2.1). As only the algorithm or data can be partitioned, we only have the following cases: *(a)* partitioning only the algorithm, *(b)* partitioning only the data, *(c)* partitioning both, algorithm and data, and *(d)* no partitioning at all. The Architectural Patterns for Parallel Programming provide different software structures for the first three cases, referring to different kinds of parallelism (functional, domain, and activity, see Sections 2.1.3 and 5.2.7). The last case, in which no partition can be achieved, refers to a sequential problem with no parallelism at all.

3. As a consequence of the previous two points, the Architectural Patterns for Parallel Programming can be selected depending on characteristics found in the algorithm and/or data, which drive the selection of a potential parallel structure by observing and studying the characteristics of order and dependence among instructions and/or datum. This selection criteria seems simple for the experienced parallel software designer. Nevertheless, it is not so for the novice or common software designer. Thus, the objective here is to help these software designers during the selection of a parallel structure, making such a selection as simple as possible (see Section 5.3). In the case of other approaches describing the overall structure of parallel programs, they do not present any selection criteria. Normally, these approaches proceed as follows: a problem is stated to be solved using parallel programming, and next, the parallel solution is described. As a result, it is not clear neither how to go from the problem description to the solution description, nor how to connect or relate both descriptions together.

4. The Architectural Patterns for Parallel Programming introduce parallel structures as forms in which software components can be assembled or arranged together, consid-

ering the different partitioning ways of the algorithm and/or data. Each form can be characterised by how the work is divided among parallel software components, and whether each component executes the same code (see Section 5.2.7). The forms represent regular organisations of software components, aiming to allow software designers to understand complex parallel software systems, and therefore, reducing the cognitive burden.

Nevertheless, even though the Architectural Patterns for Parallel Programming have these advantages, they also present disadvantages: *(a)* they do not describe, represent, or produce a complete parallel program in detail, and *(b)* they do not produce performance information (see Section 5.1.4).

It is important to consider here that at the time this PhD project was originally developed, there were neither architectural patterns discovered for parallel programming, nor an available method able to transform such kind of architectural description into a simulation program for performance estimation. Since then, there have been several efforts trying to address the lack of performance estimation features in architectural descriptions, such as those presented in Chapter 3. Moreover, the aim of this PhD project was to produce a method that allows software performance estimation to be obtained from an architectural pattern specification. Therefore, to achieve this goal, first it was necessary to discover and describe the various overall structures used in parallel programming in a pattern form, and then to propose a method that should be able to generate simulation programs from such architectural pattern descriptions. The results of this work are the Architectural Patterns for Parallel Programming, as originally presented by Ortega-Arjona and Roberts (1998a), and summarised from Section 5.2.8 to Section 5.2.12.

The architectural patterns here are proposed as a way of helping a programmer to select a starting point when designing the coordination organisation of a parallel program. The architectural patterns in this work are introduced using the POSA form (Buschmann *et al.*, 1996), presenting only the relevant sections with information for the Architectural Performance Modelling Method. Such sections are *Problem, Forces, Solution, Structure, Participants, Dynamics*, and *Implementation*. Since all the Architectural Patterns for Parallel Programming are starting points for designing parallel programs, also a *general context* and *general implementation* sections are presented in the following sections. Nevertheless, for a complete exposition of the Architectural Patterns for

Parallel Programming, refer to Ortega-Arjona & Roberts (1998a), Ortega-Arjona (2000), Ortega-Arjona (2003), and Ortega-Arjona (2004).

5.2.4 General Context

Start the design of the coordination organisation for a parallel system, using a specific programming language for a particular parallel hardware. Consider the following contextual assumptions (Ortega-Arjona & Roberts, 1998a; Ortega-Arjona, 2000; Ortega-Arjona, 2003; Ortega-Arjona, 2004):

- The problem to solve, expressed as an algorithm and data, involves tasks of a scale that would be unrealistic or not cost-effective for other systems to handle.
- The parallel platform and programming environment to be used are known, offering a reasonable fit to the parallelism found in the problem.
- The language that will be used, based on a certain programming paradigm, is already determined and a compiler is available for the parallel platform.

In general, the existence of an available parallel platform and a parallel programming language are considered as a basic context condition when starting the design and implementation of a parallel program. They are determinant of the performance that can be achieved (see Section 2.1.2), and also influence the design of software. Once fixed, the decision to use one architectural organisation or another relies mainly on the characteristics of order and dependence among instructions and/or data found in the problem description. This work focuses more closely on these characteristics. Each architectural pattern represents a form to identify how operations can be performed in parallel and/or how data can be operated simultaneously (Ortega-Arjona & Roberts, 1998a; Ortega-Arjona, 2000; Ortega-Arjona, 2003; Ortega-Arjona, 2004).

5.2.5 General Implementation

Also, due to the general context, the implementation of the Architectural Patterns for Parallel Programming share the same steps, intended to describe an exploratory approach to the architectural design. This method organises the implementation process of a parallel coordination based on four stages (Foster, 1994; Culler *et al.*, 1997; Ortega-Arjona & Roberts, 1998a; Ortega-Arjona, 2000; Ortega-Arjona, 2003; Ortega-Arjona, 2004):

1. *Partitioning.* The computation to be performed or the data operated are decomposed into operations or data pieces, defining possible components for the parallel program.

During this stage, practical hardware-dependent issues are ignored. The attention is focused on recognising the opportunities for parallel execution. In general, architectural pattern components are expected to be implemented by sub-components, perhaps using design patterns.

2. *Communication.* The communication to coordinate process execution is determined, defining appropriate communication structures between processing components. In general, architectural communication structures can be also based on design patterns.

3. *Agglomeration.* The components and communication structures recognised in the previous steps are evaluated in accordance with performance requirements. In the case of parallel systems, usually components are recombined several times into larger components, aiming to maximise processor utilisation and reduce communication costs.

4. *Mapping.* Components are assigned to real processors, trying to satisfy the results of the agglomeration stage. As a general rule, each component is expected to be assigned to a processor, attempting to maximise processor utilisation and minimise communication costs. Mapping can be defined static or dynamic, depending directly on hardware characteristics.

The approach presented here is intended to deal with the implementation issues from an architectural point of view. During the first two stages, attention is focused on concurrency and scalability characteristics. In the last two stages, attention is moved to locality and other performance-related issues. Nevertheless, it is preferable to present each stage as general considerations for parallel design, instead of providing details about the precise implementation of participants. These implementation details are described more precisely as references to design patterns for concurrent, parallel and distributed systems from several other authors (Schmidt, 1995; Schmidt, 1998a; Schmidt, 1998b).

Further references about features of parallel platforms and parallel languages can be found in Culler *et al.* (1997), Foster (1994), Perrot (1992), Pfister (1995), Philippsen (1995), and Skillicorn and Talia (1996). Also, good advice and guidelines about platform and language selection for performance, related to speed-up and scalability, can be found in Pancake (1996) and Pancake and Bergmark (1990).

5.2.6 A Note on Notation

In the following sections, a box-and-channel notation is used to describe the *Structure* of each architectural pattern. The box-and-channel notation consists of components with

128

named ports that are defined in terms of the connector types they provide or require. Both send and receive ends of the connectors are part of the component description, and the connectors themselves are named and typed separately as parts of the architecture description. All the different kinds of components and connectors are enclosed completely by a boundary. This boundary wraps up the complete scope of the software system, separating it from the surrounding environment. Any element outside the boundary is connected to any part of the system via a connection port. Figure 5.1 shows a key for a generic box-and-channel notation.

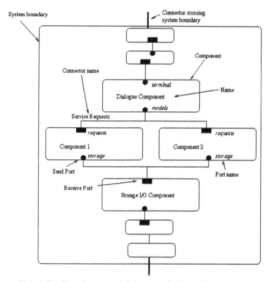

Figure 5.1 Key for a generic box-and-channel notation

Box-and-channel notations are used, for example, by Bennett (1997) and by Selic *et al.* (1994) in the ROOM method. Other similar notations were used by Magee and Kramer (1995).

5.2.7 Classification of Architectural Patterns for Parallel Programming

Our Architectural Patterns for Parallel Programming are classified following the characteristics of parallel systems as the classification criteria (Ortega-Arjona & Roberts, 1998a). Previously, Pancake (1996), Foster (1994), and Carriero & Gelernter (1988) have studied and proposed classifications according to the characteristics of parallel applications, and their performance. All of them agree that in parallel programming, the nature of the parallelisation problem (described as an algorithm and data) is tightly related to the structure and behaviour of the parallel program that solves it. Therefore, our Architectural Patterns for Parallel Programming are defined and classified according to the requirements of order of data and operations, and the nature of their processing components (Ortega & Roberts, 1998a).

Classification based on the order of data and operations

Requirements of order dictate the way in which a parallel process has to be performed, and therefore, impact on its software design. Following this, it is possible to consider that the coordination of most parallel applications fall into one of three forms of parallelism: *functional parallelism*, *domain parallelism*, and *activity parallelism* (Carriero & Gelernter, 1988; Foster, 1994; Chandy & Taylor, 1992; Pancake, 1996), which depend on the requirements of order of operations and data in the problem (Ortega-Arjona & Roberts, 1998a; Ortega-Arjona, 2000; Ortega-Arjona, 2003; Ortega-Arjona, 2004).

- *Functional parallelism* can be found in problems where a computation can be described in terms of a series of time-step ordered operations, on a series of ordered values or data with predictable organisation and interdependencies. As each step represents a change of the input for value or effect over time, a high amount of communication between components in the solution, in the form of a flow of data or operations, should be considered. Conceptually, a single data transformation is performed repeatedly (Carriero & Gelernter, 1988; Foster, 1994; Pancake, 1996).

- *Domain parallelism* involves problems in which a set of almost independent operations is to be performed on ordered local data. Because each component in the solution is expected to execute a relatively autonomous computation, the amount of communication between them can be variable, following fixed and predictable paths that can be represented as a network. It is difficult to conceive the computation as a flow of data among processing stages or sequential steps in an algorithm (Carriero & Gelernter, 1988; Foster, 1994; Pancake, 1996).

- *Activity parallelism* involves problems that apply independent operations as sets of non-deterministic transformations, perhaps repeatedly, on values of a data structure. Activity parallelism can be considered between the extremes of allowing all data to be absorbed by the components or all processes to be divided into components. Many components share access to pieces of a data structure. As each component performs independent computations, communication between processing components is not required. However, the amount of communication is not zero. Communication is required between a component that controls the access to the data structure and the properly processing components (Carriero & Gelernter, 1988; Pancake, 1996).

Classification based on the nature of processing elements

The nature of processing components is another classification criteria that can be used for parallel systems. Generally, components of parallel systems perform coordination and processing activities. Considering only the processing characteristic of the components, parallel systems are classified as *homogenous systems* and *heterogeneous systems*, according to the same or different processing nature of their components. This nature exposes properties that have tangible effects on their number in the system and the kind of communications among them (Ortega-Arjona & Roberts, 1998a; Ortega-Arjona, 2000; Ortega-Arjona, 2003; Ortega-Arjona, 2004).

- *Homogeneous systems* are based on identical components interacting in accordance with simple sets of behavioural rules. They represent instances with the same behaviour. Individually, any component can be swapped with another without noticeable change in the operation of the system. Usually, homogeneous systems have a large number of components, which communicate using data exchange operations (Ortega-Arjona & Roberts, 1998a; Ortega-Arjona, 2000; Ortega-Arjona, 2004).

- *Heterogeneous systems* are based on different components with specialised behavioural rules and relations. Basically, the operation of the system relies on the differences between components, and therefore, no component can be swapped with another. In general, heterogeneous systems are composed of fewer components than homogeneous systems, and communicate using function calls (Ortega-Arjona & Roberts, 1998a; Ortega-Arjona, 2003).

Based on these classification criteria, the five architectural patterns commonly used for defining the coordination organisation of parallel systems programming are classified as shown in Table 5.1 (Ortega & Roberts, 1998a):

	Functional Parallelism	Domain Parallelism	Activity Parallelism
Heterogeneous processing	*Pipes and Filters*		*Shared Resource*
Homogeneous processing	*Parallel Hierarchies*	*Communicating Sequential Elements*	*Manager-Workers*

Table 5.1 Classification of the Architectural Patterns for Parallel Programming

Notice that in Table 5.1, there is not a pattern considered for domain parallelism and heterogeneous processing. The reason is not that there are no architectural patterns for such classification, but more likely, that the parallel programs that would be considered under such classification simply do not have a regular structure which could be identified by a single architectural pattern. These would require to include several organisations which solve many interesting problems, such as those commonly used in simulation. So, the present thesis focuses more precisely on those categories which can be identified to be represented as a regular structure, and described using a single architectural pattern.

5.2.8 Pipes and Filters

The *Pipes and Filters* pattern extends the Pipes and Filters pattern (Buschmann *et al.,* 1996; Shaw, 1995a; Shaw & Garlan, 1996) with aspects of functional parallelism. Each parallel component performs simultaneously a different step of the computation, following a precise order of operations on ordered data that is passed from one computation stage to another as a flow through the structure. The extension presented here focuses not only on a step by step computation, but more precisely on how to exploit the simultaneity of actions present among stages, by overlapping operations through time. Thus, the extension is needed to obtain a parallel solution, based on Pipes and Filters, that executes more efficiently on a parallel platform (Ortega-Arjona & Roberts, 1998a).

Problem

The application of a series of ordered but independent computations is required, perhaps as a series of time-step operations, on ordered data. Conceptually, a single data object is transformed. If the computations were carried out serially, the output data set of the first operation would serve as input to the operations during the next step, whose output would in turn serve as input to the subsequent step-operations (Ortega-Arjona & Roberts, 1998a).

Forces

The following forces should be considered for a parallel version of the Pipes and Filters pattern (Ortega-Arjona & Roberts, 1998a):

- Maintain the correct order of operations.
- Preserve the order of shared data among all operations.
- Consider the introduction of parallelism, in which different step-operations can process different pieces of data at the same time.
- Improvement in performance is achieved when execution time decreases.

Solution

Parallelism is obtained by overlapping operations on different pieces of data through time. The operations produce data output that depend on preceding operations on its data input, as incrementally ordered steps. Data from different steps are used to generate change of the input over time. The first set of components begins to compute as soon as the first data are available, during the first time-step. When its computation is finished, the result data is passed to another set of components in the second time-step, following the order of the algorithm. Then, while this computation takes place on the data, the first set of components is free to accept more new data. The results from the second time-step components can also be passed forward, to be operated on by a set of components in a third-step, while now the first time-step can accept more new data, and the second time-step operates on the second group of data, and so on (Ortega-Arjona & Roberts, 1998a).

Structure

This pattern is called Pipes and Filters since data is passed as a flow from one computation stage to another along a pipeline of different processing elements. The key feature is that data is operated on simultaneously by different stages, and results are passed just one way through the structure. The complete parallel execution incrementally builds up, when data becomes available at each stage (Ortega-Arjona & Roberts, 1998a). Different components simultaneously exist and process during the execution time (Figure 5.2).

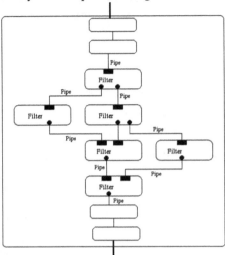

Figure 5.2 Pipes and Filters pattern

Participants

- *Filter.* The responsibilities of a filter component are to generate data or get input data from a pipe, to perform an operation on its local data, and to send output result data to one or several pipes (Ortega-Arjona & Roberts, 1998a).
- *Pipe.* The responsibilities of a pipe component are to transfer data between filters, sometimes to buffer data or to synchronise activity between neighbouring filters (Ortega-Arjona & Roberts, 1998a).

Dynamics

Due to the parallel execution of the components of the pattern, the following simple typical scenario is proposed to describe its basic run-time behaviour. As all filters and pipes are simultaneously active, they accept data, operate on it (in the case of filters), and send it to the next step. Pipes synchronize the activity between filters. This approach is based on the dynamic behaviour exposed by the Pipes and Filters pattern in Buschmann *et al.*, 1996). In this example scenario (Figure 5.3), the following steps are followed (Ortega-Arjona & Roberts, 1998a):

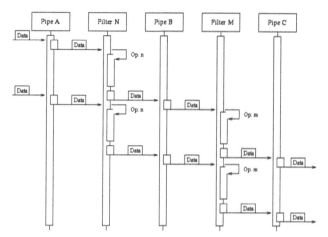

Figure 5.3 Scenario of Pipes and Filters pattern

- **Pipe A** receives data from a Data Source or another previous filter, synchronising and transferring it to the **Filter N**.

- **Filter N** receives the package of data, performs operation *Op.n* on it, and delivers the results to **Pipe B**. At the same time, new data arrives to the **Pipe A,** which delivers it as soon as it can synchronise with **Filter N**. **Pipe B** synchronises and transfers the data to **Filter M**.

- **Filter M** receives the data, performs *Op.m* on it, and delivers it to **Pipe C,** which sends it to the next filter or Data Sink. Simultaneously, **Filter N** has received the new data, performed *Op.n* on it, and synchronising with **Pipe B** to deliver it.

- The previous steps are repeated over and over until no further data is received from the initial Data Source or previous filter.

Implementation

The implementation process is based on the four stages mentioned above in the *General Implementation* (see Section 5.2.5) (Ortega-Arjona & Roberts, 1998a).

- *Partitioning.* The computation is decomposed, placing the ordered operations into a sequence of different stages, in which orderly data is received, operated on, and passed to the next stage. Attention focuses on recognising opportunities for simultaneous execution between subsequent operations, to assign and define potential filter components. Initially, filter components are defined by gathering operation stages, considering the characteristics of granularity and load-balance (Foster, 1994). As each stage represents a transformational relation between input/output data, filters can be composed of a single processing element (for instance, a process, task, function, object, etc.) or a subsystem of processing elements. Design patterns (Gamma *et al.*, 1994; Buschmann *et al.*, 1996; Coplien & Schmidt, 1995; Vlissides *et al.*, 1996) can be useful to implement the latter ones; particularly, consider the Active Object pattern (Lavender & Schmidt, 1996) and the "Ubiquitous Agent" pattern (Jezequel & Pacherie, 1997).

- *Communication.* The communication required to coordinate the simultaneous execution of stages is determined by considering communication structures and procedures to define the pipe components. Common characteristics that should be carefully considered are the type and size of the data to be passed, and the synchronous or asynchronous coordination schema, trying to reduce the costs of communication and synchronisation. A synchronous coordination is commonly used in Pipes and Filters pattern systems. The implementation of pipe components obeys the features of the programming language used. If the programming language has defined the necessary communication structures for the size and type of the data, a pipe in general can be usually defined in terms of a single communicating element (for instance, a process, a stream, a channel, etc.). However, in case more complexity in data size and type is required, a pipe component can be implemented as a subsystem of elements, using Design Patterns. Especially, patterns like the Broker pattern (Buschmann *et al.*, 1996), the Composite Messages pattern (Sane & Campbell, 1995), and those defined by Crane *et al.* (1995) can help to define and implement pipe components.

- *Agglomeration.* The filter and pipe structures defined in the previous stages should be evaluated with respect to the performance requirements and implementation costs. Once initial filters are defined, pipes are considered simply to allow data flow between filters. If an initial approach does not accomplish the expected performance, the conjecture-test approach can be used to propose another agglomeration schema. Recombining the operations by replacing pipes between them modifies the granularity and load balance, aiming to balance the workload and to reduce communication costs (Foster, 1994).

- *Mapping.* Usually, mapping is specified as static for Pipes and Filters pattern systems. As a "rule of thumb", these systems may have a good performance when implemented using shared-memory machines, or can be adapted to distributed-memory systems, if the communication network is fast enough to pipe data sets from one filter to the next (Pancake, 1996; Pfister, 1995).

5.2.9 Parallel Hierarchies

The *Parallel Hierarchies* pattern is a parallel extension of the Layers pattern approach (Buschmann *et al.*, 1996; Shaw, 1995a; Shaw & Garlan, 1996) with elements of functional parallelism. The order of operations on data is the most important feature. The extension is necessary to avoid delays due to components waiting or busy during execution. Parallelism is introduced when two or more components of a layer are able to simultaneously exist and perform the same operation. Components can be created statically, waiting for calls from higher layers, or dynamically, when a call triggers their creation (Ortega-Arjona & Roberts, 1998a).

Problem

It is necessary to perform a computation repeatedly, composed of a series of ordered operations on a set of ordered data. Consider a program whose output may be the result of just a single complex computation as a series of conceptually ordered simple operations, executed not for value but for effect, at different levels. A recurrent operation at a high level requires the execution of one or more operations at lower levels. If this program is carried out serially, it could be viewed as a chain of subroutine calls, evaluated one after another (Ortega-Arjona & Roberts, 1998a).

Forces

The following forces should be considered for the Parallel Hierarchies pattern (Ortega-Arjona & Roberts, 1998a):

- Perform the execution of ordered operations as a single computation.
- Data is shared among layers.
- The same group of operations can simultaneously be performed several times on different pieces of data.
- Operations may be different in size and level of complexity.
- Dynamic creation and destruction of components is preferred over static, to achieve load balance.

- Improvement in performance is achieved when execution time decreases.

Solution

Parallelism is obtained by allowing the simultaneous execution of more than one instance per layer through time. In a Layer pattern system, when a computation may involve the execution of several operations at different levels or layers. These operations are usually triggered by a function call, and data is shared in the form of arguments for these function calls. During the execution of operations in each layer, usually the higher layers have to wait for a result from lower layers. However, if each layer is allowed to simultaneously have more than one component, they can be executed in parallel and service other new requests. Therefore, at the same time, several ordered sets of operations can be carried out by the same system, and several computations can be overlapped in time (Ortega-Arjona & Roberts, 1998a).

Structure

This pattern is composed of conceptually-independent entities, ordered in the shape of hierarchies of layers. Each layer, as an implicit different level of abstraction, is composed of several components that perform the same operation. To communicate, layers use function calls, referring to each other as elements of some composed structure. The same computation is performed by different groups of functionally related components. Components simultaneously exist and process during the execution time (Figure 5.4) (Ortega-Arjona & Roberts, 1998a).

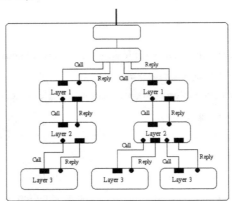

Figure 5.4 Parallel Hierarchies pattern

138

Participants

• *Layer.* The responsibilities of a layer component are to provide operations or functions to more complex level layers, and to delegate more simple subtasks to layers in
less complex levels. During run-time, more than one component per layer is allowed
to execute concurrently with others (Ortega-Arjona & Roberts, 1998a).

Dynamics

As the parallel execution of layer elements is allowed, a typical scenario is proposed to
describe its basic run-time behaviour. All layer elements are active at the same time,
accepting function calls, operating, and returning or sending another function call to elements in lower level layers. If a new function call arrives from the client, a free element
of the first layer takes it and starts a new computation (Ortega-Arjona & Roberts, 1998a).

As stated in the problem description, this pattern is used when it is necessary to
repeatedly perform a computation, as series of ordered operations. The scenario presented here takes the simple case when two computations, namely **Computation 1** and
Computation 2, have to be performed. **Computation 1** requires the operations *Op.A*,
which requires the evaluation of *Op.B*, which needs the evaluation of *Op.C*. **Computation 2** is less complex than **Computation 1**, but needs to perform the same operations
Op.A and *Op.B*. The parallel execution is as follows (Figure 5.5) (Ortega-Arjona & Roberts, 1998a):

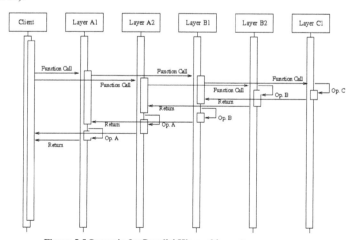

Figure 5.5 Scenario for Parallel Hierarchies pattern

- The **Client** calls a component **Layer A1** to perform **Computation 1**. This component calls to a component **Layer B1**, which similarly calls a component **Layer C1**. Both components **Layer A1** and **Layer B1** remain blocked waiting to receive a return message from their respective sub-layers. This is the same behaviour as the sequential version of the Layers pattern.
- Parallelism is introduced when the **Client** issues another call for **Computation 2**. This cannot be serviced by **Layer A1**, **Layer B1** and **Layer C1**. Another instance of the component in Layer A, called **Layer A2** —that either can be created dynamically or be waiting for requests statically— receives it and calls another instance of Layer B, **Layer B2**, to service this call. Due to the homogeneous nature of the components of each layer, every component in a layer can perform exactly the same operation. That is precisely the advantage of allowing them to operate in parallel. Therefore, any component in Layer B is capable of serving calls from components in Layer A. As the components of a layer are not exclusive resources, it is in general possible to have more than one instance to serve calls. Coordination between components of different layers is based on a kind of client/server schema. Finally, each component operates with the result of the return message. The main idea is that all computations are performed in a shorter time.

Implementation

The implementation process is based on the four stages mentioned before in *General Implementation* (see Section 5.2.5) (Ortega-Arjona & Roberts, 1998a).

- *Partitioning.* Initially, it is necessary to define a basic Layer pattern system which will be used with parallel instances: the computation to be performed is decomposed into a set of ordered operations, hierarchically defined and related, determining the number of layers. Following this decomposition, the component representative of each layer can be defined. For a concurrent execution, the number of components per-layer depends on the number of requests. Several design patterns have been proposed to deal with layered systems. Advice and guidelines to recognise and implement these systems can be found in Buschmann *et al.* (1996) and Coplien & Schmidt (1995). Also, consider the patterns used to generate hierarchies, like A Hierarchy of Control Layers (Aarsten *et al.*, 1996) and the Layered Agent Pattern (Kendall *et al.*, 1996).

- *Communication.* The communication required to coordinate the parallel execution of layer components is determined by the services that each layer provides. The idea behind this pattern is to allow for several simultaneous procedure calls, so several sequential invocations occur simultaneously. Characteristics that should be carefully considered are the type and size of the shared data to be passed as arguments and return values, the interface for layer components, and the synchronous or asynchronous coordination schema. In general, an asynchronous coordination is preferred over a synchronous one. The implementation of communication structures between components depends on the features of the programming language used. Usually, if the programming language has defined the communication structures (for instance, function calls or remote procedure calls), the implementation is very simple. However, if the language does not support communication between remote components, the construction of an extension in the form of a communication subsystem should be proposed. Design patterns can be used for this. Particularly, patterns like the Broker pattern (Buschmann *et al.*, 1996), the Composite Messages pattern (San & Campbell, 1995), the Service Configurator pattern (Jain & Schmidt, 1996) and the Visibility and Communication between Control Modules and Actions Triggered by Events (Aarsten *et al.*, 1996) can help to define and implement the required communication structures.

- *Agglomeration.* The hierarchical structure is evaluated with respect to the expected performance. Usually, systems based on identical hierarchies present a good load-balance. However, if necessary, using the conjecture-test approach, layer components can be refined by combination or decomposition of operations, modifying their granularity to improve performance or to reduce development costs.

- *Mapping.* An approach to mapping a parallel hierarchies program into a parallel platform is to execute each hierarchy on a processor, but if the number of requests is large, some hierarchies would have to block, keeping the client(s) waiting. Another mapping proposal attempts to place every layer on a processor. This simplifies the restriction about the number of requests, but if not all operations require all layers, this may overload some processors, introducing load-balance problems. The most realistic approach seems to be a combination of both, trying to maximise processor utilisation and minimise communication costs. In general, mapping of layers to processors is specified statically, allowing an internal dynamic creation of new components to serve new requests. As a "rule of thumb", a Parallel Hierarchies pattern system will perform best on a shared-memory machine, but good performance can be achieved if it can be adapted to a distributed-memory system with a fast communication network (Pancake, 1996; Pfister, 1995).

5.2.10 Communicating Sequential Elements

The *Communicating Sequential Elements* pattern is a domain parallelism pattern in which each component performs the same operations on different pieces of regular, ordered data (Foster, 1994; Chandy & Taylor, 1992). Operations in each component depend on partial results in neighbour components. Usually, this pattern is conceived as a logical structure, reflecting the particular order present in the problem (Ortega-Arjona & Roberts, 1998a; Ortega-Arjona, 2000).

Problem

A parallel computation is required that can be performed as a set of operations on ordered data. Results cannot be constrained to a one-way flow among processing stages, but each component executes its operations influenced by data values from its neighbouring components. Because of this, components are expected to intermittently exchange data. Communications between components follow fixed and predictable paths. Consider, for example, a dynamics problem simulation: the data represents a model of a real system, where any change or modification in one region influences areas above and below it, and perhaps to a different extent, those on either side. Over time, the effects propagate to other areas, extending in all directions; even the source area may experience reverberations or other changes from neighbouring regions. If this simulation was executed serially, it would require that computations be performed across all the data to obtain some intermediate state, and then, a new iteration should begin (Ortega-Arjona & Roberts, 1998a; Ortega-Arjona, 2000).

Forces

The following forces should be considered (Ortega-Arjona & Roberts, 1998a; Ortega-Arjona, 2000):

- Preserve the precise order of data distributed among processing elements. This order provides the base for result interpretation.

- Computations are performed semi-autonomously, on local pieces of data. The objective is to obtain the best possible benefit from domain parallelism.
- Every element performs the same operations, in number and complexity.
- Partial results are usually communicated among neighbour processing elements.
- Improvement in performance is achieved when execution time decreases. The main objective is to carry out the computation in the most time-efficient way.

Solution

Parallelism is introduced as multiple participating concurrent components, each one applying the same operations on a different data subset. Components communicate partial results by exchanging data, usually through communication channels. No data objects are directly shared among components; each one may access its own private data subset only. A component communicates by sending data objects from its local space to another. This communication may have different variants: synchronous or asynchronous, exchange of a single data object or a stream of data objects, and one to one, one to many, many to one or many to many communications. Often the data of the problem can be conceived in terms of an ordered logical structure. The solution is presented as a network that may reflect this logical structure in a transparent and natural form (Ortega-Arjona & Roberts, 1998a; Ortega-Arjona, 2000).

Structure

In this pattern, the same operation is simultaneously applied in effect to different pieces of data. However, operations in each element depend on the partial results of operations in other components. The structure of the solution involves a regular logical structure, conceived from the data structure of the problem. Therefore, the solution is presented as a network of elements that follows the shape imposed by this structure. Identical components simultaneously exist and process during the execution time (Figure 5.6) (Ortega-Arjona & Roberts, 1998a; Ortega-Arjona, 2000).

Participants

- *Sequential element.* The responsibilities of a processing element are to perform a set of operations on its local data, and to provide a general interface for sending and

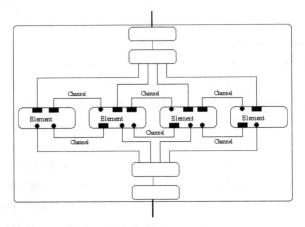

Figure 5.6 Communicating Sequential Elements

receiving messages to and from other elements (Ortega-Arjona & Roberts, 1998a; Ortega-Arjona, 2000).

- *Communication channels.* The responsibilities of a communication channel are to represent a medium to send and receive data between elements, and to synchronise communication activity between them (Ortega-Arjona & Roberts, 1998a; Ortega-Arjona, 2000).

Dynamics

A typical scenario to describe the basic run-time behaviour of this pattern is presented, where all the sequential elements are active at the same time. Every sequential element performs the same operations, as a piece of a processing network. In the most simple case (a one-dimensional structure), each one communicates only with a previous and next others (Figure 5.7). The processing and communicating scenario is as follows (Ortega-Arjona & Roberts, 1998a; Ortega-Arjona, 2000):

- Initially, all components **Element N-1**, **Element N**, **Element N+1**, etc. read different sub-sets of data. Then, every component communicates its edge data through the available communication channels (Here, **Channel A** and **Channel B**). Then all components synchronise and receive edge data from their previous and next neighbours
- The computation is started when all components **Element N-1**, **Element N**, **Element N+1**, etc. perform *Op.1* at the same time.

144

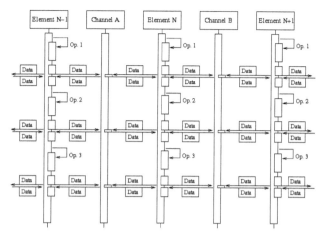

Figure 5.7 Interaction Diagram of the Communicating Sequential Elements for a one-dimensional case

- To continue the computation, all components send their partial results through the available communication channels (Here, **Channel A** and **Channel B**). Then all components synchronise again, and receive the partial results from their previous and next neighbours.

- Once synchronisation and communications are finished, each component continues computing the next operation (in this case *Op.2*). The process repeats until each component has finished its computations.

Implementation

The implementation process is based on the four stages mentioned above in the *General Implementation* (see Section 5.2.5) (Ortega-Arjona & Roberts, 1998a; Ortega-Arjona, 2000).

- *Partitioning.* The ordered logical structure of data is a natural candidate to be initially decomposed into a network of data sub-structures or pieces. In general, we can initially consider dividing the data structure into a set of data pieces in an arbitrary way, as the regular logical structure is usually considered *homogeneous* (see Section 5.2.7), and its importance relies only on its order. Thus, data pieces may have different size and shape. However, as we are aiming for an efficient computation, we normally divide the regular data structure into a set of data pieces with similar size and shape. The objective is to load-balance the processing among all the sequential elements.

145

Trying to expose the maximum concurrency, we define the basic sequential element that processes a unique sequence of operations on its assigned piece of data. Hence, computations on each sequential element present the same complexity per time step, and the total number of sequential elements is equal to the number of data pieces. Therefore, a sequential element is represented as a single processing element (for instance, a process, task, function, object, etc.) or a subsystem of processing elements, which may be designed using Design Patterns (Gamma *et al.*, 1994; Buschmann *et al.*, 1996; Coplien & Schmidt, 1995; Vlissides *et al.*, 1996). Some Design patterns that can be considered for implementing sequential components are the Active Object pattern (Lavender & Schmidt, 1996), and the "Ubiquitous Agent" pattern (Jezequel & Pacherie, 1997).

- *Communication.* The communication issues are related to the form in which processing components exchange messages. In this pattern, the sequential elements are connected using communication channels to compose a network that follows the shape of the data structure. Each sequential element is expected to exchange partial results with its neighbours from time to time through such channels. Thus, channels must perform data exchange and coordinate the operation execution appropriately. An efficient communication depends on the amount and format of the data to be exchanged, and the synchronisation schema used. Both synchronous and asynchronous schemes can be found in several domain parallel systems. However, a synchronous schema is commonly preferred in this pattern because all sequential elements are designed to perform the same operation on the same amount of data during a time step, in a synchronous way. An important issue to consider here is how communication channels are defined. In general, this decision is linked with the programming language used. Some languages define a type "channel" where it is possible to send and to receive values. Any sequential element is defined to write on the channel, and to read from it. No further implementation is necessary. Conversely, other languages do not define the channel type, or precise ways of data exchange. Thus, we must design and implement channels in such a way that allows data exchange between elements. As the use of channels depends on the language, decisions about their implementation are delayed to other refining design stages. From an architectural point of view, channels are defined whether they are implicit in the language or they must be explicitly created. Design Patterns that can help with the implementation of channel structures are the

Composite Messages pattern (Sane & Campbell, 1995) and the Service Configurator pattern (Jain & Schmidt, 1996).

- *Agglomeration.* The structure of sequential elements and channels defined in previous steps is evaluated with respect to performance. Often, in this kind of structure, agglomeration is directly related with the way data is divided among sequential elements, this is, the granularity. As each sequential element performs the same operations, changes in the granularity involve only the size of the amount of data pieces in the network to be processed per component. In the case of this pattern, performance is impacted due to redundant communications and the amount of communications in a dimension or direction.

- *Mapping.* Usually, the number of processors in a parallel platform is considerably less than the number of processing elements. Thus, a number of processing elements must be assigned to a processor. To maximise processor utilisation and minimise communication costs, the important feature to consider is load-balance. In domain parallelism, computational efficiency decreases due to load imbalances. If the design is to be used extensively, it is worthwhile to improve its load balance. Approaches include cyclic mapping or dynamic mapping. As a "rule of thumb", systems based on the Communicating Sequential Elements pattern will perform best on a SIMD (single-instruction, multiple-data) computer, if array operations are available. However, if the computations are relatively independent, a respectable performance can be achieved using a shared-memory system (Pancake, 1996).

5.2.11 Manager-Workers

The *Manager-Workers* pattern is a variant of the Master-Slave pattern (Buschmann *et al.*, 1996) for parallel systems, considering an activity parallelism approach where the same operations are performed on ordered data. The variation is based on the fact that components of this pattern are proactive rather than reactive (Chandy & Taylor, 1992). Each processing component simultaneously performs the same operations, independent of the processing activity of other components. An important feature is to preserve the order of data (Ortega-Arjona & Roberts, 1998a; Ortega-Arjona, 2004).

Problem

The same operation is required to be repeatedly performed on all elements of some ordered data. Data can be operated without a specific order. However, an important feature is to preserve the order of data. If this computation is carried out serially, it should be executed as a sequence of serial jobs, applying the same computation to each datum one after another. The goal is to take advantage of the potential simultaneity in order to carry out the whole computation as efficiently as possible (Ortega-Arjona & Roberts, 1998a; Ortega-Arjona, 2004).

Forces

The following forces are found (Ortega-Arjona & Roberts, 1998a; Ortega-Arjona, 2004):

• Preserve the order of data. However, the specific order of operation on each piece of data is not fixed.

• The operation can be performed independently on different pieces of data.

• Data pieces may have different sizes. This means that the independent computations on the pieces of data should adapt to the data size to be processed, in order to obtain automatic load-balancing.

• The solution has to scale over the number of processing elements. Changes in the number of processing elements should be reflected by the execution time.

• The coordination of the independent computations has to take up a limited amount of time in order not to impede performance of the processing elements.

• Mapping the processing elements to processors has to take into account the interconnection among the processors of the hardware platform.

• Improvement in performance is achieved when execution time decreases.

Solution

Parallelism is introduced by having multiple data sets processed at the same time. The most flexible representation of this is the Manager-Workers pattern approach. This structure is composed of a manager component and a group of identical worker components. The manager is responsible of preserving the order of data. On the other hand, each worker is capable of performing the same independent computation on different pieces of data. It repeatedly seeks a task to perform, performs it, and repeats; when no tasks remain, the program is finished. The execution model is the same, independent of the number of workers (at least one). If tasks are distributed at run time, the structure is naturally load balanced: while a worker is busy with a heavy task, another may perform several shorter tasks. This distribution of tasks at runtime copes with the fact that data pieces may exhibit different size. To preserve data integrity, the manager takes care of what part of the data has been operated on, and what remains to be computed by the workers. Also, the manager component could optionally be an active component, in order to deal with data partitioning and gathering, so such tasks can be done concurrently while receiving data requests from the workers. Hence, manager operations need capabilities for synchronisation and blocking. Moreover, the manager could be also responsible for the mapping as well, in addition to starting the appropriate number of workers. Mapping requires experiments at execution time and experience, but performing the mapping (according to a pre-determined policy) can be considered as another responsibility of the manager (Ortega-Arjona & Roberts, 1998a; Ortega-Arjona, 2004).

Structure

The Manager-Workers pattern is represented as a manager, preserving the order of data and controlling a group of processing elements or workers. Usually, only one manager and several identical worker components simultaneously exist and process during the execution time. In this pattern, the same operation is simultaneously applied in effect to different pieces of data. Operations in each worker component are independent of operations in other components. The structure of the solution involves a central manager that distributes data among workers by request. Therefore, the solution is presented as a centralised network (Figure 5.8), the manager being the central common component (Ortega-Arjona & Roberts, 1998a; Ortega-Arjona, 2004).

Participants

- *Manager.* The responsibilities of a manager are to create a number of workers, to partition work among them, to start up their execution, and to compute the overall result from the sub-results from the workers (Ortega-Arjona & Roberts, 1998a; Ortega-Arjona, 2004).
- *Worker.* The responsibility of a worker is to seek for a task, to implement the computation in the form of a set of operations required, and to perform the computation (Ortega-Arjona & Roberts, 1998a; Ortega-Arjona, 2004).

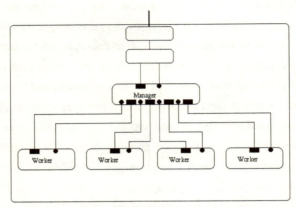

Figure 5.8 Manager-Workers pattern.

Dynamics

A typical scenario to describe the run-time behaviour of the Manager-Worker pattern is presented, where all participants are simultaneously active. Every worker performs the same operation on its available piece of data. As soon as it finishes processing, it finishes processing, it returns a result to the manager, requiring for more data. Communications are restricted to only that between the manager and each worker. No communication between workers is allowed (Figure 5.9). In this scenario, the steps to perform a set of computations are as follows (Ortega-Arjona & Roberts, 1998a; Ortega-Arjona, 2004):

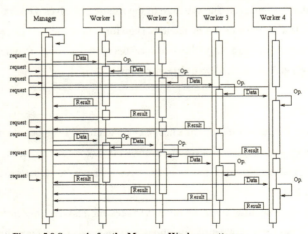

Figure 5.9 Scenario for the Manager-Workers pattern.

- All participants are created, and wait until a computation is required to the manager. When data is available to the manager, this divides it, sending data pieces by request to each waiting worker.
- Each worker receives the data and starts processing an operation *Op.* on it. This operation is independent of the operations on other workers. When the worker finishes processing, it returns a result to the manager, and then, requests for more data. If there is still data to be operated, the process repeats.
- The manager is usually replying to requests for data from the workers or receiving their partial results. Once all data pieces have been processed, the manager assembles a total result from the partial results and the program finishes. The non-serviced requests of data from the workers are ignored.

Implementation

The implementation process is based on the four stages described previously in the *General Implementation* (see Section 5.2.5) (Ortega-Arjona & Roberts, 1998a; Ortega-Arjona, 2004).

- *Partitioning.* The ordered data to be operated on by the common computation is decomposed into a set of data pieces. This partitioning criteria of the ordered data is a clear opportunity for parallel execution, and it is used to define the partitioning and gathering activity of the manager component. On the other hand, the same computation to be performed on different data pieces is used to define the structure of each one of the worker components. Sometimes, the manager is also implemented to perform the computation on data pieces as well. Usually, the structure of the manager component can be reused if it is designed to deal with different data types and sizes, delimiting its behaviour to divide, deliver, and gather data pieces to the worker components. It is possible to implement either manager or workers using a single sequential component approach (for instance, a process, a task, a function, an object, etc.), or to define a set of components that perform manager or worker activities. Usually, concurrency among these components can be used, defining different interfaces for different actions. Design Patterns (Gamma *et al.,* 1994; Buschmann *et al.*, 1996; Coplien & Schmidt, 1995; Vlissides *et al.*, 1996) can help to define and implement such interfaces. Patterns that particularly can help with the design and implementation of the manager and worker components are the Active Object pattern (Lavender & Schmidt,

1996) (which allows to create a manager and workers able to execute concurrent operations on data) and the Server Configurator pattern (Jain & Schmidt, 1996) (which allows the link and unlink of worker implementations at run-time in case that in a particular application, they are permitted to be created and destroyed dynamically). In the case of the worker components, other Design Patterns that may provide information about their implementation are the "Ubiquitous Agent" pattern (Jezequel & Pacherie, 1997) and the Object group pattern (Maffeis, 1996).

- *Communication.* The communication structure that coordinates the execution between the manager and worker should be defined. As workers are just allowed to communicate with the manager to get more work, defining an appropriate communication structure between manager and worker components is a key task. Important parameters to consider are the size and format of data, the interface to service a request of data, and the synchronisation criteria. In general, a synchronous coordination is commonly used in Manager-Worker pattern systems. The implementation of communication structures depends on the programming language used. If the language contains basic communication and synchronisation instructions, communication structures can be implemented relatively easily. However, if it is possible to reuse the design in more than one application, it would be convenient to consider a more flexible approach using configurable communication sub-systems for the exchange of different types and sizes of data. Design Patterns can help to support to the implementation of these structures; especially, consider the Composite Messages pattern (Sane & Campbell, 1995), the Service Configurator pattern (Jain & Schmidt, 1996), and the Visibility and Communication between Control Modules and Client/Server/Service patterns (Aarsten *et al.,* 1995; Aarsten *et al.,* 1996).

- *Agglomeration.* The data division and communication structure defined previously are evaluated with respect to the performance requirements. If necessary, the size of data pieces is changed, modifying the granularity of the system. Data pieces are combined or divided into larger or smaller pieces to improve performance or to reduce communication costs. Due to inherent characteristics of this pattern, the process is automatically balanced among the worker components, but granularity is modified in order to balance the process between the manager and the workers. If the operations performed by the workers are too simple or workers receive relatively small amount of data, workers may remain idle while the manager is busy trying to serve their requests. On the contrary, if worker operations are too complex, the manager will have to keep a large buffer of pending data to be processed. It is noticeable that load-balance between manager and workers can be achieved simply by modifying the granularity of data division.

- *Mapping.* In general the number of manager and worker components is a lot bigger than the number of available processors. So, it is common to place a similar number of worker components on each processor. To keep the structure as balanced as possible, the manager component can be executed on a dedicated processor, or at least on a processor with a reduced number of working components. The competing forces of maximising processor utilisation and minimising communication costs are almost totally fulfilled by this pattern. Mapping can be specified statically or determined at run-time, allowing a better load-balance. As a "rule of thumb", parallel systems based on the Manager-Workers pattern will perform reasonably well on a MIMD (multiple-instruction, multiple-data) computer, but may be difficult to adapt to a SIMD (single-instruction, multiple-data) computer (Pancake, 1996).

5.2.12 Shared Resource

The *Shared Resource* pattern is a specialisation of the Blackboard pattern (Buschmann *et al.,* 1996), lacking a control component and introducing aspects of activity parallelism. In the Shared Resource pattern, computations are performed without a prescribed order on ordered data. Commonly, components perform different computations on different data pieces simultaneously (Ortega-Arjona & Roberts, 1998a; Ortega-Arjona, 2003).

Problem

It is necessary to apply a computation on elements of a common centralised data structure. Such a computation is carried out by several sequential components executing simultaneously. The data structure should be incrementally operated and concurrently shared among the components. The details of how the data structure is constructed and maintained are irrelevant to the components. All the components know is that they can send and receive data through the data structure. The integrity of the internal representation, considered as the consistency and preservation of the data structure, is important. However, the order of operations on the data is not a central issue (Ortega-Arjona & Roberts, 1998a; Ortega-Arjona, 2003).

Forces

The following forces are found (Ortega-Arjona & Roberts, 1998a; Ortega-Arjona, 2003):

- The integrity of the data structure must be preserved. This integrity provides the base for result interpretation.
- Each component performs simultaneously and independently a computation on different pieces of data. The objective is to obtain the best possible benefit from activity parallelism.
- Every component may perform different operations, in number and complexity. However, no specific order of data access by component is defined.
- Improvement in performance is achieved when execution time decreases. Our main objective is to carry out the computation in the most time-efficient way.

Solution

Introduce parallelism as multiple participating sequential components. Each component executes simultaneously, capable of performing different and independent operations. It also accesses the data structure when needed via a shared resource component, which maintains the integrity of the data structure by defining the synchronising operations that sequential components can do. Parallelism is almost complete among components: any component can be performing different operations on a different piece data at the same time, without any prescribed order. Communication can be achieved only as function calls to require a service from the shared resource. Components communicate exclusively through the shared resource, by each one indicating its interest in a certain data. The shared resource should provide such data immediately if no other component is accessing it. Data consistency and preservation are tasks of the shared resource. The integrity of the internal representation of data is important, but the order of operations on it is not a central issue. The main restriction is that no piece of data is accessed at the same time by different components. The goal is to make sure that an operation carried out by one component goes on without interference from other components. The Shared Resource pattern is an activity parallel variation of the Blackboard pattern (Buschmann *et al.*, 1996) without a control instance that triggers the execution of the sources (the concurrent components of the Blackboard pattern). An important feature is that the execution does not follow a precise order of computations (Ortega-Arjona & Roberts, 1998a; Ortega-Arjona, 2003).

Structure

In this pattern, the different operations are applied in effect simultaneously to different pieces of data by sharer components. Operations in each sharer component are independent of operations in other components. The structure of the solution involves a shared resource that controls the access of different sharer components to the central data structure. Usually, the shared resource and several different sharer components simultaneously exist and operate during the execution time. Therefore, the solution is presented as a centralised network, with the shared resource as the central common component (Figure 5.10) (Ortega-Arjona & Roberts, 1998a; Ortega-Arjona, 2003).

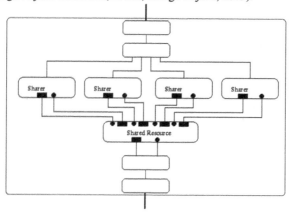

Figure 5.10 Shared resource pattern.

Participants

- *Shared resource.* The responsibility of a shared resource is to co-ordinate access of sharer components, preserving the integrity of data (Ortega-Arjona & Roberts, 1998a; Ortega-Arjona, 2003).
- *Sharer component.* The responsibilities of a sharer component are to perform its independent computation until requiring a service from the shared resource. Then, the sharer component has to cope with any access restriction imposed by the shared resource. Since its computations are independent, all sharer components are able to execute in parallel (Ortega-Arjona & Roberts, 1998a; Ortega-Arjona, 2003).

155

Dynamics

A typical scenario to describe the basic run-time behaviour of the Shared Resource pattern is presented. All participants are simultaneously active. Every sharer component performs a different operation, requiring the shared resource for data. If data is not available, the sharer can request for another piece of data. As soon as data is made available from the shared resource, the requesting sharer component continues its computations. Communications between sharer components are not allowed. The shared resource is the only common communication means among the shared components. The functionality of this general scenario is explained as follows (Figure 5.11) (Ortega-Arjona & Roberts, 1998a; Ortega-Arjona, 2003):

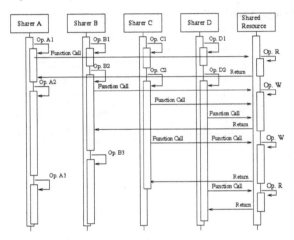

Figure 5.11 Scenario of Shared resource pattern

- For this scenario, let us consider a simple **Shared resource** which is able to perform only a couple of operations, *Op.R* and *Op.W*, in order to respectively allow reading or writing of data. Each sharer component starts processing, performing different, independent operations, and requesting the **Shared resource** to execute a read or write operation.

- Consider the basic operation: a sharer component, **Sharer A**, is performing *Op.A1*, and requests the **Shared resource** to perform a read operation *Op.R*. If no other sharer component contests for reading or writing data, the **Shared resource** is able to immediately serve the request from **Sharer A**, reading data.

- Things become more complex when one sharer component is reading or writing data of the **Shared resource,** and another sharer component requires to read or write the same data. Consider, for example, that **Sharer B** is performing *Op.B2*, which requests a writing operation *Op.W* to the **Shared resource**. If while the **Shared resource** is serving this operation, one or more other sharer components (in this scenario, **Sharer C** and **Sharer D**) issue calls to the **Shared resource**, requesting for a read or write operation, the **Shared resource** should be able to continue until completion of its actual operation, deferring the calls for later execution, or even ignoring them. If this is the case, any sharer component should be able to reissue its call, requesting for an operation on the same or other data until it is carried out.

- Another complex situation that may arise is if two or more sharer components issue calls requesting the same data to the **Shared resource** at precisely the same time. Consider, for example, the previous situation in the scenario: as the **Sharer C** and **Sharer D** calls could not be serviced by the **Shared resource**, they have to re-issue their calls, doing it at the very same time. In this particular case, the **Shared resource** should be able to resolve the situation by servicing only one call (in this scenario, the writing request from **Sharer C**), and deferring or ignoring all other calls for later (as it is the case of the reading request from **Sharer D**). Again, the sharer components whose calls were deferred or ignored should be able to reissue them, contesting again for the data piece serviced by the **Shared resource**.

Implementation

The implementation process is based on the four stages mentioned earlier in the *General Implementation* (see Section 5.2.5) (Ortega-Arjona & Roberts, 1998a; Ortega-Arjona, 2003).

- *Partitioning.* The computation to be performed can be viewed as the effect of different independent computations on the data structure. Each sharer component is defined to perform an independent computation on data from the shared resource. Sharer components can be executed simultaneously due to their independent processing nature. However, the shared resource implementation should reflect a division and integrity criteria of the data structure, following the basic assumption that no piece of data is operated at the same time by two different sharer components. Therefore, sharer components may be implemented by a single entity (for instance, a process, a task, an object, etc.) that performs a defined computation, or a sub-system of entities. Design patterns in general (Gamma *et al.*, 1994; Buschmann *et al.*, 1996; Coplien & Schmidt, 1995; Vlissides *et al.*, 1996) may help with the implementation of the sharers components as sub-systems of entities. Also, patterns used in concurrent programming like the Object group pattern (Maffeis, 1996), the Active Object pattern (Lavender & Schmidt, 1996), and Categorize Objects for Concurrency pattern (Aarsten *et al.*, 1995) can help to define and implement sharer components.

- *Communication.* The communication to co-ordinate the interaction of sharer components and shared resource is represented by an appropriate communication interface that allows access to the shared resource. This interface should reflect the form in which requests are issued to the shared resource, and the format and size of the data as argument or return value. In general, an asynchronous coordination schema is used, due to the heterogeneous behaviour of the sharer components, whose requests can be deferred or ignored by the shared resource. The implementation of a flexible interface between sharer components and shared resource can be done using Design Patterns for communication, like the Service Configurator pattern (Jain & Schmidt, 1996), the Composite Messages pattern (Sane & Campbell, 1995), and the Compatible Heterogeneous Agents and Visibility and Communication between Agents patterns (Aarsten *et al.*, 1996). Other Design Patterns like the Double-Checked Locking pattern (Schmidt & Harrison, 1996), the Thread-Specific Storage pattern (Harrison & Schmidt, 1997) and those presented by MacKenney (1996) deal with issues about the safe use of threads and locks, and may provide help to implement the expected behaviour of the shared resource component.

- *Agglomeration.* The components and communication are evaluated against performance requirements. If necessary, operations can be recombined and reassigned to create different sets of sharer components with different granularity and load-balance. Usually, due to the independent nature of the sharer components, it is difficult to achieve a good performance initially, but at the same time, it is easy to make changes on the sharer components without affecting the whole structure. The conjecture-test approach is used intensively, modifying both granularity and load-balance of sharer components to observe which combination can be used to improve performance. However, especial care should be taken with the load-balance between sharer components and a shared resource. The operations of the shared resource should be lighter than any sharer computation, to allow a fast response of the shared resource to requests. Most of the computation activity is meant to be performed by the sharer components.

- *Mapping.* As the number of processors is commonly limited and less than the number of components, any mapping strategy makes difficult and complex to load-balance the whole structure. A partial solution is to determine mapping at run-time by load-balancing algorithms. As a "rule of thumb", Shared Resource systems present a good performance when implemented on a MIMD (multiple-instruction, multiple-data) computer. Also, it would be very difficult to implement them for a SIMD (single-instruction, multiple-data) computer (Pancake, 1996; Pfister, 1995).

5.3 Selection of Architectural Patterns

The initial selection of one or several architectural patterns is guided mainly by the properties used for classifying them. However, it is important to notice that a particular architectural pattern, or its combination with others, is not a complete parallel software application. Its objective is just to describe and provide a stable coordination organisation for a software system, as a first step on the design and implementation of parallel software systems (Ortega-Arjona & Roberts, 1998a).

Based on the classification schema and the pattern description, a procedure for selecting an architectural pattern can be specified as follows (Ortega & Roberts, 1998a):

1. *Analyse the design problem and obtain its specification.* Analyse and specify, as precisely as possible, the problem in terms of its characteristics of order of data and computations, the probable nature of its processing components, and performance requirements. It is important to also consider the context conditions about the chosen parallel platform and language (see step 5) that may influence the design. This stage is crucial to set up most of the basic forces to deal with during the design.

2. *Select the category of parallelism.* In accordance with the problem specification, select the category of parallelism —functional, domain or activity parallelism— that best describes it.

3. *Select the category of the nature of the processing components.* Select the nature of the process distribution —homogeneous or heterogeneous— among components that best describes the problem specification. The nature of process distribution indirectly

reflects characteristics about the number of processing components and the amount and kind of communications between them in the solution.

4. *Compare the problem specification with the architectural pattern's Problem section.* The categories of parallelism and nature of processing components can be simply used to guide the selection of an architectural pattern. In order to verify that the selected pattern copes with the problem at hand, compare the problem specification with the *Problem* section of the selected pattern. More specific information and knowledge about the problem to be solved is required. Unless problems were encountered up to this point, the architectural pattern selection can be considered as completed. The design of the parallel software system continues using the selected architectural pattern's *Solution* section as a starting point. On the other hand, if the architectural pattern selected does not satisfactorily match aspects of the problem specification, it is possible to try to select an alternative pattern, as follows.

5. *Select an alternative architectural pattern.* If the selected pattern does not match the problem specification at hand, try to select another pattern that alternatively may provide a better approach when it is modified, specialised or combined with others. Checking the *Examples*, *Known Uses* and *Related Patterns* sections of other pattern descriptions may be helpful for this. If an alternative pattern is selected, return to the previous step to verify it copes with the problem specification.

If the previous steps do not provide a result, even after trying some alternative patterns, stop searching. The architectural patterns here do not provide a coordination organisation that can help to solve this particular problem. It is possible to look at other more general pattern languages or systems (Gamma *et al.,* 1994; Coplien & Schmidt, 1995; Buschmann *et al.,* 1996) to see if they contain a pattern that can be used. Or the alternative is trying to solve the design problem without using software patterns.

5.4 An Example of Selecting an Architectural Pattern for Parallel Programming: The Two-dimensional Wave Equation

This section introduces the Two-dimensional Wave Equation problem, as a problem used to illustrate how the selection process of an Architectural Pattern for Parallel Programming is carried out. The following sections present and describe the actual problem (the *software problem*, as explained in Sections 4.3.1 and 5.2.1), an algorithmic solution for the Two-dimensional Wave Equation (the *parallelisation problem*, as described in Sections 4.3.1 and 5.2.1), and the steps of the process towards the selection of an Architectural Pattern.

5.4.1 Problem Description — The Two-Dimensional Wave Equation

The Two-dimensional Wave Equation (Dobson & Wadsworth, 1996) is an expression to calculate the motion of a wave on the surface of a fluid medium, for example, a pressure wave on water. Let us assume that the fluid medium is homogeneous, this is, it has a uniform mass per unit of area. If a point in the area of the fluid is displaced upwards or downwards a small amount, then the tension forces will tend to return the point to its original position, producing a wave motion of the fluid surface. The mathematical equations that govern this motion can be derived from some basic principles of physics (Dobson & Wadsworth, 1996). This problem represents the *software problem*, to be solved through an algorithm and data to be processed (see Section 4.3.1).

5.4.2 Algorithmic Solution for the Two-Dimensional Wave Equation

The simplest method for deriving a numerical solution to the Two-dimensional Wave Equation is the method of finite differences. This method is based on a relaxation algorithm (see Section 5.2.2). In two-dimensions, the Two-dimensional Wave Equation has the discrete form:

$$C[i,j] = B[i,j] - A[i,j] + \frac{1}{4}(B[i+1,j] + B[i-1,j] + B[i,j+1] + B[i,j-1])$$

where three grids A, B, and C are used to hold the values of the simulation at different time steps. Grid B holds the values of points at time t; grid A at time t-1; and grid C holds the new values for time t+1. The new value of a point (i,j) is computed as a function of its past value and those of its immediate four neighbours. Thus, the proposed numerical solution to the Two-dimensional Wave Equation is now computed by simply calculating the position value for each point (i,j) in C at a given time step, and for as many time steps as desired. Notice that this numerical solution is actually a relaxation algorithm which approaches the whole solution iteratively (see Section 5.2.2).

Moreover, initially the Two-dimensional Wave Equation may seem a trivial problem, which can be solved using a simple uniprocessor system. This would normally be the case depending on the requirements of the problem. Nevertheless, a simple analysis shows that the time to solve the Two-dimensional Wave Equation rapidly grows as the requirements change. The total time required to sequentially execute this solution depends directly on the number of points in which the surface is divided, the number of time steps needed to describe the position of all points at a particular time step, and their changes of position through time. The larger number of points and number of steps, the longer it takes to compute the solution. A sequential approach than obtains a single new position for each point at each time step is not the most time-efficient way to compute the motion of all points.

Suppose, for example, that it is needed to model the position values for a surface divided into 1,000 points, considering time steps of 5 milliseconds, during a time frame of 10 seconds. The total number of operations (commonly, floating-point operations) required is 2,000,000. Simply changing the requirement for the number of points to 10,000 and the time step to 1 millisecond, the total number of operations required now is 100,000,000, that is, 50 times more. Notice that naive changes to the requirements (which are normally requested when performing this kind of simulations) produce drastic (exponential) increments of the number of operations required, which at the same time affects the time required to calculate this numerical solution.

However, we can potentially compute the numerical solution to the Two-dimensional Wave Equation in a more efficient way by *(a)* using a group of software components that exploit the two-dimensional logical structure of the surface, and *(b)* allowing each software component to simultaneously calculate the position value for all points of C at a given time step. This is the parallelisation problem to solve.

5.4.3 Selecting an Architectural Pattern for the Two-dimensional Wave Equation

Based on the problem description and algorithmic solution presented in the previous sections, the procedure for selecting an architectural pattern for a parallel solution to the Two-dimensional Wave Equation problem is presented as follows:

1. *Analyse the design problem and obtain its specification.* Analysing the problem description and the algorithmic solution provided, it is noticeable that the calculation of the Two-dimensional Wave Equation is a step-by-step process. Such a process is based on calculating the next position of each point on the surface through each time step. The calculation uses as input the actual position, the previous position, and the

actual position of the four neighbours point of the cord, and provides the position of the point at the next time step.

2. *Select the category of parallelism.* Observing the form in which the algorithmic solution partitions the problem, it is clear that the surface is partitioned into points, and a computations should be executed simultaneously on different points. Hence, the algorithmic solution description implies the category of domain parallelism (see Section 5.2.1).

3. *Select the category of the nature of the processing components.* Also, from the algorithmic description of the solution, it is clear that the position of each point of the surface is obtained using exactly the same calculations. Thus, the nature of the processing components of a probable solution for the Two-dimensional Wave Equation, using the algorithm proposed, is certainly an homogeneous one (see Section 5.2.2).

4. *Compare the problem specification with the architectural pattern's Problem section.* An Architectural Pattern that directly copes with the categories of domain parallelism and the homogeneous nature of processing components is the Communicating Sequential Elements (CSE) pattern (see Table 5.1). In order to verify that this architectural pattern actually copes with the Two-dimensional Wave Equation problem, let us compare the problem description with the *Problem* section of the CSE pattern. From the CSE pattern description, the problem is defined as *"A parallel computation is required that can be performed as a set of operations on ordered data. Results cannot be constrained to a one-way flow among processing stages, but each component executes its operations influenced by data values from its neighbouring components. Because of this, components are expected to intermittently exchange data. Communications between components follow fixed and predictable paths".* Observing the algorithmic solution for the Two-dimensional Wave Equation, it can be defined in terms of calculating the next position of the surface points as ordered data. Each point is operated almost autonomously. The exchange of data or communication should be between neighbouring points on the surface. So, the CSE is chosen as an adequate solution for the Two-dimensional Wave Equation, and the architectural pattern selection is completed. The design of the parallel software system should continue, based on the *Solution* section of the CSE pattern.

5.5 Summary

In this chapter we introduce the concept of architectural pattern, and its relation with Software Architecture and Software Performance. Also, the Architectural Patterns for Parallel Programming are introduced as part of the original work developed for this PhD thesis. These architectural patterns describe common coordination organisations in parallel software systems, as the *coordination* layer of an overall parallel software architecture. Their selection constitutes the initial step of the Architectural Performance Modelling Method.

The Architectural Patterns for Parallel Programming have the common objective of solving the *parallelisation problem*. This problem refers to describe an available algorithmic solution to a *software problem* as the simultaneous execution of communicating sequential processes. This means that, once a solution to the software problem has been found and described as an algorithm and data, the objective is to get a more efficient execution of such a solution as a parallel program.

In this chapter, the Two-dimensional Wave Equation is introduced as a case example used throughout the remaining chapters. The Two-dimensional Wave Equation represents a problem whose solution *(a)* mainly depends on the requirements of resolution in time (number of steps) and space (number of points), and *(b)* is developed as a relaxation algorithm. Even though at first sight it may seem a trivial problem, our purpose here is to introduce an example to illustrate and evaluate the Architectural Performance Modelling Method. Hence, the criteria used to select this problem is that it actually shows how to apply architectural patterns within the Architectural Performance Modelling Method, and not whether it is a complex large-scale problem.

The architectural patterns are presented here along with the guidelines on their classification and selection, in order to help the software designer with deciding which coordination organisation is potentially useful to solve a given problem. The architectural patterns described here are (Ortega-Arjona & Roberts, 1998a): Pipes and Filters, Parallel Hierarchies, Communicating Sequential Elements (Ortega-Arjona, 2000), Manager-Workers (Ortega-Arjona, 2004), and Shared Resource (Ortega-Arjona 2003).

Chapter 6

Architectural Performance Model Construction

"When we mean to build, we first survey the plot, then draw the model"

Shakespeare

Following after the selection of an Architectural Pattern for Parallel Programming, the Architectural Performance Modelling Method continues with the construction of an Architectural Performance Model. This model is used to simulate the behaviour of a parallel program, based on the generic description of parallel programs provided in Section 4.3.1.

An Architectural Performance Model is composed of two types of simulations: Coordination Simulation and Component Simulation. These simulation models reflect the basic supposition of considering that communication and processing are activities sharply separated among coordination and processing components (see Sections 1.4 and 4.3.2). Even though this may not be always the case, our objective is to prove that such a supposition does not introduce a considerable error for performance estimation. So, our scale-model can effectively be used to estimate the performance of a parallel program with the proposed constraints (see Section 4.3.1).

The Coordination Simulation captures the essential communication aspects of the parallel software behaviour, and it is based on a selected architectural pattern (see Chapter 5). The Component Simulation represents the processing behaviour of components, and it is developed based on the Active Object pattern (Lavender and Schmidt, 1996; JOLT, 1999; Schmidt et al., 2000) and elements of Queuing Theory (Kleinrock, 1975; Lazowska et al., 1984; Law & Kelton, 1991).

It is important to mention that, for the actual purposes of the present thesis, all simulation models are developed and executed on a cluster of sixteen computers, using the

JPVM environment (Ferrari, 1997; Geist, *et al.*, 1994), representing the available hardware and software resources. Also, all simulation models are programmed using the Java programming language (Smith, 2000). However, these conditions do not prevent that modelling and simulation as proposed by the method could be developed for a different hardware and software platform, in order to estimate the performance of a parallel solution on such a platform.

6.1 Coordination Simulation

6.1.1 Definition

For the actual purposes, a Coordination Simulation is defined as *a scale-model implementation of functional execution of a parallel application to the level of creation of independent communicating software components, and the coordination among them.* A Coordination Simulation is considered a partial, runnable implementation of a parallel program that exhibit only the communication and coordination among software components, based on a selected architectural pattern. The previous selection of such architectural pattern reflects the characteristics of order and precedence of steps in the algorithm and/or data found in the problem at hand, which directly affect its parallelisation (see Chapter 5).

6.1.2 Description

The Coordination Simulation consists of interactions that reflect the top-most communication level used to capture essential aspects of the parallel execution, and to derive parameters for the execution of an Architectural Performance Model. As part of the Architectural Performance Modelling Method (see Section 4.3.3), it is constructed using information from the selected architectural pattern (see Chapter 5), whose *Structure* and *Dynamics* sections define the communication structure of the prospective parallel program. Moreover, the *Participants* and *Implementation* sections of the architectural pattern provide information to develop the parallel program's communicating software components (see Sections 2.1 and 2.2). The Coordination Simulation is used to obtain initial estimates of the time spent in communication and synchronisation activities of its software components, as well as to derive parameters for the (sequential) processing components in a workload scenario.

166

6.1.3 Implementation

The Coordination Simulation is constructed from the *Implementation* section of the selected architectural pattern (see Section 5.2.5). It is created as a skeleton of code representing the structural communication relations among parallel components, and executed using the given data and available hardware an software resources only to show the communication and synchronisation interactions among sequential software components.

The implementation of a Coordination Simulation is based on an exploratory approach to design, in which hardware-independent features are early considered, and hardware-specific issues are delayed in the process (Foster, 1994). The Coordination Simulation, as a runnable implementation, is constructed through four stages of *Partitioning, Communicating, Agglomeration* and *Mapping* (see Section 5.2.5).

6.1.4 Operation

In general, the Coordination Simulation operates for a typical workload scenario, which specifies the basic partitioning and communication operations of the data to be processed by the (sequential) processing components. It also specifies the frequency with which those operations occur, representing the flow of data through a parallel program that executes on a particular platform. Thus, it is possible to measure from the Coordination Simulation the actual time it requires *only* to coordinate and communicate data among components. This time represents a lower bound on the response time due exclusively to the coordination activity of a parallel program. It is an initial indicator of whether the proposed parallel system will meet performance goals.

The Coordination Simulation also allows simulation parameters to be obtained for the execution of the Architectural Performance Model. As the workload scenario specifies the frequency with which operations occur, it is possible to measure the inter-arrival times, and thereby obtain their average (expressed as $1/\lambda$, where λ is the arrival rate, see Section 6.2.2) between request for operation that coordination components issue. These values are used later, when obtaining the parameters for the Component Simulation (see Section 6.2.2).

6.1.5 Example: CSE and the Two-dimensional Wave Equation

In this section, we continue developing the Two-Dimensional Wave Equation example introduced in Chapter 5, using the Communicating Sequential Elements architectural pattern as a selected organisation for its coordination layer (see Section 5.4). The objective now is to show how the information from the architectural pattern is used to develop the Coordination Simulation.

In the example, the main idea of the Communicating Sequential Elements pattern is that all data (representing the position of each point on the surface) is partitioned and assigned to a group of communicating sequential elements (see Section 5.2.10).

The construction of the Coordination Simulation for this problem is carried out following the steps provided in the *Implementation* section of the Communicating Sequential Elements Pattern (see Section 5.2.10), as follows:

- *Partitioning.* The Communication Sequential Elements pattern describes a cooperation between identical sequential elements, which communicate partial results by exchanging values through channels with their neighbours. In our example, the data structure (representing the surface) is the natural candidate to be initially decomposed into a two-dimensional array of points. As defined by the pattern, all communicating elements will have the same structure, which is expected to perform the same computation (in this case, the position of each point). However, for the actual purposes of Coordination Simulation construction, the basic communicating element implementation only focuses on partitioning the data structure and on referencing to its neighbouring elements, and not on the processing activity to be carried out. The code for class TwoDWave is shown in Figure 6.1, and developed in Java. TwoDWave uses several declarations of data types within the JPVM environment (Ferrari,1997). According with the description of the CSE pattern (see Section 5.2.10), the class TwoDWave is in charge of partitioning the two-dimensional array. Hence, this should be reflected by the Coordination Simulation, due to it exhibiting only the communication and coordination among software components, based on the selected architectural pattern (see Section 6.1.1). So, its most relevant attributes used to organise and perform the partitioning activities are described as follows (Ferrari, 1997):

  - nprocs. An int value, whose purpose is to define the number of processes to be created into the JPVM environment.
  - procdim. An int value that specifies the size of the two-dimensional mesh of processes.
  - tids and childTids. Two arrays of jpvmTaskId values, which are used to store the task identifiers of all workers.

168

```
import jpvm.*;

class TwoDWave{
    . . .
    static int      nprocs   = DEFAULT_NUM_PROCS;
    static int      procdim;
    static jpvmTaskId   tids[];
    static jpvmTaskId   childTids[];
    static int      my_id = -1, my_x = -1, my_y = -1;
    static int      east_id,  west_id;
    static int      north_id, south_id;
    static int      N;
    static int      Np;
    static double   X[][];
    static double   B[][];
    static double   tmpBorder[];
    static int      iteration = 0;
    static double   start_time, end_time;
    . . .
}
```

Figure 6.1 Relevant attributes of the class TwoDWave

- my_id, my_x, and my_y. Three int values which specify the location of the local two-dimensional array in the mesh of processes.

- east_id, west_id, north_id, and south_id. Four int values holding the numbers of the process neighbours on each side.

- N. An int value defining the size of the total square grid of points (N×N).

- Np. An int value defining the size of the square sub-grid of points (Np×Np).

- X. A two-dimensional array of double values, holding the present and next values of the points within the local sub-grid.

- B. A two-dimensional array of double values, holding the past values of the points within the local sub-grid.

- tmpBorder. An array of double values, which temporary hold the values to be sent to or received from the neighbouring sub-grids.

- iteration. An array of int value, which keeps record of the number of iterations so far.

- start_time and end_time. Two double values, which hold the timing information of the program's execution.

- *Communication.* Communication is defined using JPVM methods for sending and receiving data to and from the neighbouring elements. Two methods of the code of the class TwoDWave shown in Figure 6.2, carry out these communication activities, based on the JPVM environment (Ferrari, 1997).

```
import jpvm.*;

class TwoDWave{
    ...
    static void send_borders(double x[])throws jpvmException{
        ...
        jpvmBuffer buf;
        if(north_id!=NOBODY) {
            ...
            /* Send out northern border */
            for(i=0;i<how_many;i++)tmpBorder[i] = x[Np];
            buf = new jpvmBuffer();
            buf.pack(tmpBorder,how_many,1);
            jpvm.pvm_send(buf,tids[north_id],RED_SOUTH_TAG);
        }
        ...
    }
    static void recv_borders(double x[])throws jpvmException{
        ...
        jpvmMessage m;
        if(north_id!=NOBODY) {
            ...
            m = jpvm.pvm_recv(tids[north_id],RED_NORTH_TAG);
            m.buffer.unpack(tmpBorder,how_many,1);
            for(i=0;i<how_many;i++)x[Np+1] = tmpBorder[i];
        }
        else {
        if(iteration<=1)
            for(i=0;i<(Np+2);i++) x[Np+1]=0.0;
        }
        ...
    }
    ...
}
```

Figure 6.2 Communication methods for the Two-dimensional Wave Equation

The methods that implement the communication between sequential elements (see Section 5.2.10) as described by the CSE architectural pattern are described as follows:

- void send_borders(). This method is used to send the array x to the four neighbouring elements. Notice that the code used for the northern neighbour has to be repeated for the rest of the neighbours, considering the adequate values for the array x. The method makes use of jpvm.pvm_send(), to actually send the array.

- void recv_borders(). This method is used to receive data from the four neighbouring elements, and store it in the array x. Notice again that the code used for the northern neighbour has to be repeated for the rest of the neighbour, considering the adequate values for the array x. The method makes use of jpvm.pvm_recv(), to actually receive the array.

- *Agglomeration and Mapping.* Finally, for the Coordination Simulation execution, tasks are created and connected as determined by the data structure representing the complete surface. Each communicating element considers four neighbours with which exchange partial results. The Coordination Simulation is executed on the given platform, representing how the data is divided among the communicating elements, how the communicating elements exchange data, and how they iteratively carry out the whole computation. The parts of the Java code in the main() function of the parallel application, which creates and spawns the elements within the JPVM environment (Ferrari, 1997), is presented in Figure 6.3.

```java
import jpvm.*;

class TwoDWave{
    ...
    public static void main(String args[]) {
        try {
            jpvm = new jpvmEnvironment();
            ...
            tids = new jpvmTaskId[nprocs];
            childTids = new jpvmTaskId[nprocs-1];
            tids[0] = my_tid;
            my_id = my_x = my_y = 0;

            /* Spawn workers */
            if(nprocs>1) {
                jpvm.pvm_spawn("TwoDWave",nprocs-1,tids);
                tids[nprocs-1] = tids[0];
                for(i=0;i<(nprocs-1);i++)childTids[i] = tids[i];
                tids[0] = my_tid;
                ...
            }
            ...
        }
        catch (jpvmException jpe) {
            error("jpvm Exception - "+jpe.toString());
        }
        catch (Exception e) {
            error("Exception - "+e.toString());
        }
    }
    ...
}
```

Figure 6.3 Main elements of the main function for the Two-dimensional Wave Equation

The main() function starts creating a jpvmEnvironment declared as jpvm. This is the basic component for creating the rest of the tasks within JPVM (Ferrari, 1997). From jpvm, all the services of the environment can be obtained, like the creation and spawning of elements (using the method pvm_spawn()). From this point onwards, the software components are expected to execute.

In summary, these implementation steps set up the Coordination Simulation for the Two-dimensional Wave Equation, using the Communicating Sequential Elements pattern. The Coordination Simulation will be used later, for the development of the Architectural Performance Model (see Section 6.3). The Coordination Simulation only carries out the partitioning of the data, and allows for the communication exchange among instances of the class TwoDWave as described by the Communicating Sequential Elements pattern, but actually does not perform any processing on the values that describe the motion of the points on the surface. This is a consequence of the basic supposition that communication and processing are activities sharply separated among coordination and processing components (see Sections 1.4 and 4.3.2). Hence, the execution of the Coordination Simulation is used to measure the actual time it takes to coordinate and communicate data among components (see Section 7.2, "Coordination Simulation Execution"). This time represents a lower bound on the response time due exclusively to the coordination activity, and it is an initial indicator of whether the proposed parallel software architecture will meet performance goals (see Section 6.1.4). Moreover, the execution of the Coordination Simulation also allows to obtain measurements to derive the simulation parameters for the Component Simulations (see Section 7.2), and thus, for the execution of the Architectural Performance Model (see Section 7.3). As the workload scenario specifies the frequency with which operations occur, it is possible to measure the inter-arrival times between request for operation that coordination components issue, and obtain their average (expressed as $1/\lambda$) (see Section 7.3.1, "Obtaining the Simulation Parameters for the Component Simulations"). The processing activity triggered by such requests is expected to be simulated, using the Component Simulation model, which is explained as follows.

6.2 Component Simulation

6.2.1 Definition

The Component Simulation is defined as *a representation of the time in which a free-standing sequential and operational unit of the application provides functionally.* The Component Simulation is considered as the representation of the time that would take to a processing (sequential) component of a parallel software system to use the input data in order to produce an output result.

6.2.2 Description

The Component Simulation is an executable simulation of the time behaviour of a single component, representing only its processing time. As part of a parallel program, it represents the time consumed by a sequential software component, according with the definition of a parallel program (see Section 2.1.5). One way in which the Component Simulation could represent the time consumed by a sequential processing component is implementing it using the structure of an active object (Agha, 1990; Agha *et al.*,1993a; Agha *et al.*, 1993c, Frolund, 1996). Hence, for our purposes the Component Simulation will only reflect the sequential behaviour of a software component through time, using the Active Object pattern (Lavender and Schmidt, 1996; JOLT, 1999; Schmidt *et al.*, 2000) as a structural base for its implementation. This pattern represents the elements of an active object, whose behaviour depends on the messages exchanged by the participants of the pattern, and the configuration used to compose them as an active object.

Nevertheless, in order to simulate the sequential execution through time, some parameters for the Component Simulation are needed. These parameters are obtained from elements of Queuing Theory (Kleinrock, 1975; Lazowska *et al.*, 1984; Law & Kelton, 1991; Bolch *et al.*, 1998). In the following sections, the description of the Active Object pattern and its combination with elements of Queuing Theory is described, in order to develop the Component Simulation.

The Active Object Behavioral Pattern

The Active Object Behavioral Pattern (or simply, Active Object pattern) was originally proposed by Lavender and Schmidt (1996), latter extended as part of the JOLT project (JOLT, 1999), and finally introduced as part of the software patterns presented in the POSA 2 book (Schmidt *et al.*, 2000). This design pattern is proposed and used to implement active objects. In essence, the Active Object pattern decouples method execution from method invocation, allowing one or more independent objects to interleave their access to a single object. Using the Active Object pattern, a method is executed in another sequence of method calls, separated from the one that originally invoked it. In this section, a brief description of the Active Object pattern is presented, using the POSA form (Buschmann *et al.*, 1996).

Context

Use the Active Object pattern during the design and implementation of a concurrent program, where objects are required to execute using separate sequences of method calls (Lavender & Schmidt, 1996; JOLT, 1999; Schmidt *et al.*, 2000).

Problem

The concurrent execution of several objects is required in a software program. Each object is expected to execute at its own rate, residing in an individual thread of control, and communicating with other objects. As several objects execute simultaneously, each object has to guarantee a synchronised execution of its methods, controlling access to its state by methods invoked by other objects (Lavender & Schmidt, 1996; JOLT, 1999; Schmidt *et al.*, 2000).

Solution

A set of objects performs the activities of the Active Object pattern, decoupling method invocation from method execution: when a message is sent to an active object, it is received through its *client interface,* which accepts messages to be processed by the active object. The *scheduler*, a scheduling mechanism, is in charge of the queue of incoming messages in the active object's associated *activation queue*, in which messages are stored in the form of *method objects* until they can be dispatched. A *method object* is a representation of the method invoked by a message. In general, if no other criteria is specified, messages are dispatched based on an arrival order criteria. When a message can be dispatched, the *scheduler* removes its associated *method object* from the *activation queue* and invokes the real method in the object *resource representation*. This performs the expected behaviour in response to the message, manipulating the instance variables that represent the state of the active object (Lavender & Schmidt, 1996; Schmidt *et al.*, 2000).

Class Diagram and Participants

The class diagram of the Active Object pattern is illustrated in Figure 6.4.

The participants of the Active Object pattern are (Lavender & Schmidt, 1996; Schmidt *et al.*, 2000):

- *Client interface.* The client interface is a method interface presented to client applica-

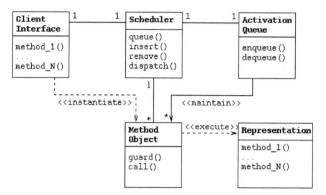

Figure 6.4 Class diagram of the components of a generic Active Object.

tions. When a method defined by the client interface is invoked, this triggers the construction and queuing of a method object.

- *Method objects.* A method object is constructed by the scheduler for any input message requiring a synchronised method execution. Each method object contains the context information necessary to execute an invoked method operation and return any result of that execution through the client interface.

- *Activation queue.* The activation queue is a priority queue, storing input messages as method invocations represented by method objects. The activation queue is controlled and managed by the scheduler.

- *Scheduler.* The scheduler is an object that manages the activation of method objects requiring execution. It is in charge of inserting and removing method objects from the activation queue, and deciding which method object is to be executed at certain time. The execution of a method object is based on mutual exclusion and condition synchronisation constraints.

- *Resource representation.* The resource representation object is the implementation of the methods defined in the client interface. It represents the resource modelled as an active object. It may also contain other methods used by the scheduler to compute runtime synchronisation conditions that determine the execution order.

Dynamics

The collaborations in the Active Object pattern are shown in Figure 6.5.

175

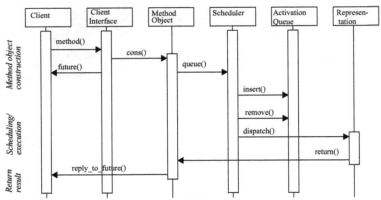

Figure 6.5 Dynamics in the Active Object pattern

The collaborations between objects are defined based on three stages, as follows (Lavender & Schmidt, 1996; Schmidt *et al.*,2000):

1. *Method object construction*. In this stage, the client application invokes a method defined by the client interface. This triggers the construction of a method object, which maintains context value information about the method as well as anything else required to execute the method and return a result. After its creation, the method object requests the scheduler to be queued on the active object's activation queue, waiting for its eventual execution. The scheduler inserts it and a result handle, or future, is returned to the client.

2. *Scheduling/execution*. In this phase, the scheduler consults the activation queue to determine which method object matches established synchronisation constraints. The scheduler removes the method object from the activation queue, and calls the resource representation to dispatch it. A call is made to the actual method of the resource representation with the information contained in the method object. The method is executed, updating the state of the resource representation to create a result.

3. *Return result*. Finally, the result value is returned when the method finishes executing. Again, using the information contained in the method object, the result is passed to the future that returns it to the client. The future and method object involved will be garbage-collected when they are no longer needed.

This completes a brief description of the essential structural and behavioural details about the Active Object pattern. This information is used later to implement the Component Simulation. However, for a more complete description, refer to the original work by

Lavender & Schmidt (1996), the extended work by the JOLT project (JOLT, 1999), or the latest description of this pattern, which can be found in the POSA 2 book (Schmidt *et al.*, 2000).

Some Basics on Queuing Theory — Stochastic Queue Models

A simple description of an active object, based exclusively on the active object's structure, does not provide a complete picture of the behaviour through time of a sequential software component. It is also necessary to address the underlying stochastic nature of its elements. Requests for service arriving at the active object's message queue can often be modelled as a random process. The amount of computation required each time by a processing activity (or job) can also be commonly modelled as a random process.

The area of mathematics known as Queuing Theory encompasses the set of analytical models that most adequately can describe this kind of random processes (Kleinrock, 1975; Law & Kelton, 1991; Lazowska *et al.*, 1984; Bolch, *et al.*, 1998). Queuing Theory analyses structures in many areas where real systems are very complex mechanisms, and tractable mathematical models must often be simplified approximations to the real system. Simulation models are used in conjunction with queuing structures to accurately model these systems, describing the performance as a function of a number of parameters, and providing approximate quantitative answers about the behaviour of a system (Lazowska *et al.*, 1984; see also Sections 3.1 and 3.2). Both queuing and simulation models play an essential role in the behaviour modelling of several systems. However, to get information through simulation often takes many hours of computation, and even then, the behaviour of a complex system over a range of configurations is still not as clear as when an analytical solution is available (Law & Kelton, 1991).

This section analyses in detail a fundamental queuing structure that has a wide application in the analysis of sequential computing systems. This structure is known as a *single station queueing system* (Bolch, *et al.*, 1998), which consists of a *queueing buffer* of finite or infinite size, and one (or more) identical *servers*. Such an elementary queueing system is also referred to as a *service station*, or simply, as a *node*. As any queueing structure, this structure has the following elements (Kleinrock, 1975; Law & Kelton, 1991; Stone *et al.*, 1975; Bolch, *et al.*, 1998):

- *An arrival mechanism.* In general, this is a process that generates requests to be serviced by the active object, modelling the time between the arrival of different requests, or interarrival time. The model discussed in this section assumes that the interarrival times are random variables, drawn from an arrival-time distribution function.

- *Service mechanisms.* After a request arrives, the primary objective of the active object is to service it. This service requires some time, and like interarrival times, the time to service a request or service time can also be modelled as random variables with a service-time distribution function.

- *Queuing discipline.* When requests for a service arrive at an active object faster that they can be serviced, a line or queue forms, and a policy is needed to determine the order in which outstanding requests will be processed.

In the following subsections we make a number of assumptions concerning these characteristics, in order to develop the Component Simulation that describes the sequential software component's behaviour through time.

Interarrival-time Distribution —The Poisson Arrival Process

The simplest arrival mechanism to mathematically model interarrival times, in a single processor/single process computing system, is the Poisson (completely random) arrival process (Law & Kelton, 1991; Stone *et al.,* 1975; Bolch, *et al.,* 1998). The most important property of this process is that events are taken from a very large population, where each member is independent of the others. This means for our purpose that the arrival at a present instant does not depend on the arrival, or non-arrival, at past or future instants. This lack of dependence on the past and future is commonly called *Markovian* or memoryless property. The simplicity of the mathematical analysis of the Poisson arrival process relies precisely on this property. To analyse a Poisson process, let λ be the average arrival rate of the Poisson process. Consider a time line with marks at several epochs or points in time that denote arrivals. The fundamental assumption that during a gap of time δt an arrival is independent of all other arrivals can be stated with the following two postulates (Lazowska *et al.,* 1984; Stone *et al.,* 1975):

- The probability of an arrival between the epochs t and $t + \delta t$ is $\lambda \delta t + o(\delta t)$, where $o(\delta t)$ denotes a quantity of smaller order of magnitude than δt. (More precisely,

$$\lim_{\delta t \to 0} \frac{o(\delta t)}{\delta t} = 0 \ .)$$

- The probability of more than one arrival between epochs t and $t + \delta t$ is $o(\delta t)$.

A mathematically derived expression for $P_n(t)$, as the probability of n arrivals during an interval of duration t, is (Lazowska *et al.*, 1984; Stone *et al.*, 1975):

$$P_n(t) = \frac{(\lambda t)^n}{n!} e^{-\lambda t}$$

From this expression, it can be observed that the exponential function can be used to model the required Markovian property of the Poisson arrival process, based exclusively on the average arrival rate λ.

Service-time Distributions — The Exponential Service-time Distribution

Following the same consideration about the memoryless or Markovian property that the Poisson process enjoys, an expression for service-time distributions for a single processor/single process computing system can be obtained (Law & Kelton, 1991; Stone *et al.*, 1975). Let μ be the average rate of service completions by an active object. Making a similar assumption to the one used in the Poisson arrival process, consider $f(t)$ as the probability of the completion of service between epochs t and $t + \delta t$. Similarly to the interarrival-time distribution, the mathematical expression derived for this probability is (Lazowska *et al.*, 1984; Stone *et al.*, 1975):

$$f(t) = \mu e^{-\mu t} \qquad t > 0$$

Again, it can be observed that using the exponential function as the service-time distribution of an active object maintains the required Markovian property.

Modelling an Active Object as a Simple Queue Structure

The Active Object is a simple programming structure whose behaviour through time can be modelled using a simple queue structure (Ortega-Arjona & Roberts, 2001). The queue structure proposed to model the behaviour through time of an active object is simple: a Poisson arrival process, and a single active object with exponential service time (Bolch *et al.*, 1998). Figure 6.6 represents this case.

The fact that the model is simple does not imply it is of little use. On the contrary, this model should be considered as a good initial approximation to the modelling of a sequential software component. The basic assumptions for the model development are (Ortega-Arjona & Roberts, 2001):

1. the arrival of messages forms a Poisson process with an average arrival rate of λ mes-

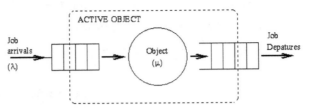

Figure 6.6 Simple queuing structure: a single active object with exponential inter-arrival and service times

sages per second;

2. the processing time per message is an exponentially distributed random variable with a service time average of μ messages per second; and

3. for simplicity, a first-in, first-out (FIFO) queue discipline is considered.

Using this information, the model must answer a number of questions when describing the time behaviour of a sequential software component, for instance (Ortega-Arjona & Roberts, 2001):

• How much time can the sequential software component spend processing a number of messages?

• What fraction of time will the software component be idle?

• What is the average response time seen by requests that are handled by the sequential software component?

To analyse this simple queuing structure, and answer the previous questions, it is necessary to develop an expression (in terms of λ and μ) for the probability of the component to be in certain state. This expression should be based on the basic considerations of the Poisson process and the exponential service-time distribution (Ortega-Arjona & Roberts, 2001).

Let p_n be the probability of the active object being in state E_n at epoch t, that is, having n messages in service or waiting for service. The expression for p_n is as follows (Law & Kelton, 1991; Stone *et al.,* 1975), where $\rho = \lambda / \mu$:

$$p_n = \rho^n(1-\rho) \qquad n = 1, 2, \ldots$$

It is possible to make some observations about this expression (Ortega-Arjona & Roberts, 2001). For instance, observe that this equation is not useful for $\rho = 1$. Furthermore, as the analysis of this queuing structure is performed for the steady state behaviour, this equation is meaningful only for $\rho < 1$: as ρ is defined as the relation λ / μ, when $\lambda > \mu$, requests arrive at a faster rate than the active object can service them. This means that there is no steady state solution for $\rho > 1$, because the arrival process is considered to saturate the active object, and its message queue grows without bound. The ratio ρ has an important role in general Queuing Theory, and it is commonly referred to as the traffic intensity of the queuing system (Kleinrock, 1975; Bolch *et al.*, 1998).

Applying this result to the questions about the active object's performance, it can be observed that the expression for p_n is considered to directly answer the first question about the probable time required to process a number of messages. The second question can be answered considering that the active object is idle when $n = 0$. Since p_0 indicates the active object has no outstanding messages to process it is idle for $(1 - \rho)$ of the time. The third question can be answered by the important fact that the active object is NOT idle with probability ρ. This result transcends the simple queuing case: in any single queuing structure, the average response or utilization equals the ratio of the arrival rate to the service rate (Ortega-Arjona & Roberts, 2001).

This completes out a brief introduction to the description of a simple queuing structure that models the behaviour through time of a sequential software component. This description is used as follows for the implementation of the Component Simulation.

6.2.3 Implementation

The implementation of the Component Simulation is based on elements related to the information of structure and behaviour from the Active Object pattern, and the steps to take for a discrete-event simulation. These elements are summarised as follows (Ortega-Arjona & Roberts, 2001):

Structure and Behaviour from the Active Object pattern
For our actual purposes, the Component Simulation should be able to simulate the processing behaviour through time of the Active Object's participants. This is achieved by taking the behaviour from the Active Object pattern (see Section 6.2.2), and proposing attributes and methods that represent the behaviour through time of its participants.

Let us state some general characteristics of execution that the Component Simulation will have, reflecting an active object's behaviour (Ortega-Arjona & Roberts, 2001):
1. At any specific time, only one job is serviced by the sequential component. If jobs arrive for service and there is already a job being serviced, the arriving jobs enter a FIFO queue.

2. Once a job is being processed, the sequential component's processing time can be calculated, simulating that the job receives service or, if the component is "busy", an idle time is obtained.

3. Upon receiving the total amount of simulated processing and idling time for a particular job, another job is serviced if the job queue is not empty.

From these characteristics, let us consider the following basic elements for the Component Simulation implementation (Ortega-Arjona & Roberts, 2001):

- The arriving jobs form a Poisson process with mean arrival rate `lambda`.
- The computation time required by a job is a exponentially distributed random variable with mean `mu`.
- All queuing in the implementation is FIFO.

These basic elements are used in the Component Simulation implementation, when defining the attributes of the simulation.

Discrete-event Simulation

The type of simulation considered to be appropriate for the study and modelling of sequential computing systems is the discrete-event simulation (Law & Kelton, 1991; Bolch *et al.*, 1998). Its most important feature is precisely that time is not considered a continuous variable incremented by uniform intervals. The execution of an event is represented by updating only the state of the simulation to reflect the occurrence of the event. After the event has occurred, the simulation is advanced to the time of the next event, and the process is repeated. Hence, the value obtained from the simulation commonly has no direct correspondence with the actual simulation time.

For the implementation of the Component Simulation, let us consider the use of discrete-event simulation to model a queuing structure (Ortega-Arjona & Roberts, 2001). Usually, when simulating a queue structure, its parameters —inter-arrival time of jobs, length of processing time required by jobs, and so on— are considered as random variables. Therefore, an important point for a discrete-event simulation of a queue structure is to generate a random variate from an arbitrary distribution. So, the simulation is carried out by the following steps (Stone *et al.*, 1975):

- Generate random variates.
- Create, modify and generally describe jobs that move through the simulation.
- Delimit and sequence the phases of a job.

- Facilitate the queuing of jobs.
- Collect, generate and display summary statistics.

These steps are used in the Component Simulation implementation, defining the methods of the simulation (Ortega-Arjona & Roberts, 2001).

The Implementation of the Component Simulation

Based on previous considerations, a Component Simulation is implemented consisting of two classes: `ActiveObjectSimulator` and `Markovian`, as shown in Figure 6.7 (Ortega-Arjona & Roberts, 2001). The interaction between these two classes allows the simula-

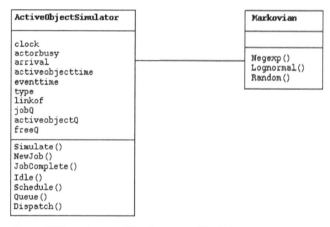

Figure 6.7 Class diagram of the Component Simulation.

tion of the time taken by the processing behaviour of a sequential software component, but executing event-time simulations instead of actual execution of the methods defined for the Active Object pattern.

The class `ActiveObjectSimulator` simulates the processing behaviour of a sequential software component as a simple queuing structure with exponential interarrival and service times (Bolch *et al.*, 1998; see also Section 6.2.2). Its most relevant attributes and methods are (Ortega-Arjona & Roberts, 2001):

- `clock` indicates the current epoch in time being simulated.
- `actorbusy` is a boolean variable that is true if the active object is busy servicing a job.
- `arrival` is an array of the times when each job arrived to the active object for service.
- `activeobjecttime` is an array that stores the total amount of processing time required to complete servicing each job.

183

- `eventtime` is an array of times in which the event associated with the job is scheduled to occur. Some jobs will not have an event time if they are queued waiting to be serviced on the active object.
- `type` is an array which specifies the state for jobs that have an event pending.
- `linkof` is an array used to link the state of each job with the next state.
- The job queue `jobQ` and the active object queue `activeobjectQ` are the FIFO queues. Internally, in the class, there are pointers to their heads as well as their tails to facilitate respectively the addition and deletion of jobs, from these queues.
- The queue `freeQ` is simply a list of unused job descriptions. Jobs are taken from this queue scheduling them upon arrival, or adding them to the free queue upon departure. For simplicity, this queue is implemented here as a stack, or last-in, first-out queue.
- The method `Simulate()` constitutes the main loop of the simulation model, initialising the state of the simulation and beginning the simulation by scheduling the arrival of the first job. The major operations of the simulation are called from this method. For each event, the simulation updates the state of the model, schedules a future event or queues a request when the unit is busy, and collects summary statistics.
- The following methods are used to control the execution of the simulation, reflecting the different events when the active object is processing or idling, and considering how time is spent on each event. There are three types of events: `NewJob()` represents the arrival of a new job to the active object; `JobComplete()` expresses that the job has completed all its processing time, and the active object searches for more queued jobs or it remains idle waiting for new jobs; `Idle()` is a special method that can be invoked in any situation in which the active object is not found in a processing state.
- A set of procedures facilitates the maintenance of the queues in the model. The `Schedule()` method adds a job to the queue of pending events; the `Queue()` method adds a job to one of the three FIFO queues `jobQ` and `activeobjectQ`. The `Dispatch()` method simulates the processing of a job on the processor.

The class `Markovian` represents the stochastical and memoryless property of the behaviour through time of a sequential software component, and its members are presented as follows (Ortega-Arjona & Roberts, 2001):
- The methods `Negexp()` and `Lognormal()` generate random variates with the indicated distributions. The kernel of each of these procedures is a uniform random number generator `Random()`. The random number generator is not defined since it is

generally machine dependent.

As the class `Markovian` is used to obtain distributed random variables with the indicated distributions, it is important to understand how it generates exponentially distributed random variables for the interarrival and service times. Let $\{e_i\}$ be a sequence of number randomly distributed with the distribution function $F(x)$:

$$F(x) = 1 - e^{-\lambda x}$$

If $\{v_i\}$ is a sequence of uniformly distributed random variables obtained from a random generator, then it is possible to generate $\{e_i\}$ as a sequence of exponentially distributed random variables with distribution function $F(x)$ with the relation (Ortega-Arjona & Roberts, 2001):

$$e_i = -\lambda^{-1} \ln v_i$$

6.2.4 Operation

A Component Simulation is an implementation that simulates the behaviour of a sequential software component based on the structure of an active object as a queueing system, which provides statistical-based information about its execution through time. It produces probable processing times, based on mean inter-arrival times and mean service time (Ortega-Arjona & Roberts, 2001).

The Component Simulation is developed considering the simulation of active objects, in Object-Oriented terms. So, a sequential software component is represented by one object that simulates the time of processing activity (and potential idling) of such a component. The simulation per sequential software component is event-driven, which means that time is not considered as a continuous variable incremented in uniform intervals, but is always *advanced* to the time of the next event (see Section 6.2.3). There is no need to wait long periods of time during the actual simulation time of a single sequential software component, since its objective is only to obtain a probabilistic value which represents it. Thus, the Component Simulation is able to produce simple values of probable residence time (processing times plus potential delays). This values are used later in Chapter 7, when calculating the overall response times of the Architectural Performance Model (see Section 7.4).

6.2.5 Summary

For the purposes of this thesis, the basic supposition is that communication and processing are activities sharply separated among coordination and processing components (see Sections 1.4 and 4.3.2). The coordination components are represented by the Coordination Simulation, which represents the main simultaneous activities carried out by a parallel program (see Sections 2.1.5 and 5.2). On the other hand, the Component Simulation is a probabilistic queueing implementation, whose solely purpose is to represent the processing time of a sequential software component (see Section 2.1.5, 2.2 and 5.2). Since such a software components is defined to execute sequentially, it can be modelled as a single processor/single process queuing system, known as a *single station queueing system* (Bolch *et al.*, 1998). In Queueing Theory terms, a Component Simulation is a M/M/1 queueing system (Law & Kelton, 1991; Stone *et al.,* 1975; Bolch, *et al.*, 1998), used to simulate the processing time of a sequential software component.

6.3 Architectural Performance Model

Once the Coordination Simulation and the Component Simulation have been described and implemented, it is possible to introduce the concept of an Architectural Performance Model, which relies on both types of simulations to early estimate the performance of parallel software designs.

6.3.1 Definition

An Architectural Performance Model is considered as a *scale-model representing a parallel software system, whose communication organisation is based on an architectural pattern, and in which the time taken by the behaviour of each of its sequential software component is simulated as a queueing system.* This is achieved by using several Component Simulation instances, whose implementation is inserted into the Coordination Simulation. Hence, Component Simulations are used to simulate the sequential behaviour of processing components (see Section 6.2), while the communication and coordination activities (and therefore the architectural pattern used, and thus, the characteristics of order and precedence of steps in the algorithm and/or data found in the problem at hand) are taken into account by the Coordination Simulation (see Section 6.1). Thus, an Architectural Performance Model is obtained from pre-defined coordinating components sharing the same physical platform, and simulated processing components which generate a statistical response time of the parallel system (see Section 1.3, "The Hypothesis").

6.3.2 Description

The Architectural Performance Model is based on the Architectural Description of Software (see Section 2.3.2), which is used to determine simulations that represent the activities of software components. The term "software components" refers to pieces of software, put together in a "container", representing code that takes some time to be (sequentially) processed by a processor, in the Software Architecture sense (see Section 2.2). Moreover, the Architectural Performance Model reflects the basic supposition of considering that communication and processing are activities sharply separated among coordination and processing components (see Sections 1.4 and 4.3.2). Hence, the performance (response time) of a parallel software system depends mainly on the times taken by its software components to carry out their coordinating or processing activities. Such a classification of software components allow us mostly to consider the simultaneity and separation of those coordination and processing activities. Even though this may not be always the case, our objective is to prove that such a supposition does not introduce a considerable error for performance estimation. So, the Architectural Performance Modelling Method can effectively be used to estimate the performance of a parallel program with the proposed constraints (see Section 4.3.1).

Based on the Architectural Description of Software (see Section 2.3.2), the Architectural Performance Model is described as the composition in code terms of the Coordination Simulation and the Component Simulation (as shown in Figure 6.8) considering that:

- The Coordination Simulation is a partial, runnable implementations that represent the top-level information of a particular parallel software system (see Section 6.1), and
- The Component Simulation is a representation of the time taken by the behaviour of constituent processing components of a particular parallel software system (see Section 6.2).

6.3.3 Implementation

The Architectural Performance Model for a particular parallel program is directly constructed by gathering together the code implementations of a Coordination Simulation

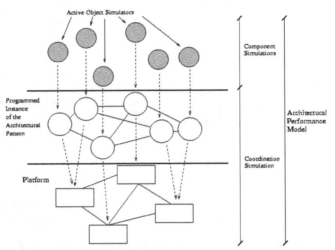

Figure 6.8 The Architectural Performance Model described in terms of the Architectural Description of Software.

(see Section 6.1.3) and several Component Simulations (see Section 6.2.3). For example, in the case of the Two-dimensional Wave Equation, the Architectural Performance Model is created by inserting a call to the method `Simulate()` of the class `ActiveObjectSimulator` at the point where the operation to obtain the new value of a point on the surface should be placed. This simple implementation procedure using both simulations produces Architectural Performance Models that are flexible enough for experimentation, easy to understand and modify, with a high potential for reuse.

6.3.4 Operation

Executing the Architectural Performance Model means executing the code of a Coordination Simulation together with several instances of Components Simulations. Already, the Coordination Simulation execution have produced a particular response time ($T_{Coord-Sim}$, see Section 4.3.2) due to the flow of data through the coordination structure, which only distributes and exchanges data (see Section 6.1). Furthermore, from this execution, it is possible to obtain the performance parameters (λ and Q, see Section 7.3.1) required for the simulation within each instance of Component Simulation.

On the other hand, instances of the Component Simulation are used to simulate the time taken by sequential processing components (see Section 6.2). The simulation results produced only represent the time taken by each sequential software component, and they are used to calculate the response time ($T_{CompSim}$, see Section 4.3.2) due to a simulated execution of the sequential parts of the parallel program.

Thus, executing the Architectural Performance Model is like executing a representation (which executes the coordination and simulates the processing) of the prospective *real* parallel program. Measurements from this model can be operated and used, then, to obtain performance estimates of the execution of such a *real* parallel program. This issue is explained in the following Chapter 7.

6.3.5 Example: CSE and the Two-dimensional Wave Equation

Continuing the example based on the Two-dimensional Wave Equation, its Architectural Performance Model is implemented. As it is mentioned in Section 6.3.3, the implementation of the Architectural Performance Model consists of inserting in the code of the class TwoDWave a call to the method Simulate() of the class ActiveObjectSimulator, at the point where the operation to obtain the new value of a point on the surface should be placed. Hence, an invocation to the code for the Component Simulation, using the class ActiveObjectSimulator and the class Markovian, is inserted into the skeleton of code provided by the Coordination Simulation for the CSE pattern, in order to simulate the processing behaviour of sequential software components.

Notice that the Architectural Performance Model is developed based on the supposition of considering that communication and processing are activities sharply separated among coordination and processing components (see Sections 1.4 and 4.3.2). Our objective here is to test that such a supposition does not introduce a considerable error for performance estimation. If this is so, then the Architectural Performance Model can effectively considered as a scale-model, used to estimate the performance of a parallel program with the proposed constraints (see Section 4.3.1).

During execution, the Coordination Simulation produces a particular flow of data through the coordination structure, distributing data and requests for processing. Each time data or requests are issued to a Component Simulation, this triggers its execution, generating a statistical value of residence time (processing times plus expected queuing delays). This value is considered as part of the total processing time of the parallel program. However, there is still a problem for setting up the parameters lambda and mu for the Component Simulations, so they can produce an adequate processing time. This problem is addressed by observing certain characteristics and relations between these two parameters. The proposed solution is presented in the Architectural Performance Model execution, in Chapter 7.

6.4 Summary

The Architectural Performance Modelling Method requires the construction of an Architectural Performance Model for parallel performance estimation. This model is composed of two types of simulations: Coordination Simulation and Component Simulation.

The Coordination Simulation captures essential communication and coordination aspects of the organisation of the parallel program. It is defined as a scale-model implementation of functional execution of a parallel application to the level of creation of independent communicating software components, and the coordination among them. During execution, the Coordination Simulation represents the set of interactions that reflect the top-most organisation of communication and coordination level of the parallel program In general, the Coordination Simulation is defined and constructed using the information contained in a selected architectural pattern.

The Component Simulation represents a simple but useful form to simulate the time behaviour of any sequential software component, based on the Active Object pattern, and introducing elements of Queuing Theory for processing simulation. The Active Object pattern is proposed as a structural base for the development of a Component Simulation, describing a sequential software component's behaviour in terms of processing and idling times. In order to introduce time parameters, the Component Simulation is based on the implementation of a simple queuing structure.

Finally, an Architectural Performance Model is implemented from inserting the code implementation of the Component Simulation into the skeleton of code provided by the Coordination Simulation. This way, both simulations can be executed together as a representation of the parallel program to be simulated. The actual process of executing the Architectural Performance Model to obtain performance estimations is presented in Chapter 8.

Chapter 7

Performance Simulation
and Calculation

"Tous les Problèmes de Géométrie se peuvent facilement réduire a tels termes, qu'il
n'est besoin paraprés que de connoistre la longeur de quelques lignes droites, pour les
construire"

*"Any problem in geometry can easily be reduced to such terms that a knowledge of
the lengths of certain straight lines is sufficient for its construction"*

Descartes

After the Architectural Performance Model construction, the Architectural Performance
Modelling Method continues with two steps: the performance simulation, and the performance calculation. The performance simulation is carried out by first executing the
Coordination Simulation, and second the Architectural Performance Model, for gathering measurements from the coordination and data from the processing simulation. The
performance calculation uses such measurements and data in order to actually calculate
the performance estimates, as the final outcome of the Architectural Performance Modelling Method.

Again, both performance simulation and calculation activities are carried out based
on the supposition of considering that communication and processing activities are
sharply separated among software components (see Sections 1.4 and 4.3.3). The objective is to test that such a supposition does not introduce a considerable error for performance estimation. So, the Architectural Performance Modelling Method can effectively be
used to obtain the best performing architectural pattern by estimating the performance of
a parallel program, based on the description provided in Section 4.3.1.

7.1 Performance Simulation

During performance simulation, the implementations of the Coordination Simulation and the Architectural Performance Model are executed, so data and measurements can be gathered for the performance calculation. The reasons for carrying out the performance simulation in two steps are *(a)* to obtain the time required for coordination among components from the Coordination Simulation, and *(b)* to solve the problem of obtaining the simulation parameters (`lambda` and `mu`) for the Component Simulations.

During the performance simulation, and for a given configuration of the parallel system, a single performance estimate is obtained by first executing the Coordination Simulation, and second, executing the Architectural Performance Model. The following sections present a description of each execution, as well as its outcome as part of the Architectural Performance Modelling Method.

7.1.1 Coordination Simulation Execution

Executing the Coordination Simulation means exclusively to compile and run the code of the Coordination Simulation. The Coordination Simulation execution is carried out considering typical workload scenarios, which specify the number of operations to be executed in response to pre-defined events, and the type and amount of data to be processed. Thus, a workload scenario also specifies the frequency with which those operations occur, representing the flow of data through a parallel program executing on a particular platform. This makes it possible to measure from the Coordination Simulation execution the actual time it takes to coordinate and communicate data among components. This coordination time represents a lower bound on the response time due exclusively to the coordination activity, along with initial indications of whether the proposed architecture will meet performance goals.

During the Coordination Simulation execution, the code of the Coordination Simulation is executed a number of times. From each execution, the time required for coordination among components and the arrival rate of requests to each component are measured. By performing a number of executions, it is possible to statistically obtain an average coordination time ($T_{CoordSim}$) and an average arrival rate of requests to each coordination software component ($1/\lambda$). $T_{CoordSim}$ is used later for performance calculation (see Section 7.2.3), and $1/\lambda$ is used for obtaining simulation parameters for the Architectural Performance Model execution (see Section 7.1.4).

7.1.2 Example: CSE and the Two-dimensional Wave Equation

Continuing with the example using CSE and the Two-dimensional Wave Equation, this section briefly describes the Coordination Simulation execution. The measurements obtained from executing the CSE Coordination Simulation are shown: $T_{CoordSim}$ and $1/\lambda$ are calculated, using a simple statistical procedure.

In this example, $T_{CoordSim}$ is considered as the lowest time required to execute a CSE-based parallel program on the platform provided, due only to the partitioning and communication activities among coordination components. Also, because the Coordination Simulation is executed using a particular data workload, the inter-arrival times between request for operation can be measured per component, in which any processing operations have to occur, and therefore, imply a limit for service times (see Section 7.1.4). Actually, the average inter-arrival time is commonly expressed as $1/\lambda$, where λ is the average arrival rate of messages per second.

For the Two-dimensional Wave Equation example, and using the CSE pattern, Table 7.1 summarises $T_{CoordSim}$ and $1/\lambda$, obtained from experimenting and measuring on the Coordination Simulation execution. Several measurements are taken for different amounts of data (256×256, 304×304, and 336×336), executing on an available platform of a JPVM environment (Ferrari, 1997; Geist *et al.*, 1994) on a cluster of sixteen processors (computers), considering the execution on 1, 2, 4, 8, and 16 processors. The mapping relation between processes and processors is one process (software component) per processor. The measurements are operated using the *t*-test statistical technique for small samples (Weiss, 1999) considering samples of 10 executions and a confidence interval of 95%.

No. of Procs	256×256		304×304		336×336	
	$T_{CoordSim}$ (milliseconds)	$1/\lambda$ (msecs.)	$T_{CoordSim}$ (milliseconds)	$1/\lambda$ (msecs.)	$T_{CoordSim}$ (milliseconds)	$1/\lambda$ (msecs.)
1	921120.2±1275.469	35.9±1.22	1441497±17270.65	35.3±1.33	2925767±19558.71	36.3±0.828
2	818376.5±1066.469	35.8±1.33	1407031±15504.74	35.9±1.384	2495871±20860.18	35.8±1.161
4	457638.4±816.729	34.7±1.09	801649.3±2082.392	35.7±1.628	1395761±19198.88	35.0±1.489
8	281449.7±1606.1	35.3±0.78	505780.6±2281.59	35.5±0.73	854484.7±1740.182	36.7±1.575
16	238785.5±2016.597	35.1±1.5	446920.7±2377.028	36.1±1.788	718673.6±2653.318	36.2±1.484

Table 7.1 Average coordination times and $1/\lambda$ values from the Coordination Simulation execution

These $T_{CoordSim}$ and $1/\lambda$ (for each parallel configuration and data amount) are used in the following sections for performance calculation and for setting up the Component Simulations' parameters during the Architectural Performance Model execution.

7.1.3 Architectural Performance Model Execution

Executing the Architectural Performance Model means to compile and run together the code of the Coordination Simulation (representing coordination and platform components) and several instances of Components Simulations (representing processing components). Nevertheless, the objective of this execution is to observe and record the probable execution time due only to sequential software components, which will have to perform the processing, but are not actually available. Thus, executing the Architectural Performance Model is like executing a kind of representation of the prospective *real* parallel program. Data and measurements from this execution can be used as performance estimates of the execution of the sequential components of the *real* parallel program.

However, for the Architectural Performance Model execution, it is first necessary to derive some parameters for the Component Simulations. For this, the average arrival rate of requests $(1/\lambda)$ from the Coordination Simulation execution is used along with information from the selected architectural pattern to derive the parameters for each Component Simulation. So, the Architectural Performance Model execution can be carried out a number of times, in order to obtain the simulated processing times per sequential component $(t_{CompSim})$ that are used later to derive the simulated average processing time $(T_{CompSim})$. Finally, $T_{CompSim}$ is added to $T_{CoordSim}$ (obtained from the Coordination Simulation execution, see Section 7.1.1), in order to calculate a single performance estimate (T) (see Sections 4.3.3 and 7.2.3), as an average approximation of the time taken by the parallel program execution given some constraints (see Sections 1.3 and 4.3.1).

7.1.4 Obtaining the Simulation Parameters for the Component Simulations

In the Architectural Performance Modelling Method, the time taken by each sequential software component is simulated by a Component Simulation, which take into account time parameters such as the mean arrival rate (λ) and the mean service rate (μ) (see Sections 6.2.2 and 6.2.3). In order to carry out a precise performance estimation, the method requires parameter values for both λ and μ to be set up.

In the case of λ, it has been pointed out that during Coordination Simulation execution, it is possible to measure the time intervals between requests for processing $(1/\lambda)$ that coordination components issue (see Section 7.1.1). Moreover, according to the calculation of performance estimates (see Section 4.3.3), these time intervals are independent of the processing components, and in fact, represent "time slots" in which all sequential processing activity has to be carried out (see Section 4.3.1). The average of all these time intervals is actually $1/\lambda$, and therefore, λ can be directly obtained from the Coordination Simulation execution by measuring the interval times between requests from the coordination components (see Section 7.1.1). Notice that such "time slots" are actually provided by and dependent of the architectural pattern used.

In the case of μ, the procedure is not so simple, because at this stage there is no sequential processing code, and thus, without information about the activity of processing components, it is simply not possible to propose a value for μ beforehand. Nevertheless, as λ has already been obtained from measuring the Coordination Simulation, two relations between μ and λ can be useful for restricting the set of values that can be considered as possible sequential processing times (see Section 6.2.2):

$$\lambda < \mu \qquad \text{and} \qquad \rho = \frac{\lambda}{\mu}$$

From the simple queue structure used for the Component Simulation implementation (see Section 6.2.2), the relation $\lambda < \mu$, guarantees that the activity of the processing structure is stable. In operational terms, this means that the processing component can safely carry out its sequential processing activity, because it is able to provide a result before another request is issued. If this is the case, then it means that the mean service time for sequentially processing a request is less than the mean arrival time of the requests (this is, $\frac{1}{\lambda} > \frac{1}{\mu}$). This relation implies that any sequential processing activity should "*fit*" into the available "time slot" between requests. If this is the case, this relation between λ and μ ensures that the processing and communicating activities, in which a sequential software component is involved, are independent from each other. In any other case, the component would tend to indefinitely increase the queue of requests (if $\frac{1}{\lambda} < \frac{1}{\mu}$) or

present an undefined activity (if $\frac{1}{\lambda} = \frac{1}{\mu}$). Moreover, it may be obvious, but it seems necessary to state that any processing activity would produce a mean service time for sequential processing, which is always greater than zero (this is, $\frac{1}{\mu} > 0$).

From the previous analysis, two limits for the mean service time are set up for the stable case:

$$0 < \frac{1}{\mu} < \frac{1}{\lambda}$$

Thus, for the stable operation of the sequential processing component, the mean service time for processing $(1/\mu)$ is always between zero and the average of time intervals between requests $(1/\lambda)$, which has been already measured from the Coordination Simulation execution (se Section 7.1.1). This is an important result, because it means that if stable processing is expected from a sequential software component, its processing code should be made in such a way that its average processing time $(1/\mu)$ must not exceed the time between request arrivals. Moreover, this average processing time $1/\mu$ can be manipulated through changing the granularity relation at the processing, coordination, or platform layer of the parallel program. This is further explained in Section 8.4.

By now, given this relation between λ and μ, it is noticeable that it is always possible to express $1/\mu$ as a fraction of $1/\lambda$. Notice that this fraction is actually the given definition of ρ (see Section 6.2.2). Multiplying each term of the relation by λ allows to expresses the relation in terms of ρ as:

$$0 < \rho < 1$$

This means that the processing time of a sequential software component can be taken into consideration by obtaining a value of ρ that is between 0 and 1, which means that μ is always a fraction of λ. The problem now is to propose a value of ρ for the Architectural Performance Model execution, such that the Component Simulations actually reflect the behaviour of the sequential software components.

It is already known (see Section 6.2.2) that for any queuing system, the number of messages in service or waiting for service at any moment (n) is a probabilistic function of λ and μ. This means that it is not possible to know before the code is available how much time a processing service requires to be completed, but actually, we know that it is related to the number of messages in service or waiting for service in the queue. This number of messages is related to another element of Queuing Theory: the average queue length Q. Moreover, this average queue length Q is not arbitrarily chosen, but it can be observed and taken from the expected dynamic behaviour of the coordination, expressed by the selected architectural pattern.

An expression for Q is found in terms of ρ from the expression of p_n (see Section 6.2.2) as follows (Stone *et al.*, 1975):

$$Q = \sum_{0 \le n < \infty} np_n$$

$$= (1-\rho) \sum_{1 \le n < \infty} n\rho^n$$

$$= \rho(1-\rho) \sum_{1 \le n < \infty} n\rho^{n-1}$$

$$= \rho(1-\rho) \sum_{1 \le n < \infty} \frac{d}{d\rho}(\rho^n)$$

$$= \rho(1-\rho)\frac{d}{d\rho}\left(\sum_{1 \le n < \infty} \rho^n \right)$$

$$= \rho(1-\rho)\frac{d}{d\rho}\left(\frac{\rho}{1-\rho} \right)$$

$$Q = \frac{\rho}{1-\rho}$$

From this expression, a value of ρ can be obtained from Q:

$$Q = \frac{\rho}{1-\rho}$$

$$Q(1-\rho) = \rho$$

$$Q - Q\rho = \rho$$

$$Q = \rho + Q\rho$$

$$Q = (1+Q)\rho$$

$$\rho = \frac{Q}{1+Q}$$

By obtaining the number of Q messages in service or possibly waiting for service by each sequential software component, it is possible to calculate a value of ρ. This value represents an approximation that can be used to obtain potential values of μ, based on the measured values of λ, for that sequential software component. The time taken to process a service, then, is only a fraction of the time between requests, and also depends on the number of requests issued during such a period of time. Furthermore, the average queue length Q is the number of messages that arrive to a processing component at any time during execution, and depends on the way the coordination components cooperate, and therefore, depends on the architectural pattern selected.

In summary, we can obtain the parameters λ and μ for the Component Simulations by:

- measuring λ from the Coordination Simulation execution, considering the interarrival time between requests as $1/\lambda$, and

- observing from the dynamic behaviour of the architectural patterns the average queue length Q as the number of messages in service or waiting for service in each processing component. Using this value, a probable ρ is calculated and used to obtain μ

Both simulation parameters λ and μ are used by the Component Simulations during the Architectural Performance Model execution.

7.1.5 Example: CSE and the Two-dimensional Wave Equation

In this section, the simulation parameters λ and μ are obtained by continuing with the example of the Two-dimensional Wave Equation. From the Coordination Simulation execution, using the interval times between requests $(1/\lambda)$ in Table 7.1, the value of λ for each configuration and amount of data is obtained.

The value of μ is obtained by considering $\mu = \lambda/\rho$, or, in terms of the actual Component Simulation parameters, mu = plambda. At this point, the task is to find an approximation to the value of ρ, in such a way that the Component Simulations actually simulate the behaviour of the processing components. Analysing the interaction diagram in the *Dynamics* section for a two-dimensional case of the CSE pattern (see Figure 5.7 in Section 5.2.10), observe that for each processing component (the participants of this architectural pattern) the average queue length Q should be at least four messages at any time. These four messages represent the data exchange between neighbouring components, which have to be performed before *any* processing is started (see Section 6.1.5). The rationale is as follows: if less than three message arrive, the sequential element cannot continue its normal operation; if more than four messages arrive, this means that there is a problem with the coordination, which is not operating as it should be.

Considering a normal operation, at least four messages are in service or waiting for service during the execution of the Coordination Simulation. Thus, the approximate value of ρ for this coordination structure is as follows:

$$\rho = \frac{Q}{Q+1} = \frac{4}{5}$$

198

This means that from the total time between requests $(1/\lambda)$ to a sequential software component, and since at most 4 messages can be in service or waiting for service, the total service time $(1/\mu)$ could be at most 4/5 of $1/\lambda$ for such a component. The rest of the time, the component remains idle (see Section 4.3.1). So, using this approximation value of ρ for the Architectural Performance Model execution, the simulated processing times per each sequential component ($t_{CompSim}$) are obtained, considering the different cases of data size, number of processors, and number of software components. These times are used in the performance estimate calculation to obtain the average processing time $T_{CompSim}$, as described in the next step of the Architectural Performance Modelling Method.

7.2 Performance Estimate Calculation

The performance estimate calculation consists of taking the average coordination times ($T_{CoordSim}$) measured from the Coordination Simulation execution, and adding them with the average processing times ($T_{CompSim}$) simulated in the Architectural Performance Model execution (see Section 4.3.3). Nevertheless, in order to carry out this operation, it is necessary to calculate $T_{CompSim}$ from the simulated processing times per each sequential component ($t_{CompSim}$) of the parallel program.

7.2.1 Calculating the simulated average processing time ($T_{CompSim}$)

The calculation of the simulated average processing time ($T_{CompSim}$) from the simulated processing times per each sequential component ($t_{CompSim}$) requires further clarification. Obviously, the way in which $T_{CompSim}$ is calculated depends on the selected architectural pattern, since the distinction among architectural patterns is based on the form in which each pattern distributes and allows the execution of the sequential processes that compose the parallel program (see Sections 4.3.1 and 5.2.3). Moreover, the selected architectural pattern imposes how and how many requests for service arrive to each sequential component, since it is used to develop a coordination which distributes and communicates among the sequential components (see Sections 2.1, 4.3.1, 5.2 and 5.2.3). Notice that both these actions depend on the classification of the Architectural Patterns for Parallel Programming, regarding the type of parallelism they exhibit (see Section 5.2.7). Hence, the calculation of $T_{CompSim}$ depends on the order of data and operations that describe each architectural pattern:

- *Functional Parallelism.* Architectural Patterns based on a functional parallelism approach base the simultaneous execution of their sequential software components on the overlapping of sequential actions. Both, Pipes and Filters (see Section 5.2.8) and Parallel Hierarchies (see Section 5.2.9), depend on allowing simultaneous execution of operations on different data items. Thus, based on such a description, the following expression is proposed for calculating $T_{CompSim}$ from the simulated processing times of a kth sequential component $(t_{CompSim-k})$:

$$T_{CompSim} = \sum_{i=1}^{n} (t_i)_{CompSim-k}$$

where $(t_i)_{CompSim-k}$ represents the ith simulated processing time of the kth sequential component. The sum of the n simulated processing times provides of a representation of the time for sequential execution (the only kind of execution at the processing component level, see Section 2.3.2) of the kth component. Such kth component is selected from the set of N sequential software components, by considering the sequential component whose sum of simulated processing times is the maximum value. So, it is considered that this kth component is a representative of the worst case for functional parallelism, in which the performance of the whole parallel process is as fast as its slowest component (Ortega-Arjona & Roberts, 1998a).

- *Domain Parallelism.* Communicating Sequential Elements is the only domain parallelism Architectural Pattern (see Section 5.2.10), and it is based on the simultaneous execution of its sequential software components performing the same sequential action on different pieces of data. Hence, the calculation of $T_{CompSim}$ from a simulated processing time of a kth sequential component $(t_{CompSim-k})$ for the CSE pattern is expressed as:

$$T_{CompSim} = timeSteps(t_{CompSim-k})$$

where $(t_{CompSim-k})$ represents the maximum simulated processing time of the kth sequential component, which is obtained from the set of all simulated processing times of all N sequential software components. Commonly, due to the defined behaviour of this pattern, the coordination and synchronisation of sequential components yield that the sum of simulated processing times of a given sequential software component tend to have a very similar value. Hence, the approach here is to consider that all simulated processing times have the same magnitude, equal to the longest $t_{Comp\text{-}Sim\text{-}k}$, which reflects the worst case representation of the sequential execution (the only kind of execution at the processing component level, see Section 2.3.2) (Ortega-Arjona & Roberts, 1998a; Ortega-Arjona, 2000) of such a kth component. Notice that, in the case of domain parallelism, the total sum of the simulated processing times depends on the number of time steps (*timeSteps*) that the sequential components are allowed to carry out their operations. However, since we are considering only one simulated processing time for the worst case, a simplification is possible in which it is only necessary to multiply the simulated time $t_{CompSim\text{-}k}$ by the number of time steps.

- *Activity Parallelism.* Architectural Patterns that expose activity parallelism are based on the simultaneous overlapping execution of their sequential software components on different data. Manager-Workers (see Section 5.2.11) and Shared Resource (see Section 5.2.12) organise their sequential software components so they simultaneously and independently execute their operations on different data items. Based on such a description, the following expression is proposed for calculating $T_{CompSim}$ from the simulated processing times of a kth sequential component ($t_{CompSim\text{-}k}$):

$$T_{CompSim} = timeSteps \left(\sum_{i=1}^{n} (t_i)_{CompSim-k} \right)$$

where $(t_i)_{CompSim-k}$ represents the ith simulated processing time of the kth sequential component. As with functional parallelism, the sum of the n simulated processing times provides of a representation of the sequential execution (the only kind of execution at the processing component level, see Section 2.3.2) of the kth component. This kth component is chosen from the set of N sequential software components, considering to be the sequential component whose sum of simulated processing times results the maximum value. Hence, this simulated processing time of the kth component represents the worst case for executing simultaneous operations. So, commonly the performance of the whole parallel process is initially considered as fast as its slowest component (Ortega-Arjona & Roberts, 1998a). Nevertheless, notice that in activity parallelism, a sequential software component is allowed to execute its operations on different data a certain number of times (*timeSteps*). So, such a worst case execution is considered to be sequentially carried out a number of times, increasing the time for sequential execution. This is reflected in the expression by multiplying the sum of the n simulated times by the number of times such kth sequential software component executes.

7.2.2 Calculating $T_{CompSim}$ for the Two-dimensional Wave Equation

The Architectural Performance Model developed for the Two-dimensional Wave Equation is executed, and the simulated processing times are obtained and stored into a file, so they can be used to calculate the average processing times ($T_{CompSim}$). The simulated processing times are obtained executing the Architectural Performance Model on a cluster of sixteen computers, considering each time 1, 2, 4, 8, and 16 processors, and different amounts of data (256×256, 304×304, and 336×336). Notice that, as part of the Architectural Performance Model, each Component Simulation model is set to use a $1/\mu$ value derived from the $1/\lambda$ values obtained from measuring the coordination simulation (see Table 7.1) and Q = 4/5 (see Section 7.1.5). Table 7.2 shows the values of $T_{CompSim}$ obtained from the simulated processing times.

No. of Processors	256×256	304×304	336×336
	$T_{CompSim}$ (milliseconds)	$T_{CompSim}$ (milliseconds)	$T_{CompSim}$ (milliseconds)
1	1125715.4±20157.9	2662864±22889.97	3256332±17300.12
2	563161.2±2354.831	1335341±23620.32	1622570±15311.73
4	281639.8±1737.596	665380.5±2668.964	812512.8±2558.968
8	141131.2±2739.212	332583.2±2540.849	496460.5±2896.881
16	70707.5±2358.05	166357.1±2395.897	203565.3±1738.195

Table 7.2 Average (simulated) processing times from the Architectural Performance Model execution

For this example, the calculation of $T_{CompSim}$ depends on the order of data and operations that describe the CSE pattern (see Section 5.2.10), as it is explained above. So, calculating $T_{CompSim}$ depends on the maximum simulated processing time of the kth sequential component ($t_{CompSim-k}$). Using this value, $T_{CompSim}$ is statistically obtained for the different combinations of number of processors and amounts of data.

7.2.3 Calculating estimates of the Total Execution Time

A single performance estimate is a time value that represents an approximation to the total execution time for a given and particular configuration of the parallel system in question. As the result of the Architectural Performance Modelling Method, it is finally calculated by adding the average coordination time ($T_{CoordSim}$) and the simulated average processing time ($T_{CompSim}$). Let T be one approximation of the total execution time for a given and particular configuration of the parallel system in question. In the Architectural Performance Modelling Method, T is defined from the expressions for Coordination Simulation time and Component Simulation time as follows (see Section 4.3.3):

$$T \approx T_{CoordSim} + T_{CompSim}$$

This expression considers and contains the contributions of each one of the groups of components (*platform, coordination,* and *processing,* see Section 2.3.2), and it is used for the final performance estimate calculation. Nevertheless, all the time values for $T_{CoordSim}$ and $T_{CompSim}$ are probabilistic values (see Section 4.3.1), so such addition should be carried out using the following statistical sum expression (Weiss, 1999):

$$T \approx (T_{CoordSim} + T_{CompSim}) \pm (\sqrt{\sigma^2_{CoordSim} + \sigma^2_{CompSim}})$$

This mathematical expression takes into consideration our basic supposition that the coordination and processing times are the probabilistic values (or more precisely, parameters) of two independent populations (Weiss, 1999).

The Architectural Performance Modelling Method concludes with this step, producing performance estimates that are obtained from the Coordination Simulation execution and the Architectural Performance Model execution.

7.2.4 Calculating estimates T for the Two-dimensional Wave Equation

For the example of the Two-dimensional Wave Equation, the performance estimate calculation is carried out for each configuration and amount of data. The result is a set of performance estimates, as approximations to the performance behaviour of the *real* parallel program. Table 7.3 shows the results of adding $T_{CoordSim}$ (from Table 7.1) and $T_{CompSim}$ (from Table 7.2), for each parallel configuration proposed.

7.3 Summary

This chapter presents the two steps of the Architectural Performance Modelling Method: the performance simulation and the performance calculation. The performance simula-

No. of Processors	256×256 T (milliseconds)	304×304 T (milliseconds)	336×336 T (milliseconds)
1	2046835.6±20254.79	4104361±39803.13	6182099±36194.96
2	1381537.7±2956.032	2742371±38290.13	4118442±35692.21
4	739278.2±2418.911	1467030±4610.96	2208274±21593.9
8	422580.9±4281.527	838363.8±4743.892	1260945±4336.072
16	309493±4226.21	613277.8±4703.481	922238.9±4130.285

Table 7.3 Average total execution times (estimates) for the Two-dimensional Wave Equation

tion is actually the execution of the simulations and model obtained in the previous step, in order to gather data and make measurements. The performance calculation takes such data and measurements, and actually calculates the performance estimates as the final outcome of the Architectural Performance Modelling Method.

Nevertheless, now it arises the question whether the Architectural Performance Modelling Method actually obtains performance estimates that are approximations to the execution times of a real implementation of the parallel program executing on the parallel hardware, and based on the organisation described by the same architectural pattern. Hence, it is required to evaluate the Architectural Performance Modelling Method against what it is supposed to model, this is, the real parallel program (see Section 4.3.1). In order to do this, a statistical procedure is carried out between the obtained estimates and measurements of the execution time from the real parallel program. This is discussed and shown in the following Chapter 8.

Chapter 8

Evaluation of the Method

"E cosi' si possono fare un numero infinito di esperimenti. E plasmare le propie regole."

"And thus you can make an infinite number of experiments. And form your rule."

Leonardo Da Vinci.

This chapter presents an evaluation of the Architectural Performance Modelling Method for estimating the performance of a parallel program that behaves as described in Section 4.3.1. First, some considerations and assumptions are defined for the evaluations. Second, the performance estimates of the Architectural Performance Modelling Method are evaluated for the Two-dimensional Wave Equation example. Third, the method is evaluated for the early selection of an architectural pattern, when comparing potential parallel solutions. Three experimental examples are used to compare three different architectural patterns. Finally, some conclusions, a comparison with the related work (presented in Chapter 3), an evaluation of the cost, and an analysis of applicability of the method in the general case are discussed.

8.1 Considerations and Assumptions for the Evaluations

The objective of this evaluation is to verify if the Architectural Performance Modelling Method produces estimates that are accurate enough to describe the performance behaviour of a parallel software system. More precisely, the aim is to verify how accurate the estimates are, when compared with the actual performance values measured from the *real* parallel software system. The objective is to test if the method provides an acceptable accuracy. Remember that our basic consideration is that processing and communication are activities sharply separated among coordination and processing components (see Sections 1.4 and 4.3.2). Even though this may not be always the case, our objective in this research work is to prove that such a supposition does not introduce a considerable error for performance estimation. So, the scale-models developed using the Architectural Performance Modelling Method can effectively be used to estimate the performance of a parallel program with the proposed constraints (see Section 1.3).

In all the evaluations presented here, some considerations and assumptions have been taken in order to reduce their complexity and make them easier to be understood. Such considerations and assumptions are derived from the basic constraints: the method has as input *(a)* given parallel hardware and software resources, and *(b)* an architectural pattern that describes the overall coordination of the parallel program (see Section 1.3):

- Architectural Performance Models and real parallel programs are executed using the Java Parallel Virtual Machine (JPVM) standard (Ferrari, 1997; Geist *et al.*, 1994). Low-level hardware details such as memory hierarchies and the topology of the processor interconnection network are considered to be solved by the JPVM environment, executing on a cluster of computers.

- Time measurements and observations on the Coordination Simulation execution and the Architectural Performance Model execution are carried out using the method `System.currentTimeMillis()`, available from the libraries of the Java programming language (Smith, 2000; Hartley, 1998). This method actually reads the time stamp of the hardware real time clock, allowing to measure overall execution times of the simulation and the real program, when executing on the given cluster platform.

8.2 Evaluating the Architectural Performance Modelling Method for the Two-dimensional Wave Equation

8.2.1 Execution Time

For the Two-dimensional Wave Equation problem, the evaluation is carried out by comparing the estimates of the Architectural Performance Modelling Method (see Section 7.2.4) against real average execution times. So, in order to do this, an implementation of the real parallel program has to be created. As the process to obtain and develop a coordination based on the selection of an architectural pattern for parallel programming (see Sections 5.2.3, and 5.3) is the same than that used as part of the method (see Section 4.3.3), it would be redundant to start the whole process once more. Hence, we use the Coordination Simulation already coded, only replacing the Component Simulations by real processing components. This way, the real program is executed a number of times, so the real average execution time can be statistically obtained from the measured execution times. For the Two-dimensional Wave Equation problem, Tables 8.1, 8.2, and 8.3 present the numerical values of the performance estimates, and compares them with the real average execution times, obtained from the real parallel system.

No. of Processors	Estimate ($\rho = 0.75$) (milliseconds)	Real System (milliseconds)
1	2047158±21357.52	2046886±3771.24
2	1381029±4404.319	1380765±15508.46
4	738894.6±3099.292	738850.1±1368.391
8	421802.4±4524.241	422684.5±2293.336
16	309014±4367.925	309678.6±1748.871

Table 8.1 Performance estimates and real average execution times for the Two-dimensional Wave Equation example (using a 256×256 array).

No. of Processors	Estimate ($\rho = 0.75$) (milliseconds)	Real System (milliseconds)
1	4104361±39803.13	4104664±19475.29
2	2742371±38290.13	2742885±9524.33
4	1467030±4610.96	1466505±23778.03
8	838363.8±4743.892	838641.2±2255.117
16	613277.8±4703.481	613625.6±2359.494

Table 8.2 Performance estimates and real average execution times for the Two-dimensional Wave Equation example (using a 304×304 array).

No. of Processors	Estimate ($\rho = 0.75$) (milliseconds)	Real System (milliseconds)
1	6182099±36194.96	6181554±16267.74
2	4118442±35692.21	4117611±21311.85
4	2208274±21593.9	2207884±13553.03
8	1260945±4336.072	1259470±13176.48
16	922238.9±4130.285	922352.3±2774.776

Table 8.3 Performance estimates and real average execution times for the Two-dimensional Wave Equation example (using a 336×336 array).

Figure 8.1 shows a graphical comparison of the estimates and the real average execution times.

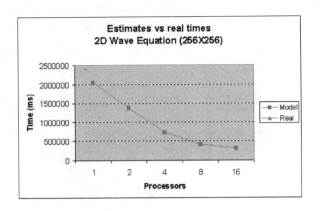

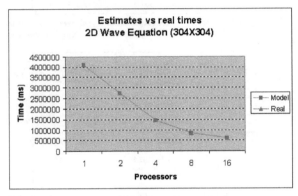

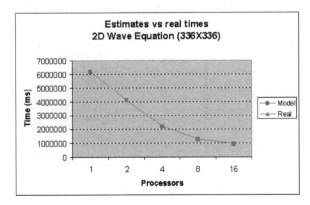

Figure 8.1 Comparisons between performance estimates and real average execution times for the Two-dimensional Wave Equation problem.

Graphically, from Figure 8.1 is clear that all perfornce estimates and real average execution times are not distinguisable. Hence, it is necessary to carry out a further statistical comparison, in order to evaluate how accurate the method is. Thus, for comparison purposes, the error between each estimate and each real average execution time is obtained, using a t-test criteria (Weiss, 1999). Tables 8.4 shows the errors between performance estimates and real average execution times. Each error is calculated for a confidence interval of 95%, using the expression:

$$Error = |\bar{y}_1 - \bar{y}_2| \pm t_{(\alpha/2),(n_1 + n_2 - 2)} S_p \sqrt{\frac{1}{n_1} + \frac{1}{n_2}}$$

where $\bar{y}_1$ and $\bar{y}_2$ are the means of the samples, $t_{(\alpha/2),(n_1 + n_2 - 2)}$ is the superior percentile point $\alpha/2$ of the t distribution with $n_1 + n_2 - 2$ degrees of freedom, n_1 and n_2 are the sample's sizes, and S_p^2 is an estimate of the common variance $\sigma_1^2 = \sigma_2^2 = \sigma^2$ calculated by:

$$S_p^2 = \frac{(n_1 - 1)S_1^2 + (n_2 - 1)S_2^2}{n_1 + n_2 - 2}$$

where S_1^2 and S_2^2 are the individual sample variances.

A statistical test t_0 commonly used to compare two sets of samples is (Montgomery, 1991):

$$t_0 = \frac{|\bar{y}_1 - \bar{y}_2|}{S_p \sqrt{\frac{1}{n_1} + \frac{1}{n_2}}}$$

In order to use this statistical test, it is necessary to compare the value of t_0 with the t distribution with $n_1 + n_2 - 2$ degrees of freedom, allowing a decision on whether the equivalence between the performance estimates and real average execution times is rejected. The equivalence should be rejected if:

$$t_0 > t_{(\alpha/2),(n_1 + n_2 - 2)}$$

The use of this procedure is justified by Montgomery (1991). In this example, the superior percentile point for a confidence interval of 95% ($\alpha/2 = 0.025$) of the t distribution with $10 + 10 - 2 = 18$ degrees of freedom is $t_{0.025,18} = 2.101$.

No. of Procs	256×256		304×304		336×336	
	Error (milliseconds)	t_0	Error (milliseconds)	t_0	Error (milliseconds)	t_0
1	271.5±133.7776	0.85279	302.5±205.469	0.618636	545.5±193.2962	1.185844
2	264.4±119.0869	0.93294	513.8±184.5345	1.169964	830.7±201.4888	1.732405
4	44.5±56.4078	0.331495	525±142.1913	1.551466	389.2±158.2128	1.033682
8	882.1±69.68078	5.319378*	277.4±70.60188	1.650997	1474.9±111.6793	5.549398*
16	664.6±66.00244	4.23113*	347.8±70.92377	2.0606	113.4±70.12644	0.679497

Table 8.4 Errors between the estimates and real average execution times, and values of their statistical test t_0 for the Two-dimensional Wave Equation example

Notice that the range between the best and the worst estimates is about 44.5 millisenconds (for the smallest error) to 1474.9 milliseconds (for the largest error). From this observation, we conclude that for the present example, the estimates are actually a close representation of the real average execution times. However, from the statistical comparison, some estimates have to be rejected, since they do meet the rejection criteria. The rejected estimates are those whose t_0 value is marked with (*). As a result, from a total of 15 comparisons, 3 results should be rejected. That is, there is actual equivalence in 80% of the experiments. Therefore, the Architectural Performance Modelling Method produces representative performance estimates of the real parallel program's average execution times. The conclusion from this example is that they can be used to support performance modelling during early parallel software design.

8.2.2 Speed-up and Efficiency

From the results obtained in the previous section between performance estimates and real execution times, in this section the values for speed-up and efficiency are derived as further measures of the performance analysis for the Two-dimensional Wave Equation example. Such measures are commonly calculated from the execution times in order to analyse the performance of a parallel program as the number of processors increase (see Section 2.1.5). Tables 8.5, 8.6, and 8.7 present the values of speed-up and efficiency for the estimates and the real time measures for the Two-dimensional Wave Equation, using respectively two-dimensional arrays of 256×256, 304×304, and 336×336.

No. of Processors	Estimate Speed-up	Real System Speedup	Estimate Efficiency (%)	Real System Efficiency (%)
1	1.0±0.0	1.0±0.0	100.0±0.0	100.0±0.0
2	1.48234172±0.011412	1.4824289±0.016001	74.117086±0.5706201	74.121447±0.800064
4	2.7705676±0.020278	2.7703671±0.006456	69.264192±0.506952	69.259177±0.161399
8	4.8533536±0.021521	4.8425859±0.024843	60.666958±0.269021	60.53232±0.3105453
16	6.624805±0.064121	6.6097108±0.035931	41.405031±0.400762	41.3106928±0.22457

Table 8.5 Speed-up and efficiency values for estimates and real time execution times for the Two-dimensional Wave Equation example (using a 256×256 array).

No. of Processors	Estimate Speed-up	Real System Speedup	Estimate Efficiency (%)	Real System Efficiency (%)
1	1.0±0.0	1.0±0.0	100.0±0.0	100.0±0.0
2	1.4966466±0.007712	1.4964766±0.004191	74.832333±0.385612	74.823829±0.209594
4	2.7977352±0.018851	2.79894311±0.033027	69.943382±0.471282	69.973577±0.825697
8	4.8956801±0.020974	4.89442148±0.011496	61.196002±0.262182	61.179576±0.14371
16	6.692499±0.0179432	6.6891986±0.0119357	41.8281181±0.112145	41.807271±0.074598

Table 8.6 Speed-up and efficiency values for estimates and real time execution times for the Two-dimensional Wave Equation example (using a 304×304 array).

No. of Processors	Estimate Speed-up	Real System Speedup	Estimate Efficiency (%)	Real System Efficiency (%)
1	1.0±0.0	1.0±0.0	100.0±0.0	100.0±0.0
2	1.501167±0.00502	1.5013102±0.00596	75.05838±0.2510022	75.065513±0.298039
4	2.799776±0.0121156	2.7999312±0.012709	69.99441±0.3028912	69.998281±0.317736
8	4.9026593±0.012432	4.909067±0.0421138	61.283242±0.155404	61.363338±0.526423
16	6.7032864±0.014608	6.7020172±0.017904	41.89554±0.0913038	41.887607±0.111904

Table 8.7 Speed-up and efficiency values for estimates and real time execution times for the Two-dimensional Wave Equation example (using a 336×336 array).

Figure 8.2 shows the comparisons between the speed-up and efficiency for the estimates and real average execution times for the Two-dimensional Wave Equation problem.

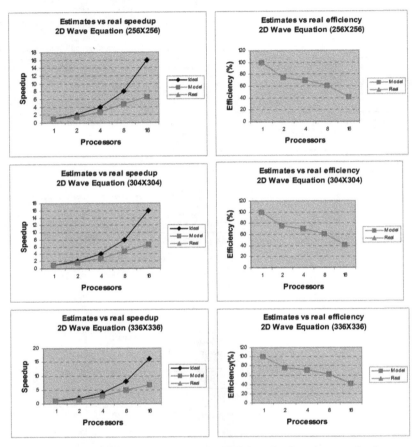

Figure 8.2 Comparisons between speed-up and efficiency for the estimates and real average execution times for the Two-dimensional Wave Equation problem.

From Figure 8.2, it is noticeable that, graphically, no difference is perceptible. Hence, the comparison is carried out using the same statistical procedure based on a *t*-test criteria (Weiss, 1999) as in the previous section, the errors between the speed-up and efficiency for each estimate and each real average execution time is obtained. Thus, Tables 8.8 shows the errors between the speed-up values of the performance estimates and real average execution times, whereas Table 8.9 shows the errors between the efficiency values of the performance estimates and real average execution times.

No. of Procs	256×256		304×304		336×336	
	Speed-up Error	t_0	Speed-up Error	t_0	Speed-up Error	t_0
1	0.0±0.0	-	0.0±0.0	-	0.0±0.0	-
2	0.0005691±0.13972	0.00171163	0.000392±0.09207	0.00178922	0.0001425±0.08843	0.00067745
4	0.0000632±0.13798	0.00019268	0.002566±0.192218	0.00561045	0.0001546±0.13296	0.00048872
8	0.010616±0.181716	0.02454885	0.001069±0.152071	0.00295526	0.006407±0.197097	0.01366076
16	0.016037±0.266939	0.02524487	0.003120±0.145875	0.00898912	0.001269±0.152170	0.00350474

Table 8.8 Errors between the speed-up values of estimates and real average execution times, and their respective statistical test t_0 for the Two-dimensional Wave Equation example

No. of Procs	256×256		304×304		336×336	
	Efficiency Error	t_0	Efficiency Error	t_0	Efficiency Error	t_0
1	0.0±0.0	-	0.0±0.0	-	0.0±0.0	-
2	0.02845±0.988022	0.01210308	0.01960±0.651076	0.01265167	0.007128±0.625317	0.00479028
4	0.001581±0.689922	0.00096342	0.06416±0.961091	0.02805226	0.003866±0.664834	0.00244359
8	0.132702±0.642465	0.08679329	0.0133±0.537655	0.01044841	0.080095±0.696843	0.04829808
16	0.10023±0.667349	0.06311218	0.019503±0.364687	0.02247279	0.007932±0.380425	0.00876186

Table 8.9 Errors between the efficiency of estimates and real average execution times, and their respective statistical test t_0 for the Two-dimensional Wave Equation example

From both, Tables 8.8 and Table 8.9, it can be observed that there is no value for t_0 greater than 2.101, which (in terms of the t-test criteria) means that the speed-up and efficiency produced by the Architectural Performance Model are statistically similar to the actual speed-up and efficiency of the real parallel system. The performance analysis based on obtaining speed-up and efficiency for the Architectural Performance Model reforces the fact that this model can be used as a representative performance estimates of the real parallel program's average execution times. Both, speed-up and efficiency of the model can be used as a complementary criteria for selecting a parallel solution among several potential solutions, as it is presented in the following sections.

8.3 Evaluating the Architectural Performance Modelling Method for Comparing Architectural Patterns

In this section, another evaluation is proposed for the Architectural Performance Modelling Method. The objective of this evaluation is to show the application of the method for

selecting a parallel solution among several potential solutions, using performance estimates as the comparative criteria. Each potential solution is based on a different architectural pattern.

To evaluate the Architectural Performance Modelling Method for comparing potential solutions, the following steps are taken:

1. *Obtaining the Performance Estimates.* For each architectural pattern, the Architectural Performance Modelling Method is applied, and the performance estimates are
   obtained for different configurations of the parallel system.
2. *Comparative Analysis.* By comparing the performance estimates for different configurations, it is possible to select the architectural pattern that presents the most adequate solution.
3. *Validating the Comparative Analysis.* The comparison is validated by developing the
   real parallel programs, obtaining the real average execution times, and checking if the
   pattern with the best performance using real average execution times is also the
   selected pattern by comparing performance estimates.

In order to show the Architectural Performance Modelling Method applied for
selecting a parallel solution using performance estimates as the comparative criteria,
three examples are used, developing three potential solutions for each one. Each potential solution is based on a different architectural pattern.

The codes implementing the Coordination Simulation as a framework programmed
using the Java programming Languaje (Smith, 2000; Hartley, 1998) using a JPVM environment (Ferrari, 1997; Geist *et al.*, 1994) on a cluster of sixteen processors, executing
on 1, 2, 4, 8, and 16 processors. The used frameworks are presented in Appendix B.

8.3.1 Example of Comparing Architectural Patterns — The Matrix Multipli-
cation Problem

The experimental example, developed for the Matrix Multiplication problem (Hoare,
1978; Andrews, 1991; Freeman & Phillips, 1992; Foster, 1994; Kleiman, *et al.*, 1996;
Hartley, 1998; Andrews, 2000), is described as follows.

Problem Description
The Matrix Multiplication problem is to calculate the product of two square matrixes A
and B, with n rows and n columns each one. This requires computing n^2 inner products,

214

one for each combination of row and column (Foster, 1994). Let us consider a specific case, in which the product $C = AB$ is obtained for two square matrixes A and B with 512 rows and 512 columns each. The parallel program is to be developed and executed into a JPVM environment (Ferrari, 1997; Geist *et al.*, 1994), on a cluster of sixteen computers (see Section 8.1).

Algorithmic Solution for the Matrix Multiplication problem

The elements of the matrix product C are obtained using the algorithm shown in Figure 8.3 (Andrews, 1991). The matrix product can be computed in parallel since the inner products are disjoint. This algorithmic solution may not be the optimal one, but it is a good enough example to evaluate the Architectural Performance Modelling Method.

```
for i = 1:n, j = 1:n;
    C[i,j] = 0;
    for k = 1:n;
        C[i,j] = C[i,j]+A[i,k]*B[k,j];
    end
end
```

Figure 8.3 Pseudocode for the matrix multiplication computation

The CSE Solution for the Matrix Multiplication

A solution to the Matrix Multiplication problem is proposed based on the CSE pattern (see Section 5.2.10). The strategy is that all data is distributed among a group of communicating elements. Communications between neighbouring elements are restricted to the exchange of data only (Figure 8.4).

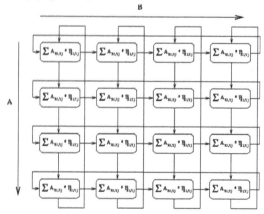

Figure 8.4 The Communicating Sequential Elements Solution to the Matrix Multiplication problem

In order to use the CSE pattern for solving the Matrix Multiplication problem, every element of the matrix C is computed by assigning a set of rows from matrix A and a set of columns from matrix B to each communicating element. Each communicating element is then responsible for computing the product elements of matrix C that involve these two sets of rows and columns. Finally, after all computations are finished, results are gathered and ordered to represent the product matrix C. Such an implementation is based on Cannon's algorithm (Freeman & Phillips, 1992).

The MW Solution for the Matrix Multiplication
Matrix Multiplication is a problem that exhibits characteristics of order of data and a regular homogeneous computation, and therefore, its parallel solution could be based on the MW pattern (see Section 5.2.11). The main idea is that all data is divided by the manager into smaller pieces that can be handled by the workers. The only communication allowed is that between each worker and the manager, receiving or sending data (Figure 8.5).

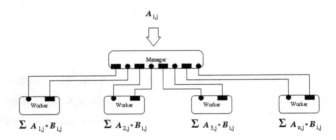

Figure 8.5 Manager-Workers solution to the Matrix Multiplication problem

This parallel solution simply divides the operation into inner products. The manager is in charge of distributing the rows of matrix A among the workers, and each worker has a complete copy of matrix B. The solution goes through each worker computing all inner products per a single row in matrix A, returning the result to the manager, and requesting if there are more rows to be multiplied. The key to efficiency is to limit the part of matrix B that has to be looked at to carry out the multiplication. Once processing is finished, the manager is sent the results by the workers (Kleiman, *et al.*, 1996).

The PF Solution for the Matrix Multiplication

Another solution to the Matrix Multiplication problem is proposed, based on the PF pattern (see Section 5.2.8). This architectural pattern takes advantage of the overlapping of operations through time, in which all data is operated by each filter, producing intermediate results as output. Pipes make sure that the output of a filter is used as the input of the next filter, allowing the flow of data through the filters (Figure 8.6).

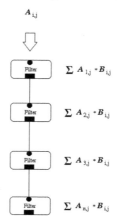

Figure 8.6 Pipes and Filters Solution for the Matrix Multiplication problem

Taking advantage of operation overlapping in this solution, each filter is defined so it has a complete copy of matrix B, and receives the rows of matrix A. The solution goes through each filter computing all inner products per a single row in matrix A. Since these inner products are disjoint, every filter can operate locally, overlapping operations to simultaneously obtain different inner products. Finally, after finishing all filter operations, every filter has stored a group of intermediate results that represent the product of the two square matrixes (Andrews, 2000).

Obtaining the Performance Estimates

Applying the Architectural Performance Modelling Method, the performance estimates for each potential solution are obtained. Table 8.10 presents the numerical values of the performance estimates for different configurations, and for different values of ρ. This value is obtained from observing the behaviour of the parallel software coordination (see Section 7.1.4). The numerical values of the performance estimates are statistically calcu-

lated using the *t*-test technique for small samples (Weiss, 1999; see also Section 8.2) of
10 executions and a confidence interval of 95%.

No. of Processors	Communicating Sequential Elements ($\rho = 0.66$) (milliseconds)	Manager-Workers ($\rho = 0.75$) (milliseconds)	Pipes and Filters ($\rho = 0.75$) (milliseconds)
1	18027959±90084.63	9906419±219400.7	13647634.7±63424
2	11991416±202470.5	5838507±54682.24	8039670±208346
4	6450871±99412.9	3320815±100411.5	4596345±253389.7
8	3677507.7±70343.4	1779525±294748	2530492±190842
16	2693465.3±76162.06	1169512±124073.2	1810181±172642.6

Table 8.10 Performance estimates for the Matrix Multiplication problem (with matrices of 1024×1024 elements), using different architectural patterns.

Comparative Analysis

Figure 8.7 shows a graphical comparison of the estimates of the three solutions for the
Matrix Multiplication, based on CSE, MW, and PF. Each graph represents the estimated
times for each model executing on different configurations of a cluster of computers with
1, 2, 4, 8, and 16 processors.

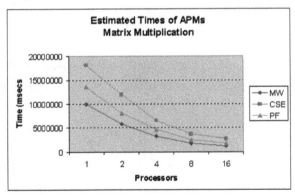

Figure 8.7 Comparison of the estimated times of the three solutions for the Matrix Multiplication problem

From observing the performance estimates in Table 8.10 and their representation in
Figure 8.7, notice that the solution based on MW produces the shorter time estimates for
Matrix Multiplication. Even though the solutions based on CSE and PF can also be used
to carry out Matrix Multiplication, the estimates obtained by these solutions are in every
case larger than the MW solution. The reason for this is that even though the CSE and PF

solutions produce the same processing effect, they require larger times for communicating and coordinating their components. It is clear that both CSE and PF solutions do not represent a viable solution for Matrix Multiplication.

For every configuration, the estimates of the MW solution are always smaller because this solution has less communication overhead by data exchange, and this is reflected by the performance estimates. Therefore, the MW solution is considered as the most viable candidate for solving Matrix Multiplication, using the available resources of a JPVM environment on a cluster of sixteen computers.

Validating the Comparative Analysis

To validate the comparative analysis, the real parallel programs are implemented, and the real average execution times for each architectural pattern are statistically calculated, measuring execution times. Table 8.11 presents the numerical values for the real average execution times for different configurations.

No. of Processors	Communicating Sequential Elements (milliseconds)	Manager-Workers (milliseconds)	Pipes and Filters (milliseconds)
1	18028684±125607.3	9907734±31214.72	13646605±52136.5
2	11991057±456307.4	5839202±48165.42	8041677±101541.1
4	6449274±60252.29	3320537±35616.13	4595789±55375.04
8	3677042±55153.66	1783757±95323.96	2533818±177565.8
16	2691156±64614.96	1170663±82602.59	1814142±103150.9

Table 8.11 Real average execution times for the Matrix Multiplication problem (with matrices of 1024×1024 elements), using different architectural patterns.

Figure 8.8 shows the graphical comparison of the real average execution values. Observe the similarity between the graphical representations of estimates and real average execution times in Figures 8.7 and 8.8. From Figure 8.8, the real average execution times for solving the Matrix Multiplication show that the MW solution has the shortest execution times. Even though there are differences between estimates and real average execution times, analysing both groups of values leads to the same conclusion: the MW solution is the best option for Matrix Multiplication, using the available resources of a JPVM environment on a cluster of sixteen computers. The relationships among the performance estimates for CSE, MW and PF are mostly preserved among the real average execution times for each parallel program based on the same patterns.

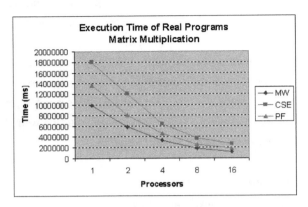

Figure 8.8 Comparison of the execution times of the three real parallel programs for the Matrix Multiplication

Furthermore, comparing the values in Table 8.10 and Table 8.11, it can be observed that there are differences (errors) between the performance estimates and real average execution times. For comparison purposes, the error between each estimate and each real average execution time is obtained, using again the t-test criteria (see Section 8.2). Table 8.12 shows the error calculated between each performance estimate and each real average execution time, as well as the statistical test used to compare two sets of samples. The equivalence between estimates and real average execution times should be rejected, with the conclusion that at the average level the values are different, if $t_0 > 2.0101$.

No. of Processors	Communicating Sequential Elements		Manager-Workers		Pipes and Filters	
	Error (milliseconds)	t_0	Error (secs.)	t_0	Error (secs.)	t_0
1	724.6±391.9359	0.776854	1314.8±422.475	1.307717	1029.1±286.881	1.507339
2	359±684.9637	0.220233	694.5±270.642	1.078284	2007.3±469.785	1.79543
4	1597.3±337.212	1.990396	278±311.2516	0.375309	556.2±468.9341	0.498397
8	466±298.9612	0.654979	4231.6±527.072	3.373574*	3325.5±512.227	2.728039*
16	2309.5±316.638	3.064856*	1150.2±383.656	1.259757	3961.8±443.190	3.756285*

Table 8.12 Errors between the estimates and real average execution times, and values of their statistical test t_0 for the Matrix Multiplication problem.

Notice that in this example, most of the calculated errors are small enough (between 359 milliseconds and 4231.6 milliseconds). This means that the estimates are close values to the real average execution times. However, some equivalencies have to be rejected, since they meet the rejection criteria. The rejected results are those experiments whose t_0 value is marked with (*). From a total of 15 experimental results, 4 should be rejected. That is, there is actual equivalence between performance estimates and real average execution times in 73.33% of the experiments. Therefore, in this case, the conclusion is that the Architectural Performance Modelling Method produces representative performance estimates of a real parallel program's average execution times, and it can be used to support performance modelling during early parallel software design.

Speed-up and Efficiency

In order to compare the performance estimates and real execution times, in this section the values for speed-up and efficiency (see Section 2.1.5) are derived as measures of the performance analysis for the Matrix Multiplication problem. Tables 8.13, 8.14, and 8.15 present the values of speed-up and efficiency for the estimates and the real time measures for the Matrix Multiplication problem, based respectively on CSE, MW, and PF.

No. of Processors	Estimate Speed-up	Real System Speedup	Estimate Efficiency (%)	Real System Efficiency (%)
1	1.0±0.0	1.0±0.0	100.0±0.0	100.0±0.0
2	1.697183±0.042378	1.697052±0.015959	84.83692±2.118944	84.83809±0.7979634
4	2.9831288±0.141297	2.984460±0.028512	74.578219±3.532446	74.59436±0.7128056
8	5.5668897±0.963165	5.552716±0.306726	69.586121±12.03957	69.43026±3.8340854
16	8.4705553±0.748538	8.467161±0.630299	52.94097±4.6783686	52.89597±3.9393730

Table 8.13 Speed-up and efficiency values for estimates and real execution times for the Matrix Multiplication problem using MW.

No. of Processors	Estimate Speed-up	Real System Speedup	Estimate Efficiency (%)	Real System Efficiency (%)
1	1.0±0.0	1.0±0.0	100.0±0.0	100.0±0.0
2	1.5034053±0.027924	1.5035108±0.050937	75.17027±1.3962222	75.175538±2.546856
4	2.7946551±0.044898	2.7954597±0.030647	69.866378±1.122459	69.886491±0.766183
8	4.9022222±0.099488	4.9030405±0.080377	61.277777±1.243605	61.288006±1.004716
16	6.6932215±0.203554	6.6992347±0.173028	41.832634±1.2722118	41.870217±8.100572

Table 8.14 Speed-up and efficiency values for estimates and real execution times for the Matrix Multiplication problem using CSE.

No. of Processors	Estimate Speed-up	Real System Speedup	Estimate Efficiency (%)	Real System Efficiency (%)
1	1.0±0.0	1.0±0.0	100.0±0.0	100.0±0.0
2	1.6975368±0.041317	1.69698509±0.02169	84.876839±2.065851	84.849254±1.084400
4	2.969236±0.1631035	2.9693715±0.031819	74.230903±4.077587	74.234288±0.795471
8	5.3932732±0.391404	5.3857887±0.408278	67.415915±4.892551	67.322358±5.103477
16	7.5393770±0.695645	7.52234491±0.38082	47.121106±4.3477785	47.014656±2.380099

Table 8.15 Speed-up and efficiency values for estimates and real execution times for the Matrix Multiplication problem using PF.

Figure 8.9 shows the speed-up achieved by the different solutions based on MW, CSE, and PF for the estimates and real average execution times when solving the Matrix Multiplication problem. On the other hand, Figure 8.10 shows the efficiency of the different solutions based on MW, CSE, and PF for the estimates and real average execution times when solving the Matrix Multiplication problem.

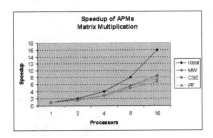
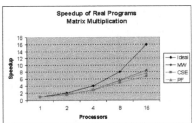

Figure 8.9 Speed-up of the performance estimates and real execution times for the Matrix Multiplication problem using different parallel solutions based on MW, CSE, and PF.

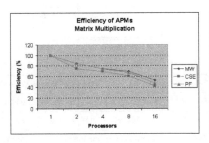
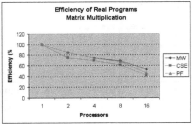

Figure 8.10 Efficiency of the performance estimates and real execution times for the Matrix Multiplication problem using different parallel solutions based on MW, CSE, and PF.

From the graphical comparisons in Figures 8.9 and 8.10, the speed-up and efficiency for MW, CSE, and PF are extremely similar. Nevertheless, to ensure a statistical similarity, an error analysis using the t-test criteria (Weiss, 1999) is carried out between the speed-up and efficiency for each estimate and each real average execution time. Table 8.16 shows the errors between the speed-up values of the performance estimates and real average execution times, whereas Table 8.17 shows the errors between the efficiency values of the performance estimates and real average execution times..

No. of Procs	MW		CSE		PF	
	Speed-up Error	t_0	Speed-up Error	t_0	Speed-up Error	t_0
1	0.0±0.0	-	0.0±0.0	-	0.0±0.0	-
2	0.000130±0.203833	0.00026956	0.0035124±0.23699	0.00622768	0.002408±0.211829	0.00477721
4	0.007899±0.347760	0.00954507	0.0002079±0.23195	0.00037663	0.020047±0.372588	0.02260922
8	0.339316±0.951002	0.14992680	0.0009614±0.35791	0.001128747	0.009231±0.754669	0.00513979
16	0.085477±0.990957	0.03624525	0.0021732±0.51788	0.00176330	0.120901±0.875582	0.05802158

Table 8.16 Errors between the speed-up values of estimates and real average execution times, and their respective statistical test t_0 for the Matrix Multiplication problem.

No. of Procs	MW		CSE		PF	
	Efficiency Error	t_0	Efficiency Error	t_0	Efficiency Error	t_0
1	0.0±0.0	-	0.0±0.0	-	0.0±0.0	-
2	0.0065380±1.44132	0.00190608	0.175619±1.675775	0.04403632	0.120413±1.497858	0.03377995
4	0.197489±1.738801	0.04772535	0.005197±1.159773	0.00188313	0.501185±1.862940	0.113046107
8	4.241454±3.362301	0.53007127	0.012018±1.265398	0.00399072	0.115387±2.668159	0.01817189
16	0.53423±2.4773921	0.090613114	4.126833±2.583642	0.671182497	0.755632±2.188956	0.14505395

Table 8.17 Errors between the efficiency of estimates and real average execution times, and their respective statistical test t_0 for the Matrix Multiplication problem.

Notice that in both tables there is no value for t_0 greater than 2.101, which means that in speed-up and efficiency terms, the Architectural Performance Model produces values completely similar to the actual speed-up and efficiency of the real parallel system. So, the speed-up and efficiency information obtained from the model is a representative of the speed-up and efficiency of the real system. This means that by only using the information from the model, it is possible to have a criteria to select an architectural pattern.

8.3.2 Example of Comparing Architectural Patterns — A Prime Numbers Sieve

A second example is presented to compare three different architectural patterns for solving the Prime Numbers Sieve problem (Hoare, 1978; Andrews, 1991; Nevison *et al.*, 1994; Hartley, 1998; Andrews, 2000).

Problem Description

The Prime Numbers Sieve problem is to find all primes less than or equal to a given target number (Nevison *et al.*, 1994). The parallel program is to be developed and executed using a JPVM environment (Ferrari,1997; Geist *et al.*, 1994) on a cluster of sixteen computers (see Section 8.1).

Algorithmic Solution for a Prime Numbers Sieve problem

An algorithm to find the prime numbers less than or equal to a target number tests each candidate number to see if it is prime by dividing it by all primes smaller than its square root. The division by composite numbers is not needed, since every composite number has prime factors; also, the division by primes greater than the square root is not needed, since such a factor would have a corresponding factor less than the square root. Thus, all the primes less than a given target are tested by first finding all primes less than the square root, and then, testing all numbers by dividing out by these primes. This is done sequentially for a serial algorithm. Also, using the knowledge that all even numbers greater than two are composite, only odd numbers are considered as input (Nevison *et al.*, 1994; Hartley, 1998). In this algorithm, each test of a candidate value is independent of any checks of other candidates. Conceptually, many of the tests can be done in parallel (Hoare, 1978; Nevison *et al.*, 1994).

The CSE Solution for the Prime Numbers Sieve

A potential solution to the Prime Numbers Sieve problem can be based on the CSE pattern (see Section 5.2.10). The strategy is that all available data is divided among a group of communicating elements, which are able to exchange data through channels.

The CSE solution for solving the Prime Numbers Sieve problem uses data distribution, by dividing the set of odd numbers into subsets, and assigning each subset to a communicating element (Figure 8.11). Each communicating element searches for local

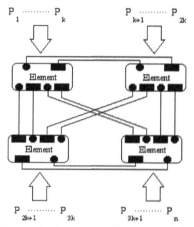

Figure 8.11 The Communicating Sequential Elements Solution to the Prime Numbers Sieve problem

candidates in its assigned subset. However, to improve the efficiency of the search, if an element finds a new prime number, it communicates this result to all other elements. Finally, the set of all prime numbers less or equal to the target number is found after all searches are finished.

The MW Solution for the Prime Numbers Sieve

Another potential solution to the Prime Numbers Sieve problem is based on the MW pattern (see Section 5.2.11). This pattern takes advantage of the characteristics of a regular homogeneous computation, so all data is divided and assigned by the manager to a group of workers. Each worker can only receive and send data to the manager (Figure 8.12).

Solving the Prime Number Sieve problem using the MW pattern, the set of odd numbers to test is passed by the manager to the workers. Each worker goes on testing its subset of numbers, and each time it finds a prime number, sending the result to the manager. When all workers have finished testing their assigned subset of numbers, the manager has the set of all prime numbers found.

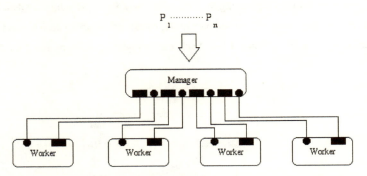

Figure 8.12 The Manager-Workers Solution to the Prime Numbers Sieve problem

The PF Solution for the Prime Numbers Sieve

The computations required by the Prime Numbers Sieve problem present characteristics of order of data and a regular homogeneous computation, so its solution can be developed using the PF pattern (see Section 5.2.8). The main strategy is to allow a data flow from one filter to another, each of which carries out a part of the computation (Figure 8.13).

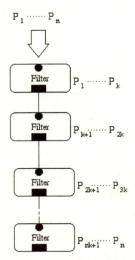

Figure 8.13 Pipes and Filters Solution for the Prime Number Sieve problem

Each filter tests the data stream, eliminating those values that it divides evenly. For finding a prime number, all the previous prime numbers will be assigned to the previous filters, and are therefore passed through. Each filter searches for a prime, or a group of

226

primes, and after that point, the filter starts checking each number as it passes through. The effect of the test is to pass the number on to the next filter if it is not evenly divisible by the prime tested on this filter. However, the algorithm avoids a division step and takes advantage of the fact that the stream of candidate numbers is increasing. Thus, as long as the candidate number is less than the current odd multiple of the prime, it is passed on. When a candidate number exceeds the test value, the test value is increased to the next odd multiple of the prime, and the process continues until all input odd numbers have been tested (Hoare, 1978; Andrews, 1991; Nevison, *et al.*, 1994; Andrews, 2000).

Obtaining the Performance Estimates

Applying the Architectural Performance Modelling Method, the performance estimates for different configurations and for observed values of ρ are shown in Table 8.18. Again, this value is obtained from observing the behaviour of the parallel software coordination (see Section 7.1.4). Each estimate is calculated using the t-test technique (Weiss, 1999; see also Section 8.2) for small samples considering samples of 10 executions and a confidence interval of 95%.

No. of Processors	Communicating Sequential Elements ($\rho \propto$ No. Procs) (milliseconds)	Manager-Workers ($\rho = 0.66$) (milliseconds)	Pipes and Filters ($\rho = 0.5$) (milliseconds)
1	12244482±39162.79	13319844±42475.6	10081013±120019
2	8158154±44012.72	8331713±29993.41	5933422±32018.78
4	4370036±35794.46	4594682±33024.68	3363190±42588.2
8	2502092±38833.4	2422643±40605.26	1922279±8193.58
16	1832465±38886.78	1628265±17751.85	1383901±28542.74

Table 8.18 Performance estimates for the Prime Numbers Sieve problem (for 1048576 primes), using different architectural patterns.

Comparative Analysis

Figure 8.14 shows a graphical comparison of the estimates of the three solutions for the Prime Numbers Sieve, based on CSE, MW, and PF. Each graph represents the estimated times for each model executing on different configurations of a cluster of sixteen computers, with 1, 2, 4, 8, and 16 processors.

Observing the performance estimates in Table 8.18 and their graphical representation in Figure 8.14, it is noticeable that in most cases the PF solution gives the lower estimates for carrying out the proposed Prime Numbers Sieve algorithm. However, in some

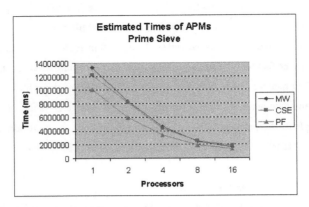

Figure 8.14 Comparison of the estimated times of the three solutions for the Prime Numbers Sieve problem

cases the CSE and MW solutions produce lower estimates than the PF solution for a small number of components. From considering this, the CSE and MW solutions would represent viable solutions for solving the Prime Numbers Sieve problem. However, the PF solution tends to produce lower estimate values as the number of processing components increase. The reason is that the PF solution requires less communications between components, because it exploits the characteristic of order among prime numbers that the CSE and MW solutions do not consider. As the number of components increase, the overhead due to communication in the PF solution tends to decrease faster than in the CSE or MW solutions. Therefore, the conclusion is that for larger numbers of processing components, the PF solution seems to be the best candidate for solving the Prime Numbers Sieve problem, using the available resources of a JPVM environment on a cluster of sixteen computers.

Validating the Comparative Analysis

The real parallel programs are implemented, and the real average execution times for each architectural pattern are statistically calculated to validate the comparative analysis. Table 8.19 shows the numerical values of the real average execution times for different configurations.

Figure 8.15 shows the graphical comparison of these execution values. Comparing the performance estimates and the real average execution times shown in Figures 8.14 and 8.15, there is a strong similarity. Based on this similarity, a comparative analysis can

No. of Processors	Communicating Sequential Elements (milliseconds)	Manager-Workers (milliseconds)	Pipes and Filters (milliseconds)
1	12245581±138019.8	13321116±222773	10082070±24857.3
2	8156974±123741	8331034±16601.1	5932584±23430.17
4	4368366±174610.1	4594617±27185.35	3363697±12061.68
8	2500831±15980.34	2423165±13763.41	1923410±20759.17
16	1830680±14195.66	1626502±16499.58	1383763±22591.46

Table 8.19 Real average execution times for the Prime Number Sieve problem (for 1047586 primes), using different architectural patterns.

be carried out using the real average execution times. From Figure 8.15, notice that in most cases the PF solution has the shorter execution times for solving the Prime Numbers Sieve problem. Again, considering performance properties of the different solutions for solving the Prime Numbers Sieve problem, CSE and MW solutions represent viable solutions. However, as it is the case with the estimates, the PF solution tends to produce shorter execution times as the number of processing components increase. Based on this observation, a similar conclusion to that obtained from the performance estimates can be drawn from analysing the execution times. Again, for larger numbers of processing components the PF solution is the most viable solution for solving the Prime Numbers Sieve problem using the available resources of a JPVM environment on a cluster of sixteen computers. The relationships among the performance estimates for CSE, MW and PF are preserved among the real average execution times for each parallel program based on the same patterns.

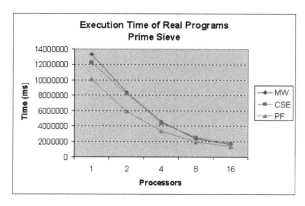

Figure 8.15 Comparison of the execution times of the three real parallel programs for the Prime Numbers Sieve problem

229

Comparing the values in Table 8.18 and Table 8.19, differences (errors) are observed between the performance estimates and real average execution times. The error between each estimate and each real average execution time is obtained, again using the t-test criteria (see Section 8.2). Table 8.20 shows the error calculated between each performance estimate and each real average execution time, as well as the statistical test t_0 used to compare two sets of samples. The equivalence between estimates and real average execution times should be rejected if $t_0 > 2.101$.

No. of Processors	Communicating Sequential Elements		Manager-Workers		Pipes and Filters	
	Error (milliseconds)	t_0	Error (secs.)	t_0	Error (secs.)	t_0
1	1099±355.2291	1.300006	1272.8±434.635	1.230528	1057±321.216	1.382719
2	1180.3±345.648	1.434876	678.9±182.1652	1.566017	838.4±198.7214	1.772812
4	1670.3±387.102	1.813113	64.7±207.0773	0.131289	506.5±197.2843	1.078805
8	1261±197.5799	2.681813*	522.2±196.7761	1.115117	1131±143.5962	3.309602*
16	1785.4±194.434	3.858497*	1763±156.1843	4.743195*	137.7±190.8331	0.303205

Table 8.20 Errors between the estimates and real average execution times, and values of their statistical test t_0 for the Prime Numbers Sieve problem.

In this example, most of the calculated errors show are between 64.7 milliseconds and 1785.4 milliseconds, which means that the estimates are close to the real average execution times. However, some equivalencies have to be rejected, since they meet the rejection criteria. The rejected results are those experiments whose t_0 value is marked with (*). From a total of 15 experimental results, 4 should be rejected. That is, there is actual equivalence between performance estimates and real average execution times in 73.33% of the experiments. Therefore, in this case, the conclusion is that the Architectural Performance Modelling Method produces representative performance estimates of the real parallel program's average execution times, and it can be used to support performance modelling during early parallel software design.

Speed-up and Efficiency
For comparison purposes, the values for speed-up and efficiency (see Section 2.1.5) are obtained from the estimates and the real execution times of the Prime Numbers Sieve problem. Tables 8.21, 8.22, and 8.23 respectively show the speed-up and efficiency for the estimates and the real time measures using a solution based on CSE, MW, and PF.

No. of Processors	Estimate Speed-up	Real System Speedup	Estimate Efficiency (%)	Real System Efficiency (%)
1	1.0±0.0	1.0±0.0	100.0±0.0	100.0±0.0
2	1.598692±0.0026513	1.598975±0.0246546	79.9346±0.1325672	79.94876±1,2327301
4	2.89897±0.0126687	2.89928±0.0399261	72.47425±0.3167193	72.48219±0.998153
8	5.498062±0.0739425	5.497403±0.074623	68.72578±0.9242818	68.71754±0.9327991
16	8.180391±0.0985265	8.190040±0.0880906	51.1274±0.6157906	51.18775±0.5505663

Table 8.21 Speed-up and efficiency values for estimates and real execution times for the Prime Number Sieve problem using MW.

No. of Processors	Estimate Speed-up	Real System Speedup	Estimate Efficiency (%)	Real System Efficiency (%)
1	1.0±0.0	1.0±0.0	100.0±0.0	100.0±0.0
2	1.500889±0.0038454	1.50124±0.01434606	75.04444±0.1922701	75.06204±0.717303
4	2.801918±0.014153	2.803241±0.082383	70.04795±0.3538253	70.08102±2.0595751
8	4.89369±0.05969827	4.896606±0.0350946	61.17123±0.7462283	61.20757±0.4386820
16	6.681973±0.1183307	6.689090±0.0421489	41.7623±8.03937995	41.80682±8.0169825

Table 8.22 Speed-up and efficiency values for estimates and real execution times for the Prime Numbers Sieve problem using CSE.

No. of Processors	Estimate Speed-up	Real System Speedup	Estimate Efficiency (%)	Real System Efficiency (%)
1	1.0±0.0	1.0±0.0	100.0±0.0	100.0±0.0
2	1.699022±0.0267391	1.699440±0.0058005	84.95109±1.3369547	84.97200±0.2900256
4	2.997456±0.0626522	2.997318±0.0084920	74.93639±1.5663050	74.93296±0.2122997
8	5.244303±0.0738036	5.241769±0.0614618	65.55379±0.9225456	65.52211±0.7682733
16	7.284490±0.1900587	7.285979±0.1012461	45.52807±1.1878668	45.5374±0.63278838

Table 8.23 Speed-up and efficiency values for estimates and real execution times for the Prime Numbers Sieve problem using PF.

The speed-up achieved by the different solutions (for the estimates and real average execution times) is graphically shown in Figure 8.16. Also, the efficiency of the different solutions is presented in Figure 8.17.

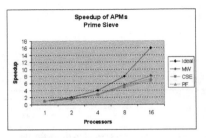
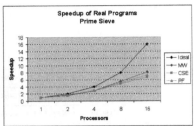

Figure 8.16 Speed-up of the performance estimates and real execution times for the Prime Numbers Sieve problem using different parallel solutions based on MW, CSE, and PF.

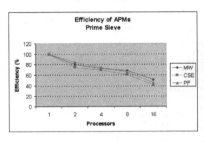
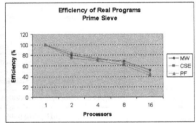

Figure 8.17 Efficiency of the performance estimates and real execution times for the Prime Numbers Sieve problem using different parallel solutions based on MW, CSE, and PF.

The comparisons between the graphics for speed-up and for efficiency show that both measures are very similar. However to ensure this similarity, an statistical error analysis between the speed-up and efficiency for each estimate and each real average execution time is carried out using the t-test criteria (Weiss, 1999). Table 8.24 presents the errors between the speed-up values of the performance estimates and real average execution times. Also, Table 8.25 presents the errors between the efficiency values of the performance estimates and real average execution times.

No. of Procs	MW		CSE		PF	
	Speed-up Error	t_0	Speed-up Error	t_0	Speed-up Error	t_0
1	0.0±0.0	-	0.0±0.0	-	0.0±0.0	-
2	0.0002028±0.13945	0.000611057	0.000649±0.113823	0.00239748	0.000182±0.152231	0.00050225
4	6.53101E05±0.1935	0.00014180	0.00856±0.2622060	0.01372149	0.001726±0.225096	0.00322259

Table 8.24 Errors between the speed-up values of estimates and real average execution times, and their respective statistical test t_0 for the Prime Numbers Sieve problem.

No. of Procs	MW			CSE			PF		
	Speed-up Error	t_0		Speed-up Error	t_0		Speed-up Error	t_0	
8	0.003948±0.325281	0.00509954		0.000552±0.259828	0.00089222		0.001478±0.310378	0.00200131	
16	0.006658±0.364564	0.00767366		0.001056±0.338071	0.00131219		0.002974±0.455483	0.00274363	

Table 8.24 Errors between the speed-up values of estimates and real average execution times, and their respective statistical test t_0 for the Prime Numbers Sieve problem.

No. of Procs	MW		CSE		PF	
	Efficiency Error	t_0	Efficiency Error	t_0	Efficiency Error	t_0
1	0.0±0.0	-	0.0±0.0	-	0.0±0.0	-
2	0.010139±0.986079	0.00432083	0.032471±0.804853	0.01695274	0.009098±1.076438	0.00355147
4	0.001633±0.967698	0.00070898	0.214056±1.311030	0.06860745	0.043158±1.125480	0.016112959
8	0.049345±1.150041	0.01802958	0.006896±0.918630	0.00315447	0.018478±1.097354	0.00707569
16	0.041610±0.911410	0.01918416	0.040710±3.381595	0.00505868	0.018588±1.138707	0.00685908

Table 8.25 Errors between the efficiency of estimates and real average execution times, and their respective statistical test t_0 for the Prime Numbers Sieve problem.

There is no value for t_0 greater than 2.101 in both tables. This means that in terms of speed-up and efficiency, the Architectural Performance Model generates speed-up and efficiency values extremely similar to the actual values obtained for the real parallel system. So, the model can be effectively used to get speed-up and efficiency information representative of the speed-up and efficiency of the real system. Hence, the model estimates can be used as a selection criteria for choosing an architectural pattern.

8.3.3 Example of Comparing Architectural Patterns — The Heat Equation

Our last experimental example for comparing architectural patterns is based on the Heat Equation problem (Freeman & Phillips, 1992; Geist et al., 1994; Ortega-Arjona, 2000).

Problem Description

The Heat Equation problem is to calculate the heat diffusion through a substrate, using a parallel program (Geist et al., 1994; Ortega-Arjona, 2000). Let us consider the simplest case, in which the Heat Equation is used to model the heat distribution on a one-dimensional body, a thin substrate, such as a wire (Figure 8.18). Different intervals expose a different temperature, determining a particular distribution at different times. The heat diffusion is obtained as data representing the way in which the temperature of each interval varies through time, tending to increase or decrease depending on the exchange of heat with other intervals (Ortega-Arjona, 2000). The parallel program is to be developed and executed using a JPVM environment (Ferrari, 1997; Geist, *et al.*, 1994), on a cluster of sixteen computers (see Section 8.1).

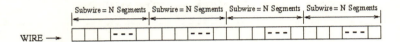

Figure 8.18 Dividing the segments of a wire into intervals

Algorithmic Solution for the Heat Equation

A simple method developed for deriving a numerical solution to the Heat Equation is the method of finite differences (Geist *et al.*, 1994; Ortega-Arjona, 2000). Consider the discrete form for the one-dimensional heat equation:

$$A(i+1,j) = A(i,j) + \frac{\Delta t}{\Delta x^2}(A(i,j+1) - 2(A(i,j)) + A(i,j-1))$$

where i represents time steps and j indicates wire subintervals.

The numerical solution is now computed simply by calculating the value for each interval at a given time frame, considering the temperature from both its previous and its next intervals (Ortega-Arjona, 2000).

The CSE Solution for the Heat Equation

The algorithmic solution to the Heat Equation exhibits characteristics of order of data and a regular homogeneous computation, and therefore, a parallel solution is likely based on the CSE pattern (see Section 5.2.10). The main idea is that all data (representing the temperature of each subwire in the wire) is divided and assigned to a group of communicating elements. Communications between neighbouring elements are restricted only to the exchange of data representing temperatures at the boundaries (Figure 8.19).

The Heat Equation computation starts with simultaneous communications between neighbouring elements. As many intervals of data are assigned to each communicating element, only data from the boundaries must be exchanged through channels. After data

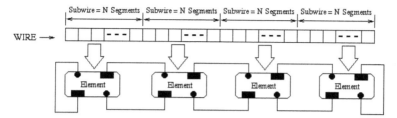

Figure 8.19 The Communicating Sequential Elements Solution to the Heat Equation

exchange is finished, each communicating element proceeds to operate on the data representing its subwire. Once all communicating elements have operated on all their data, they write the results as an intermediate value representing the heat diffusion for that particular time step. The computation starts over again, repeating the communications and operations using the intermediate result as input for the next time step. After finishing all time step iterations, all intermediate results are grouped in order, representing the heat diffusion in the wire through different time steps (Ortega-Arjona, 2000).

The MW Solution for the Heat Equation

Another solution to the Heat Equation is based on the MW pattern (see Section 5.2.11). This architectural pattern also takes advantage of the characteristics of order of data and a regular homogeneous computation. The main idea is that all data (representing the temperature of each subwire in the wire) is divided by the manager into smaller pieces that can be handled by the workers. Communications between workers is restricted: each worker can only receive and send data to the manager (Figure 8.20).

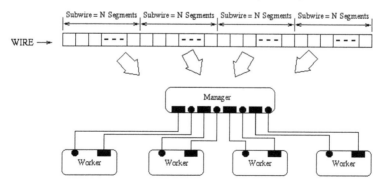

Figure 8.20 The Manager-Workers Solution to the Heat Equation

In order to use the MW pattern for solving the Heat Equation, the computation is carried out each time step, in which the manager divides the data representing the wire among the workers, and these operate on their assigned subwire and return the results. These results are grouped by the manager as an intermediate result for that time step, which will be used as input for the next time step. After finishing all time step iterations, all intermediate results are grouped in order, representing the heat diffusion through the wire in different time steps.

The PF Solution for the Heat Equation

A third solution to the Heat Equation is based on the PF pattern (see Section 5.2.8). Compared to the two previous solution approaches, this architectural pattern takes advantage of the overlapping of operations through time. The main idea is that all data (representing the temperature of each segment in the wire) is operated on by each filter, producing intermediate results as output for each time step. Pipes allow the flow of data through filters, making sure that the output of a filter is used as the input of the next filter (Figure 8.21).

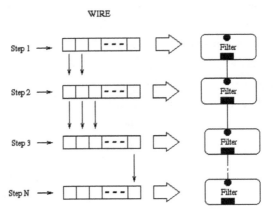

Figure 8.21 Pipes and Filters Solution for the Heat Equation

In order to take advantage of operation overlapping in this solution, each filter is defined so it operates on just a segment at a time, producing the intermediate result for the present segment. However, once operated on, this intermediate result can be stored, and communicated as input to the next filter, which can start producing the intermediate result for the next time step. So, for solving the Heat Equation, the PF solution is based on overlapping operations on segments rather than dividing all data among processing components. Finally, after finishing all filter operations, every filter has stored a group of intermediate results that represent the heat diffusion in the wire at each different time step.

Obtaining the Performance Estimates

The Architectural Performance Modelling Method is applied for the three architectural pattern solutions, obtaining performance estimates. Table 8.26 presents the numerical values of the performance estimates for different configurations, and for observed values of ρ. As with the previous examples, this value is obtained from observing the behaviour of the parallel software coordination (see Section 7.1.4). The estimates are collected by using the t-test technique for small samples (Weiss, 1999; see also Section 8.2) considering samples of 10 executions and a confidence interval of 95%.

No. of Processors	Communicating Sequential Elements ($\rho = 0.66$) (milliseconds)	Manager-Workers ($\rho = 0.75$) (milliseconds)	Pipes and Filters ($\rho = 0.75$) (milliseconds)
1	14681663±154282.5	16845451±146968	18397714±165363
2	9799680±30439.72	9930470±42506.48	10828290±125152
4	5250581±28988.61	5614518±34748.58	6146556±185295
8	2998637±30060.16	2954294±16221.33	3484603±96866.84
16	2199937±21909.73	1983324±12701.85	2481815±76766.57

Table 8.26 Performance estimates for the Heat Equation problem (with 65536 elements during 32 iterations), using different architectural patterns.

Comparative Analysis

Figure 8.22 shows the graphical comparison of the estimated times of the three solutions for the Heat Equation problem, based on CSE, MW, and PF. Each graph represents the estimated times for each model executing on a cluster of sixteen computers with 1, 2, 4, 8, and 16 processors.

Observing the performance estimates in Table 8.26 and their representation in Figure 8.22, it is clear that for solving the Heat Equation, the CSE solution provides the shorter time estimates, followed closely by the MW solution. PF can also be used to solve the Heat Equation problem, but the estimates obtained suggest that this solution is slower compared to the CSE or MW solutions. Even though the PF solution carries out the same processing, its coordination organisation requires large times for communicating and

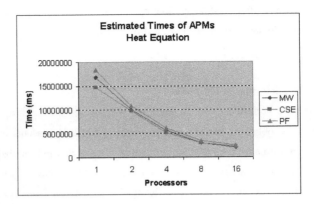

Figure 8.22 Comparing the estimates of the three architectural patterns for the Heat Equation problem

coordinating components. Noticing this, it is clear that PF would not be a viable solution for the Heat Equation.

For every configuration, the estimates of the CSE solution are always less than the estimates of the MW solution. However, the difference between the estimates from the CSE solution and the MW solution is not very large. MW barely requires a little more time to coordinate and communicate than CSE. The reason is the additional overhead introduced by the extra communications due to data exchange between manager and workers to produce each time step intermediate results. If these communications were not needed, MW would represent a feasible potential solution. Nevertheless, as the performance estimates are given for comparing the three potential solutions, the CSE solution seems to be the best candidate for solving the Heat Equation, using the available resources of a JPVM environment on a cluster of sixteen computers.

Validating the Comparative Analysis

In order to validate the comparative analysis, the real parallel programs are implemented, so the real average execution time for each architectural pattern are statistically obtained from measured execution times. Table 8.27 shows the numerical values for the real average execution times for different configurations.

Figure 8.23 shows the graphical comparison of the real average execution values. A noticeable similarity can be observed between the graphical representations of the real average execution times in Figure 8.23, and the performance estimates in Figure 8.22. Moreover, a similar comparative analysis can be carried out either using the performance

No. of Processors	Communicating Sequential Elements (milliseconds)	Manager-Workers (milliseconds)	Pipes and Filters (milliseconds)
1	14682749±104282.3	16844786±155274	18395446±165780
2	9799204±18906.37	9930628±11281.2	10830096±171361
4	5250047±20019.49	5613606±15007.76	6144707±8796.492
8	2998598±7068.558	2952807±25934.29	3487189±14680.95
16	2198400±15551.4	1983788±18733.36	2484508±17809.08

Table 8.27 Real average execution times for the Heat Equation problem (with 65536 elements during 32 iterations), using different architectural patterns.

estimates or the real average execution times. From Figure 8.23, for solving the Heat Equation, the CSE solution again provides the shortest real average execution times, followed by the MW solution. PF also shows a similar relationship with respect to the CSE or MW solutions. Again, the result of these comparison shows that the CSE solution seems to be the best candidate for solving the Heat Equation, using the available resources of a JPVM environment on a cluster of sixteen computers. The relationships among the performance estimates for CSE, MW and PF are preserved among the real average execution times for each parallel program based on the same patterns.

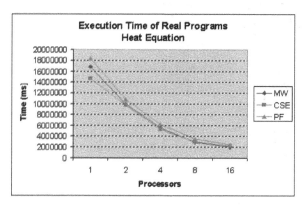

Figure 8.23 Comparison of the real average execution times of the three parallel programs for the Heat Equation problem

From comparing the values in Table 8.26 and Table 8.27, differences (errors) between the performance estimates and real average execution times can be observed. For comparing each estimate and each real average execution time, the error between them is obtained, using again the *t*-test criteria (see Section 8.2). In this criteria, two values are statistically compared by obtaining the difference between their means, and considering an adjustment for both confidence intervals (Weiss, 1999). Table 8.28 shows the error calculated between each performance estimate and each real average execution time, as well as the statistical test t_0, used to compare two sets of samples. The equivalence between estimates and real average execution times should be rejected, concluding that at the average level the values are different, if $t_0 > 2.101$.

No. of Processors	Communicating Sequential Elements		Manager-Workers		Pipes and Filters	
	Error (milliseconds)	t_0	Error (secs.)	t_0	Error (secs.)	t_0
1	1086.1±429.123	1.063514	664.4±463.9552	0.601741	2267.5±485.631	1.96199
2	475.9±187.4668	1.066712	158.1±195.7219	0.339429	1805.8±459.536	1.651223
4	534.3±186.8237	1.201737	912.2±188.2445	2.036216	1848.9±371.793	2.089624
8	39.2±162.6122	0.101295	1486.7±173.270	3.605402*	2585.2±281.856	3.854089*
16	1537±163.3384	3.954044*	464.2±149.6257	1.303632	2693.4±259.530	4.360831*

Table 8.28 Errors between the estimates and real average execution times, and values of their statistical test t_0 for the Heat Equation problem.

Notice that most of the calculated errors range between 39.2 milliseconds and 2693.4 milliseconds. This means that the estimates are close values to the real average execution times. However, some equivalencies have to be rejected, since they do meet the rejection criteria. The rejected results are those experiments whose t_0 value is marked with (*). From a total of 15 experimental results, 4 should be rejected, resulting in an actual equivalence between performance estimates and real average execution times in 73.33% of the experiments. Therefore, in this case, the conclusion is that the Architectural Performance Modelling Method produces representative performance estimates of the real parallel program's average execution times, which can be used to support performance modelling during early parallel software design.

Speed-up and Efficiency

Tables 8.29, 8.30, and 8.31 present the values of speed-up and efficiency for the estimates and the real time measures for the Heat Equation problem, based respectively on CSE, MW, and PF.

No. of Processors	Estimate Speed-up	Real System Speedup	Estimate Efficiency (%)	Real System Efficiency (%)
1	1.0±0.0	1.0±0.0	100.0±0.0	100.0±0.0
2	1.696340±0.0187918	1.696246±0.0144833	84.81699±0.9395898	84.81229±0.7241667
4	3.000338±0.0275878	3.000707±0.0296005	75.00845±0.6896955	75.01767±0.7400129
8	5.70202±0.0385492	5.704669±0.0790314	71.27529±0.4818650	71.3084±0.98789276
16	8.493545±0.0866237	8.491223±0.0277752	53.0847±0.54139831	53.07014±0.1735952

Table 8.29 Speed-up and efficiency values for estimates and real execution times for the Heat Equation problem using MW.

No. of Processors	Estimate Speed-up	Real System Speedup	Estimate Efficiency (%)	Real System Efficiency (%)
1	1.0±0.0	1.0±0.0	100.0±0.0	100.0±0.0
2	1.498178±0.0135252	1.498361±0.01103019	74.90889±0.6762597	74.91807±0.5515093
4	2.796198±0.03114967	2.796689±0.0233230	69.90494±0.7787418	69.91723±0.5830759
8	4.896112±0.05302869	4.896539±0.0373845	61.20140±0.6628586	61.20673±0.4673064
16	6.673674±0.11689837	6.678834±0.0812983	41.7105±8.03653748	41.74271±7.985726

Table 8.30 Speed-up and efficiency values for estimates and real execution times for the Heat Equation problem using CSE.

No. of Processors	Estimate Speed-up	Real System Speedup	Estimate Efficiency (%)	Real System Efficiency (%)
1	1.0±0.0	1.0±0.0	100.0±0.0	100.0±0.0
2	1.699041±0.0289936	1.698549±0.0299174	84.95207±1.4496783	84.92744±1.4958708
4	2.993174±0.0764388	2.993706±0.0276764	74.82936±1.9109691	74.84265±0.6919109
8	5.279715±0.11757735	5.27515±0.06270572	65.99644±1.4697168	65.93939±0.7838215
16	7.413009±0.2848695	7.40406±0.04521688	46.33131±1.7804342	46.2754±0.28260549

Table 8.31 Speed-up and efficiency values for estimates and real execution times for the Heat Equation problem using PF.

Figure 8.24 shows the speed-up achieved by the different solutions based on MW, CSE, and PF for the estimates and real average execution times when solving the Heat Equation problem. On the other hand, Figure 8.25 shows the efficiency of the different solutions based on MW, CSE, and PF for the estimates and real average execution times when solving the Heat Equation problem.

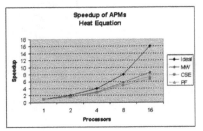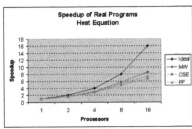

Figure 8.24 Speed-up of the performance estimates and real execution times for the Heat Equation problem using different parallel solutions based on MW, CSE, and PF.

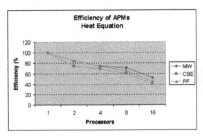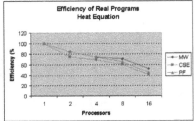

Figure 8.25 Efficiency of the performance estimates and real execution times for the Heat Equation problem using different parallel solutions based on MW, CSE, and PF.

Comparing the speed-up and efficiency for MW, CSE, and PF from Figures 8.24 and 8.25, their behaviours are quite similar. However, it is not completely clear if they prsent a similarity so the models can be considered representative of the real system. Thus, to ensure similarity, an error analysis using the t-test criteria (Weiss, 1999) is carried out between the speed-up and efficiency for each estimate and each real average execution time. Table 8.32 shows the errors between the speed-up values of the performance estimates and real average execution times, whereas Table 8.33 shows the errors between the efficiency values of the performance estimates and real average execution times..

No. of Procs	MW		CSE		PF	
	Speed-up Error	t_0	Speed-up Error	t_0	Speed-up Error	t_0
1	0.0±0.0	-	0.0±0.0	-	0.0±0.0	-
2	0.000245±0.153942	0.00066824	0.000230±0.132243	0.00073052	0.000216±0.204831	0.00044388
4	0.000278±0.201814	0.00057798	0.000455±0.196964	0.00097121	0.004626±0.272305	0.00713851

Table 8.32 Errors between the speed-up values of estimates and real average execution times, and their respective statistical test t_0 for the Heat Equation problem.

No. of Procs	MW		CSE		PF	
	Speed-up Error	t_0	Speed-up Error	t_0	Speed-up Error	t_0
8	0.003864±0.289378	0.00561024	0.000110±0.253755	0.00018258	0.011364±0.358324	0.01332579
16	0.002856±0.285436	0.00420417	0.004051±0.375704	0.00453073	0.028984±0.484855	0.025118937

Table 8.32 Errors between the speed-up values of estimates and real average execution times, and their respective statistical test t_0 for the Heat Equation problem.

No. of Procs	MW		CSE		PF	
	Efficiency Error	t_0	Efficiency Error	t_0	Efficiency Error	t_0
1	0.0±0.0	-	0.0±0.0	-	0.0±0.0	-
2	0.012241±1.088536	0.00472513	0.011495±0.935096	0.00516553	0.010819±1.448375	0.00313873
4	0.006940±1.009071	0.00288992	0.011381±0.984821	0.00485603	0.115650±1.361523	0.03569257
8	0.048295±1.023107	0.01983521	0.001378±0.897158	0.00064552	0.142044±1.266865	0.047113782
16	0.017849±0.713591	0.01051042	0.17608±3.3780024	0.02190261	0.181149±1.212137	0.06279734

Table 8.33 Errors between the efficiency of estimates and real average execution times, and their respective statistical test t_0 for the Heat Equation problem.

From both tables it is noticeable that in the column for t_0 in all cases there is no value greater than 2.101. This means that in speed-up and efficiency terms, the Architectural Performance Model produces values completely similar to the actual speed-up and efficiency of the real parallel system. So, the speed-up and efficiency information obtained from the model is a representative of the speed-up and efficiency of the real system. This means that by only using the information from the model, it is possible to have a criteria to select an architectural pattern.

8.4 Some Conclusions from the Experimental Examples

The objective of all the experimental examples is to evaluate whether the Architectural Performance Modelling Method models the behaviour through time of a parallel software system (as described in Section 4.3.1), that is, if it produces useful estimates to describe the real performance behaviour of parallel software systems. If this is the case, it can be used during the initial stages of parallel software design to estimate the performance of potential solutions with different coordination organisations.

The evaluation results of the experimental examples show that the method produced performance estimates very similar to the real average execution times obtained by running the actual program on the cluster computing environment. The main reason is that the performance a parallel software system is able to achieve depends not only on the parallel platform and the programming language used, but most importantly, it largely depends on the organisation of the coordination among the several sequential processing components that constitute such parallel software system. Such organisation is described and developed based on the Architectural Patterns for Parallel Programming (see Chapter 5), which in this thesis are used for developing models for performance estimation. Notice that for each experimental example, the performance estimates obtained from Architectural Performance Models generate curves exposing trends very similar to the actual parallel program's performance characteristics. Each curve obtained for each case study can be considered as representing the probable performance behaviour of the parallel system. Thus, the Architectural Performance Models are actually "scale-models" that describe the performance of parallel programs, and that allow early estimates about their behaviour to be made. Once developed, such models can be subjected to appropriate assessments and tests, and refined as required (making further use of other software patterns, when necessary).

An interesting conclusion is that the processing time of sequential software components (at the processing layer) depends on the "slots" allowed by the time taken for executing platform and coordination components. In a parallel program, such slots may be varied through modifying the granularity: *(a)* at the level of processing components, by changing the number of such components and their mapping into coordination components; *(b)* at the level of coordination components, by changing the number of coordination components and their mapping into processors; and *(c)* at the level of platform components, by changing the number of processors on which the parallel process takes place (this last modification is the kind of changes we aim to avoid, see Section 1.2). These three ways of modifying granularity are widely used in the parallel programming practice to improve the performance of a parallel system, with specific constraints of platform, language, and problem requirements. As the performance that a parallel program is able to achieve using a particular hardware and software environment depends on the organisation and communication among the sequential processing components, and the Architectural Performance Modelling Method allows to perform these modifications on the Architectural Performance Model, then the method permits to test an verify the result of applying such modifications on the performance of a prospective parallel system.

The differences between performance estimates and real average execution times mainly originate from the following causes:

- The Architectural Performance Modelling Method makes some assumptions to obtain the general expression for total execution time of a parallel system (see Sections 4.3.1 and 4.3.2). These assumptions represent basic errors introduced between estimates and real average execution times. The most relevant assumptions taken in this thesis are: *(a)* a parallel program specifies simultaneous processing and communication activities carried out by software components; *(b)* the given inputs for designing a parallel program are the problem statement, the amount of data to be operated on, and the parallel hardware and software resources available *(c)* the solution to the paralleli-sation problem is not directly affected by the nature of the problem itself, but more precisely, by the order and relation among instructions within the algorithm and/or datum within the data; *(d)* processing and communication are activities sharply sepa-rated among coordination and processing components of a parallel program; *(e)* soft-ware components are prone to remain idle during periods of time due to the non-deterministic parallel environment in which software components are executed; *(f)* the time required to execute a parallel program ought to be described more likely as prob-abilistic values, due to non-determinism; *(g)* a parallel program finishes only when all the software components it specifies finish; *(h)* during execution, the state of each software component of a parallel program is considered to be *processing, communi-cating,* or *idling*; *(i)* a parallel program can be described in terms of Platform, Coordi-nation and Processing components; *(j)* the performance of a parallel program mainly depends on the time it takes for all its components to carry out coordinating or processing activities; *(k)* coordination components spend most of their time coordinat-ing and communicating data between processing components; *(l)* processing compo-nents spend most of their time processing data; *(m)* the functionality of platform and coordination components can be represented by a runnable implementation of an architectural pattern, that only represents the coordination among major components on the parallel resources available; and *(n)* the functionality of processing components can be simulated by statistical components.

- The technique for measuring is only as precise as allowed by the method sys-

`tem.currentTimeMillis()`(Smith, 2000; Hartley, 1998). As the performance estimates depend strongly on measuring the coordination, they also depend on the quality
and accuracy of the measuring technique used. The Java libraries use the hardware
real time clock, obtaining measurements in the order of milliseconds. Nevertheless,
this measurement is known to have a precision, producing certain small errors in the
final measurements (Hartley, 1998).

- In the Component Simulation, the class `Markovian` makes use of a random function
  to produce the stochastic behaviour of processing components, attempting to model
  the non-deterministic execution of actual pieces of code. However, values obtained by
  simulation are only approximations: they are product of a modelling abstraction of the
  stochastic sequential behaviour of real processing components. It is precisely for this
  reason that the estimates are considered as *accurate approximations*, not exact predictions, of the execution times of the real parallel program (see Section 1.3).

Another important issue to consider as part of the conclusions is the cost of developing the Architectural Performance Modelling Method against simply building the application in several ways. The discussion here concentrates on the cost of effort, as this has
the most significant effect on general project costs (Sommerville, 1989).

At the beginning, the Architectural Performance Modelling Method gives the
impression to have a high cost of effort, since it uses simulation modelling for parallel
programming. Both activities, parallel programming and simulation modelling, represent
by themselves a considerable cost of effort (see Sections 2.1 and 3.1.2). In such a situation, the method does not seem to offer a better solution than simply building the application in several ways.

Nevertheless, even though the Architectural Performance Modelling Method
requires working on parallel programming and simulation modelling, it supports Parallel
Software Design since: *(a)* as simulation modelling is carried out using simple queuing
systems, based on Markovian chains (see Section 6.2.2), once a simulation model has
been developed, it can be reused as necessary to simulate the behaviour of later sequential processing component, hence decreasing the cost of having to re-code the simulation
model; and *(b)* as parallel coordinations are based on the Architectural Patterns for Parallel Programming, their implementation within the Architectural Performance Modelling
Method can be reused in later problems with similar characteristics of algorithm order
and/or data access (see Sections 5.2.1 and 6.1.2), thus decreasing parallel design and

implementation costs. Moreover, since the Architectural Performance Modelling Method is based on the Architectural Patterns for Parallel Programming, the experience gained in parallel design and implementation as part of the method will prove valuable and useful for later parallel applications, whose development will benefit from reusing both design and implementation of parallel coordinations (see Section 5.2.3).

Finally, building a parallel application in several ways normally tends to result in a parallel program that yields incorrect results, or executes slower than its sequential counterpart (see Section 2.1). In contrast, the Architectural Performance Modelling Method provides a systematic guide to Parallel Software Design, since it is based on the layered description of software architectures (see Section 2.3.2), in which the Architectural Patterns for Parallel Programming are used for designing the coordination layer. This is important, since the performance a parallel software system is able to achieve depends on the organisation of the coordination among the several sequential processing components that constitute such parallel software system. As a consequence, the Architectural Performance Modelling Method obtains models that provide performance estimates of the behaviour of a parallel software system. This information is valuable not only for the present parallel application, but for other later parallel applications developed from an architectural pattern, and using a given parallel platform and programming language (see Sections 1.3 and 4.3). Therefore, the cost of using the Architectural Performance Modelling Method *(a)* is worth the effort for an actual parallel development, since it provides information about the potential performance of a prospective parallel application; and *(b)* tends to decrease for future parallel applications, in contrast with just building a parallel application in several ways. The cost of the later approach is normally high, and eventually would require an extensive use of the "fix-it-later" approach, which we seek to avoid (see Sections 1.1 and 1.2).

8.5 Comparison with Related Work on Software Architecture and Performance Modelling

In Chapter 3, various approaches are described as related work, ranging from general methods to case studies. These approaches consider various types of performance models and different architectural specifications from which such performance models are derived. Also, in Chapter 3, several other approaches are also presented that generate performance models for parallel and distributed systems. In the present section, the

Architectural Performance Modelling Method (APMM) is compared with all those approaches, in order to expose their similarities and differences.

8.5.1 Deriving Models from Software Architecture Descriptions

Basically, APMM is defined as a method for deriving performance model from architectural patterns as a regular software architecture description (see Sections 2.2.3, 4.3.3, 5.1.3, and 5.1.4). In general, all approaches presented in Chapter 3 develop performance models (whether analytical or simulation) from a software architecture description. In general, APMM is similar to almost all the described approaches (particularly, those implementing performance simulation models) in the sense that they describe a method, an algorithm, or a sequence of steps to develop performance models from a software architecture description.

Several approaches consider use cases (or similar representations) as software architecture descriptions from which performance models are derived. These approaches are Jarvinen and Kurki-Sunio (1991), Luckham (1996), Smith and Williams (1997), Williams and Smith (1998), Menascé and Gomaa (1998), Balsamo, *et al.* (1998), Jonkers *et al.* (1998), El-Sayed *et al.* (1998), Huber *et al.* (1998). Most of the recent approaches consider the UML specification as a software architecture description, and make use of various UML diagrams to derive information to define and parameterise the performance model. These approaches are Arief and Speirs (1999a), Arief and Speirs (1999b), Pooley and King (1999), King and Pooley (1999), Pooley (1999), Kähkipuro (1999), Akenhurst and Waters (1999a), Akenhust *et al.* (1999), Utton *et al.* (1999). However, in these approaches, it is often considered necessary to introduce additional information to the UML diagrams through simple annotation or extensions, commonly based on stereotypes and tagged values, in order to complete the software architecture specification for deriving a performance model. Finally, and as it is the case with APMM, some other approaches refer to architectural patterns in order to develop performance models. These approaches are Petriu and Wang (1999), Ortega-Arjona and Roberts (1999c).

Nevertheless, the APMM has the advantage over these approaches of basing its performance estimations on the Architectural Patterns for Parallel Programming (Ortega-Arjona & Roberts, 1998a), which are software patterns particularly developed for parallel systems, and whose aim is to support the design of parallel software systems. Other approaches develop performance models that have to be modified in order to deal with several issues dependent of the parallel execution environment (like for example, non-determinism), whereas the Architectural Patterns for Parallel Programming are developed expressly to express and deal with such issues.

8.5.2 Describing a Software Architecture as a Layered Composition

The APMM approach models a parallel application considering different types of models (in a layered form) for describing processing, communication, and platform components (see Sections 2.3.2, and 4.3).

Describing a Software Architecture as a layered composition of models is also the case of many of the proposed methods, like Smith and Williams (1997), Williams and Smith (1998), Menascé and Gomaa (1998), Huber *et al.* (1998), Jonkers *et al.* (1998), Akenhurst and Waters (1999a), Akenhust *et al.* (1999), Utton *et al.* (1999), Petriu and Wang (1999), King and Pooley (1999), Pooley (1999), Ortega-Arjona and Roberts (1999c). The reason of such a similarity seems to be that APMM, as all the other methods, is deeply influenced by the SPE methodology, originally developed and introduced by C.U. Smith (Smith, 1990).

However, the APMM has the advantage that it attempts to confine all parallel design decisions at the communication layer, solving parallel issues only at this level, and making the design based on Architectural Patterns for Parallel Programming reusable between applications. Moreover, the objective is to keep sequential code at the processing level, allowing the reuse of design at the communication layer as frameworks, representing the architectural patterns.

8.5.3 Simulation based on Queuing Models

The APMM simulates processing based on simple queuing models (see Section 6.2). This is also the case of several approaches described as related work, which are based on queuing models, and refer to a higher abstraction level that could make the feedback at the software architecture design easier than with more detailed stochastic models. In particular, when software architecture components can be related to queuing components (i.e., service centres or sub-networks), performance results of the performance models can be directly interpreted at the software architecture design level. The approaches based on simple queuing models like APMM are Menascé and Gomaa (1998), Balsamo, *et al.* (1998), Pooley and King (1999), Kähkipuro (1999), Ortega-Arjona and Roberts (1999c).

About the use of derivations of queuing models, we have that:

- Layered Queuing Networks (LQN) are used by El-Sayed *et al.* (1998), Petriu and Wang (1999);

- Augmented Queuing Networks (AQN) are used by Kähkipuro (1999).

Most of these approaches refer to the entire software life cycle, whereas some others refer to the design specification stage. The later ones usually consider a formal behavioural software specification modelled by Stochastic Petri Nets —like Botti and Capra (1996), Jonkers *et al.* (1998), and King and Pooley (1999)— or Stochastic Process Algebras —such as Pooley (1999). Such models integrate functional and non-functional aspects and provide a unique reference model for software architecture specification and performance. However, from the performance evaluation point of view, the analysis usually refers to the numerical solution of the underlying Markov chain, which can easily lead to numerical problems due to state space explosion. Moreover, from the software designer point of view, it is not clear a direct and easy interpretation of the numerical performance results in terms of software architecture design. The APMM attempts to solve these problems by considering a sharp separation between communicating and processing activities. This separation simplifies the calculation of the average total execution time, which can be obtained as presented in Section 7.2.3. The average total execution time obtained is interpreted as a representative value of the time a solution based on a particular architectural pattern takes to execute on a certain parallel platform, and implemented using a certain parallel language.

8.5.4 Queuing Models based on Markov Chains

Just as it is the case with APMM (see Section 6.2), many approaches use Markovian and semi-Markovian chains for modelling purposes as the underlying analytical model of the simulation queuing models. These approaches are Pooley and King (1999), Pooley (1999), Ortega-Arjona and Roberts (1999c). A common issue of APMM and these approaches is that they all require parameters for the Markovian and semi-Markovian chain. Nevertheless, all the approaches report to have problems deriving their parameters. Hence, they propose three forms to address this problem:

- promoting feedback from one execution to another, i.e. use parameter information from experimenting with the models;

- supposing a behaviour through time of the components, and deriving parameter values from such a description (as it is the case with APMM, see Section 7.1.4), and;
- leaving the parameter definition to an expert modeller.

As different types of models are used for describing processing, communication, and platform components, APMM obtains simulation estimates (see Section 7.2.3) by combining communications and processing values obtained from measuring (see Section 7.1.1) and observed values (see Sections 7.1.3 and 7.1.4). This is also the case of many approaches, such as Luckham (1996), Howell (1996), Menascé and Gomaa (1998), Petriu and Wang (1999), King and Pooley (1999), Ortega-Arjona and Roberts (1999c). Nevertheless, the estimates obtained by APMM are processed through a performance analysis stage, based on a statistical procedure (see Section 7.2). This produces more regular and general performance estimate values. Moreover, performance estimates obtained using the APMM can be used as feedback to modify or change the parameter values supposed for the queuing model that represent processing components. Thus, the APMM has a potential use for experimentation and performance feedback to software architecture (see Section 2.2.3 and 2.3.3).

8.5.5 Describing Parallel Programs through Common Parallel Structures

During the last few years there has been tendency to apply design to parallel programming (see Section 5.2.1). These software design is represented as "outlines of the program" (Chandy & Taylor, 1992), "parallel algorithms" (Hartley, 1998), "high-level design strategies" (Lewis & Berg, 2000), "paradigms for process interaction" (Andrews, 2000). These descriptions are based on "flow" descriptions of data and/or instructions through the processing components (see Section 5.2.1), and they are basically similar to the Architectural Patterns for Parallel Programming within APMM (see Section 4.3.3 and Chapter 5). Furthermore, from the approaches for performance estimation of parallel systems, the approach by Gemund (2003) presents several parallel programming structures similar to the architectural patterns for parallel programming, which the author uses to test his approach.

Another commonality of APMM with some of the approaches to performance estimation of parallel systems is about the evaluation of the methods. As a method, APMM is evaluated by comparing simulation estimates with real parallel system measurements (see Sections 8.2 and 8.3). This is also the base of evaluation considered by Botti and Capra (1996), and Howell (1996).

Various approaches have been proposed or used tools to implement some steps of the proposed approaches in parallel and distributed programming. These tools are DisCo (Jarvinen & Kurki-Sunio, 1991), POSET (Luckham, 1996) Multi Micro Environment (Botti & Capra, 1996), Architectural Modelling Box (Jonkers *et al.*, 1998), and Autofocus (Huber *et al.*, 1998). However, none of them has been implemented yet into a complete environment for specification, performance analysis, and feedback to software designer.

An open problem and challenge is to completely automatise the process of deriving performance models from software specification and integrate the supporting tools in a unique environment. Nevertheless, the use of tools and environments for simulating parallel and distributed systems are normally expensive in terms of execution time. It tends to be time consuming to run simulations of such systems. This situation is reported for performance modelling for general software architectures in Arief and Speirs (1999a), and Arief and Speirs (1999b). The same is mentioned when simulating parallel or distributed systems by Luckham (1996), Huber *et al.* (1998), and Jonkers *et al.* (1998).

In order to deal with simulation cost, APMM is proposed so the communication of a parallel program executes on the real parallel system (see Section 7.1.1), and the processing components are actually simulated (see Section 7.1.3) to decrease simulation cost. Other approaches for performance prediction of parallel systems, such as Botti and Capra (1996) and Howell (1996), also consider similar ideas to deal with simulation costs.

8.5.6 Constraints on the Software Architecture

Some approaches introduce constraints on the software architecture, like Menascè & Gomaa (1998), which applies to client/server systems. Others are only interested in analysing software architecture, without specifying (or using information regarding) the underlying hardware platform. This is the case of Williams and Smith (1998). In the case of APMM, it is proposed here precisely to deal with the performance modelling on parallel software systems, considering the constraints included as part of the hypothesis of this thesis (see Section 1.3).

8.6 Comparison with Related Work on Architectural Design Approaches for Parallel Software

Also in chapter 3, we introduced other prior efforts that similarly identify and capture general Parallel Software Design experience and performance estimation. In this section, we summarise the similarities and differences of these efforts compared with our research work. In our work, we have considered such efforts, sometimes taking elements from them in order to obtain similar advantages, or reduce their disadvantages. The comparison with related work is carried our around four points: Description of Software Structure, Development Strategy, Performance Modelling, and Classification and Selection of Software Structures.

8.6.1 Description of Software Structure

The approaches presented in chapter 3 were considered as related work because, as with our Architectural Patterns, they represent a description of common configurations used to model Software Structure in Parallel Software Design. An Architectural Pattern represents a relation that occurs during the initial stages of Parallel Software Design between a process to be applied on data depending on certain characteristics of order, and a Software Structure that allows the execution of such a process, maintaining the characteristic of order. Archetypes, Skeletons and Structural Modelling are considered related work in the sense that they share a similar objective, which is describing and modelling Software Structure. However, even though they aim and look for structural solutions in parallelism, it is interesting that these approaches do not present a clear description of Software Structure. Instead, they seem to look for "ready-to-use" software implementations of parallel programming components, allowing programmers to code their parallel programs in terms of these software components.

The Archetypes approach is similar to our Architectural Patterns work as both use a narrative description with several similar parts, capturing structure, experience and techniques. However, the Archetypes description is more extensive, trying to cover in a single archetype all aspects of design and implementation for every case, and sometimes providing too much information to be consulted by the software developer. Although the description is extensive, Archetypes do not present a single precise description that represents the Software Structure as a whole (see section 3.4.1).

In contrast, the Skeletons approach does present precise representation of structural constructs of useful patterns of parallel computation and interaction, but these constructs are presented more commonly as functional programming language constructs, encapsulating all structural and design information. By providing only this level of information, skeleton descriptions restrict the understanding of the structural constructs they represent (see section 3.4.2).

Finally, the Structural Modelling approach does not aim to express common Software Structures in distributed systems, presenting only a over-simplified description of Software Structure based on Structural models, as developer's descriptions expressed usually in the form of pseudocode (see section 3.4.3).

8.6.2 Development Strategy

By development strategy we mean a specific formulation of plans or instructions to generate a solution as a form or structure. We used the pattern description and proposed our architectural description to guide the software developer in selecting an appropriate Architectural Pattern for parallelising a given application. In general, the brief, problem, and the solution sections are the basic information to be considered during pattern selection (see section 5.3). The other sections of the pattern description provide guidelines for the actual implementations and relationships with other patterns. However, patterns have the disadvantage that they do not provide a detailed solution: Patterns provide generic schemes for solving groups of problems, but they do not provide final complete solutions.

The development strategy of the Archetypes and Skeletons approaches are similar to our approach as they consider mainly three levels of software construction, archetypes or high-level, application or middle-level, and programs or low-level, in which Software Structure is considered just as the high-level organisation of components. Furthermore, their development strategies attempt to deliver complete software systems, using the same archetypes or skeletons for all levels of software construction, instead of deriving sub-structures for more particular cases. In particular, Archetypes focus on deriving a parallel solution from a previously developed sequential algorithm (see section 3.4.1). Even though it may be a good approach, this may reduce the potential of parallel execution, restricting the creativity of a parallel software developer, and not supporting the development of software design experience in parallel systems.

The goal of Skeletons is to "build parallel programs without programming" (see section 3.4.2), by providing a limited range of possibilities. However, the development strategy based on program transformations does not clearly expose how to proceed or use skeletons to support different design stages.

In the case of Structural Modelling, the modelling approach is focused on the development of structural models for performance prediction, and no precise structural information other than the experience of a developer is provided.

8.6.3 Performance Modelling

Performance is related to Software Structure as the execution time of a software system depends on the top-most functional organisation or configuration of their components and connectors (Bass *et al.*, 1998). In this research work, we developed an Architectural Performance Model that aims to use structural information, obtaining a performance estimate for the system as a whole. The estimate of performance is an important decision parameter when comparing parallel or distributed systems. This point is actually also present in all approaches of the related work, in which efforts have been made to obtain performance estimations based on structural characteristics.

The Archetype based performance models are similar to our approach as they simplify the process of performance analysis by exploiting commonalities in parallel programs, in the form of simple equations. However, their drawback is that the Archetype approach considers performance issues late in the program development strategy, in a "fix-it-later" form. This may work, but represents a hard last step of parallel development, as performance is closely related to structural characteristics of software which are decided during initial stages of design (see section 3.4.1).

Skeletons provide good performance modelling due to their simplicity and the use of equations based on problem and machine parameters to represent and predict performance, making them suitable for identifying improvements. However, these equations generally require machine-specific parameters to be derived reliably, which is not always possible (see section 3.4.2).

Both the Archetype and Skeletons approaches, concentrate on deriving program specifications for reasoning about correctness and performance, but not on developing models. In contrast, the goal of Structural Modelling is to obtain models for distributed performance estimation. Similarly to our work, Structural Modelling uses component models, defined recursively as arithmetic combinations of input values, selected using descriptions of where execution time is spent. Initially, these input values are estimate percentages for each component, evolving later to interval values and finally to stochastic values, which seems to be the most similar performance modelling to our work. In general, Structural Modelling presents a simple and easy way to express an application profile, but it does not consider a particular distribution of performance, considering at most a normal distribution for the stochastic values. Further, the input values are usually fixed arbitrarily, relaying on a developer's experience (see section 3.4.3).

8.6.4 Classification and Selection of Software Structures

An important characteristic, that we consider that a Software Structure modelling approach should cover, is about providing a classification schema that simplifies the selection of Software Structures. We have developed our Architectural Patterns aiming at helping the software developer select a particular Software Structure during the initial design and construction of a parallel software system (see sections 5.2 and 5.3).

In a similar form, Archetypes and Skeletons provide classification schemes used to organise their configurations, but not necessarily to address the problem of selection. This choice is left to the software developer, who judges and selects the best form of parallelism for a particular application based on examples provided by Archetypes or Skeletons. Often, these example systems have limited applicability. For example, Archetypes contains a good classification scheme based on strategies for partitioning and examples, but no precise rationale or guidance is provided to select a particular archetype. They are only identified as "appropriate solutions", selected mainly by experience (see section 3.4.1). The several Skeletons approaches provide a similar number of classifications. In the general case, design decisions are expected to be made based on a decision-tree provided by previous experience, but no precise selection rationale, in the form of when to use each skeleton, is provided (see section 3.4.2).

Finally, as the Structural Modelling approach considers only issues about performance prediction for distributed systems, no classification of common structures, selection method, or benefits and liabilities of using different structural descriptions is discussed (see section 3.4.3).

8.7 Analysis of Applicability of the Method in the General Case

The importance of an ability to estimate the performance of a (software) system during its design stage is highlighted by the existence of workshops dedicated specifically for this topic, such as the series of International Workshop on Software and Performance (WOSP). These indicate that research on the approaches for incorporating software performance into software architecture/design is still an ongoing process and deemed useful so that it may provide many benefits for the software engineering community.

In the present thesis, the Architectural Performance Modelling Method has been applied to several examples in order to obtain performance estimates for several configurations of a parallel system. In all these examples, the method has provided performance estimates that are not very different from the real average execution times of the actual parallel system. More specifically, the Two-dimensional Wave Equation is used as a case study throughout several chapters to illustrate the application of the Architectural Performance Modelling Method (see Sections 5.4, 6.1.5, 6.3.5, 7.1.2, 7.1.5, 7.2.2, and 7.2.4). The reason is that it is a problem easy to explain and describe (see Section 5.4.1). Nevertheless, even though it may seem a not so complex problem, it serves its purpose within this thesis, which is simply to provide an idea about how to use and explain the method. Moreover, the Two-dimensional Wave Equation presents characteristics and features similar to several other common problems solved using parallel programming (see for example, Hoare, 1978; Andrews, 1991; Freeman & Phillips, 1992; Foster, 1994; Geist et al., 1994; Kleiman, et al., 1996; Hartley, 1998; Andrews, 2000, and many others). For example, one of its main characteristics is that its solution is based on the concept of relaxation, as explained by Kleiman, et al., 1996 (see Section 5.2.2).

The question is now: how applicable is the Architectural Performance Modelling Method for performance estimation in the general case, beyond the Two-dimensional Wave Equation? Let us answer this question by analysing the input information and steps that are involved during the development of the Architectural Performance Modelling Method, to expose the elements of generality within the method.

8.7.1 Analysing the Input Information

The Architectural Modelling Method uses as input information (see Section 4.3.3):

- a statement of the problem, in terms of an algorithm, the data to be processed, and the performance requirements for the parallel system.
- a specification of the known parallel platform (hardware and software) to be used.

Parallel programming is concerned with obtaining a parallel program that addresses a problem, stated as a requirement of computation (see Section 4.3.1). As with any computation, it is defined in terms of an algorithm and the data to be processed. Parallelising such a computation has to consider dividing either the algorithm into steps, or the data into pieces, or both (see Section 5.2.3). Moreover, the designer has to deal explicitly with performance requirements, which are the driving factor for parallel programming (see Sections 1.1 and 1.2). In general, the designer is asked to develop a parallel program on a given parallel platform (the development of any parallel program does not usually take place without having or knowing the parallel platform to be used).

The Architectural Performance Modelling Method copes with these issues by using as input all information that is required for developing a parallel program. So, in the general case, the Architectural Performance Modelling Method can be used, since its input coincides with the input information for any parallel programming.

8.7.2 Analysing the Steps of the Architectural Performance Modelling Method

Architectural Pattern Selection

The problem statement is presented in terms of an algorithm and data (see 5.2.3). Since the classification and selection of the Architectural Patterns for Parallel Programming (see Sections 5.2.7 and 5.3) consider dividing the problem into steps, data pieces, or both, it means that they are applicable to most of the known parallel problems. In general, the solution to any of these known problems can be viewed as an instance or variation of one of the architectural patterns.

Architectural Performance Model Construction

Coordination Simulation

A Coordination Simulation is constructed based on the implementation section of an architectural pattern, for any configuration of components (see Section 6.1.1). As it is a runnable implementation of the architectural pattern, it covers all the activities at the coordination and communication level, and all the features at the platform level of the parallel system (see Sections 2.1.3 and 5.2.3). From the implementation section of a given architectural pattern, it is possible to construct a Coordination Simulation as a skeleton of code. This code executes on the parallel platform provided as part of the input.

Component Simulation

A Component Simulation can be always constructed on any platform, based on the implementation of a simple queuing structure, for representing a processing component (see Section 6.2.1). A processing component is basically seen as a closed box that has inputs, outputs, does some processing, and follows some sort of state sequence. A Component Simulation takes into consideration all these characteristics. Moreover, it produces a stochastic value of processing time, based on an exponential distribution (see Section 6.2.4). Once implemented and provided with its parameters, the Component Simulation is always able to simulate the processing behaviour of any processing component.

Architectural Performance Model

An Architectural Performance Model is an executable program that gathers together the Coordination Simulation and one or several Component Simulations (see Section 6.3.1). Given these two implementations, the Architectural Performance Model is constructed by inserting the code of the Component Simulations into the skeleton of code of the Coordination Simulation. Once assembled together, the two simulations interact within the Architectural Performance Model to run simulations and produce measurable results (see Section 6.3.4).

Performance Simulation

Coordination Simulation Execution

The Coordination Simulation is a runnable implementation of an architectural pattern. During its execution, it is necessary to measure the time required for coordination among components and the arrival rate of requests to each component (see Section 7.1.1). This requires the existence of a way to measure such execution times. In this work, this requirement is covered by the method `System.currentTimeMillis()`, which produces a reading from the real time hardware clock (see Section 8.1). Furthermore, by performing a number of executions, it is possible to obtain the average coordination time and the average arrival rate of requests to each component, which are used later for the calculation of a performance estimate (see Section 7.1.1).

Architectural Performance Model Execution

The parameters for the Component Simulations are derived from the average arrival rate of requests and from the architectural pattern. This allows for the execution of the Architectural Performance Model (see Section 7.1.3). Since this model is defined and constructed from the simulations, it is executed a number of times to obtain the simulated average processing time, which is also used later for the calculation of a performance estimate.

Performance Estimate Calculation

From the analysis presented in Section 4.3.2, a single performance estimate for the given configuration of the parallel system is calculated by simply adding the average coordination time and the simulated average processing time (see Section 7.2). This performance estimate takes into consideration all the previous assumptions about hardware and software, and can be re-produced in any case for any variation of such assumptions.

In summary, to briefly answer the question proposed, it seems still necessary to refer to some basic concepts and definitions:

- A parallel program is originally defined in the literature as a set of communicating sequential processes by Dijkstra (1968), Hoare (1978), Brinch-Hansen (1978), and many others (see Sections 2.1.1 and 5.2). Following this concept, the Architectural Patterns for Parallel Programming are considered as organisations in which such sequential processes communicate. Hence, such architectural patterns describe communication structures among sequential processes (see Section 5.2.3).
- The Architectural Performance Modelling Method makes use of architectural patterns to develop models for performance estimation (see Section 4.3). These are used to obtain performance estimates, given a platform and a programming language.

Therefore, the Architectural Performance Modelling Method is applicable for any problem as long as its solution (a parallel program) is *(a)* conceived and developed as a set of communicating sequential processes; *(b)*organised following the description of an architectural pattern; and *(c)* programmed for a parallel platform, using a particular parallel language. However, there is no description of a parallel program other than as a set of communicating sequential processes (see Chapter 2). Hence, the method is applicable for most parallel programs and systems. The Architectural Performance Modelling Method produces performance estimates that can be considered equivalent to the probable real average execution times of a prospective parallel program.

8.8 Summary

This chapter presents and discusses an evaluation of the Architectural Performance Modelling Method for estimating the performance of parallel applications. The evaluation is presented using experimental examples, comparing three potential solutions using different architectural patterns. The comparison with related work is examined and discussed. Finally, an analysis is made of the applicability of the method in the general case.

Chapter 9

Conclusion

第九章

持而盈之，不如其已；   揣而銳之，不可長保。
金玉滿堂，莫之能守；   富貴而驕，自遺其咎。
功遂身退，天之道。

"Retire. Fill a cup to its brim and it is easily spilled; temper a sword to its hardest and it is easily broken; amass the greatest treasure and it is easily stolen; claim credit and honour and you easily fall; Retire once your purpose is achieved – this is natural"

Lao-Tze

This chapter presents the conclusions of the thesis, a summary of the research work and restatements of the hypothesis and contributions. A discussion and interpretation of results is provided to critically examine and expose how the hypothesis and contributions have been addressed by the research work. Finally, a future work section summarises the next steps to follow into the research of Software Patterns and Software Architecture for Parallel Programming.

9.1 Summary of the Research Work

The main idea behind the present thesis is basically to identify the best performing architectural pattern as a coordination organisation for a parallel software architecture, by building models for performance estimation early in the design process.

The Architectural Performance Modelling Method is part of an architectural design approach applied during the initial stages of parallel software development, with the aim of modelling performance issues. Its main objective is to provide a mechanism to evaluate parallel software alternatives by estimating their performance before any further implementation takes place. The idea is to take into consideration performance issues during parallel software design from the beginning, aiming to avoid the "fix-it-latter" approach. So, the method aims to complement parallel software pattern descriptions, helping parallel designers to obtain performance information during early design, and to select between potential parallel architectural solutions based on such potential performance of the proposed application.

By considering a parallel program as an instance of a particular software architecture, the Architectural Performance Modelling Method describes such a parallel program in terms of software components, which are classified depending on their particular objective as:

- *Platform:* components representing the hardware and software environment;
- *Coordination*: components representing the fundamental organisation for coordination and communication; and
- *Processing*: components providing particular processing functionalities.

A performance estimate is the result of the times that each individual software component requires to carry out its coordinating or processing activities. Performance is understood, modelled, and analysed from an architectural point of view, using simulation models that consider the arrival rates and distributions of service requests and potential processing times.

An Architectural Performance Model is obtained as product of the method. The construction of this model is based on a Coordination Simulation (developed from an architectural pattern, describing a coordination organisation commonly used in parallel programming), and a generic Component Simulation (a queuing representation of a component's processing behaviour through time).

The Architectural Performance Modelling Method is used to simulate a partially implemented program design, using *(a)* the available information about hardware and software, *(b)* the problem description, and *(c)* the amount of data. It makes it possible to obtain estimates of the parallel program's probable performance, by constructing "scale-models" of the complete parallel software during early design phases.

The information contained in architectural patterns is used to determine characteristics and parameters for the Architectural Performance Model and its execution. Briefly, the elements retrieved from architectural patterns used in the Architectural Performance Modelling Method are:

- The description of the coordination organisation that is used to construct the Coordination Simulation of a potential solution. This construction considers sections such as *Structure, Dynamics, Participants* and *Implementation* of an Architectural Pattern for Parallel Programming. The Coordination Simulation is developed as a skeleton of code, representing the relations of coordination and communication among components.

- From the Coordination Simulation, it is possible to measure the inter-arrival times $(1/\lambda)$ between requests for operation, that coordination components issue, allowing λ parameters to be derived for the Architectural Performance Models. The λ parameters are the average arrival rate of messages to a component. These measured values are used as parameters for the Component Simulations.

- From observing the expected *Dynamics* of the architectural pattern in a scenario for solving the actual problem, it is possible to suppose an average number of messages in service or waiting for service per each processing component. Using this number of messages, a probable value for ρ is calculated and used to obtain a performance estimate. ρ is commonly referred to as the traffic intensity of the queuing system, and it is defined as the relation λ / μ, where μ is the average service time of messages per second. This calculated value is also used as parameters for each Component Simulation.

9.2 Hypothesis Restatement

Let us restate the hypothesis of this thesis, as presented in Chapter 1 as follows:

"Given a problem to be solved and a set of parallel hardware and software resources for deployment, it is possible to obtain a reasonable estimate of the performance characteristics of a parallel program during the initial stages of parallel software design in order to identify the architectural pattern that will produce the best performance for the program."

9.2.1 Discussion

Parallel software design is a complex activity, aiming for performance improvement while diminishing the high costs of parallel software development. It requires extra effort from the software designer, who has to select the most appropriate parallel software architecture to balance between these two design issues. Thus, to provide a method for early performance estimation that assists the parallel software designer to perform such a selection would be highly valuable.

The Architectural Patterns for Parallel Programming are proposed as useful solutions for initially designing a parallel software architecture. However, they do not address the problem of early performance estimation. Hence, this thesis proposes an experimental method, based on architectural patterns, in order to identify the best performing architectural pattern by early performance estimation.

The Architectural Performance Modelling Method is presented as such an experimental method. It is proposed as an initial design study, using information about the problem, hardware and software. During design, the Architectural Performance Modelling Method provides estimates of performance properties of designs, and assists in selecting from among design alternatives early in the development before more detailed coding begins.

The Architectural Performance Modelling Method starts with one or several architectural patterns, shows how to construct a simulation based on it, and obtains estimates of the execution times of a parallel application constructed using such architectural patterns. The simulation is carried out based on models, as programmed instances of the architectural patterns, which are executed to obtain the performance estimates. In this thesis, examples are developed to evaluate the method for performance estimation and to compare potential parallel software architectures.

In Chapters 5, 6, and 7, an example is developed using the Two-dimensional Wave Equation, detailing every step of the Architectural Performance Modelling Method, and obtaining performance estimates using the Communicating Sequential Elements pattern. Even though at first this problem may seem trivial, the Two-dimensional Wave Equation represents a common open ended problem for which parallel programming is used for. As other open ended problems, the Two-dimensional Wave Equation becomes as computationaly difficult as to require parallel programming for its solution, under particular requirements of number and/or complexity of operations and data. Nevertheless, it is a problem easy to explain and describe. Even though it may not seem a large-scale problem, it serves its purpose within this thesis, which is simply to illustrate and explain the Architectural Performance Modelling Method. Moreover, the Two-dimensional Wave Equation presents characteristics and features similar to several other common problems solved using parallel programming. One of such characteristics is that its solution is based on relaxation.

The Architectural Performance Modelling Method is applicable for performance estimation in the general case beyond the Two-dimensional Wave Equation, since it is based on the concept of a parallel program, and its relation with the Architectural Patterns for Parallel Programming: *(a)* a parallel program is originally defined in the literature as a set of communicating sequential processes by Dijkstra (1968), Hoare (1978), Brinch-Hansen (1978). Based on this concept, the Architectural Patterns for Parallel Programming are considered as organisations in which such sequential processes communicate, that is, architectural patterns describe communication structures among sequential processes; and *(b)* the Architectural Performance Modelling Method makes use of architectural patterns as descriptions of parallel systems, in order to develop models for performance estimation. These are used to obtain performance estimates, given particular characteristics of the platform and the programming language to be used.

Therefore, it follows that the Architectural Performance Modelling Method is applicable for any problem as long as its solution (a parallel program) is:

• conceived and developed as a set of communicating sequential processes;

• organised following the description of an architectural pattern for parallel programming; and

• programmed for a parallel platform, using a particular parallel language.

Nevertheless, there is no other description of a parallel program than as a set of communicating sequential processes, which makes the method applicable for most parallel programs and systems. The Architectural Performance Modelling Method produces performance estimates that can be considered equivalent to the probable real average execution times of a prospective parallel program.

9.2.2 Interpretation and Analysis of Results

The evaluation results of the experimental examples in Chapter 8 show that the method produced performance estimates very similar to the real average execution times obtained by running the actual program on the computing environment. The main reason is that the performance a parallel software system is able to achieve heavily depends on the organisation of the coordination among the several sequential processing components that constitute such parallel software system, and not only on the parallel platform and the programming language used. In this thesis, such organisation is described and developed based on the Architectural Patterns for Parallel Programming, which are used as a base for developing models for performance estimation.

The graphical representation of the performance estimates obtained from Architectural Performance Models showed very similar curves to the actual parallel program's performance characteristics. Each curve can be considered as the probable performance behaviour of the parallel system. From this, we conclude that the Architectural Performance Models actually identifies the best performing architectural pattern by describing the performance of parallel programs, using early estimates about their time behaviour to be obtained. Once developed, the models can be subjected to appropriate assessments and tests, and refined as required.

Another important conclusion of this thesis is that the processing time of sequential software components at the processing layer depends on the time slots allowed by the execution of platform and coordination components. In parallel programming, such time slots are varied through modifying the granularity:

- by changing the number of processing components and their mapping into coordination components, at the level of processing components;
- by changing the number of coordination components and their mapping into processors, at the level of coordination components; and
- by changing the number of processors on which the parallel process takes place, at the level of platform components. We aim to avoid this kind of modification, since it implies the use of the "fix-it-later" approach.

The Architectural Performance Modelling Method allows to test an verify the result of applying the first two kinds of modifications on the models of a prospective parallel system.

As the performance that a parallel program is able to achieve depends on the organisation and communication among the sequential processing components, and under the assumptions taken in the thesis, the method produced performance estimates that are equivalent to the real average execution times in 73.33% to 80.0% of the experiments.

These results indicate that it is possible to compare potential parallel solutions by early obtaining reasonable performance estimations with conceptually simple models. The objective of the modelling effort has been to keep these models as simple as possible. This is achieved by considering that processing and communication are activities sharply separated among coordination and processing components. Even though this may not be always the case, the results show that such a supposition does not introduce a considerable error for performance estimation. So, our models can effectively be used to select the best performing architectural pattern by estimating the performance of a parallel program with the proposed constraints.

The results also indicate that these simple models are sufficient to compare different potential parallel designs. In all experimental examples, performance estimates set up a probable performance characteristic of a parallel program, which can be used as an initial reference to be considered when making design decisions, before an actual program implementation is available.

From the description of problem addressed by this thesis, the main goal has been to consider and include performance information as early as possible during parallel software design. Based on the experimental results, it can be seen that it is possible to obtain reasonable performance estimates during the initial stages of parallel software design, by creating and analysing representative "scale-models", based on the coordination and communication organisation, to estimate the performance of a parallel system.

9.2.3 Cost

Parallel programming, by itself, represents a high cost of effort. As it relies on the coordination of computing resources, so that they simultaneously work towards a common objective, it requires extra effort from the software designer because of the increased complexity involved. Moreover, as it is considered a means to improve performance, the software designer should consider sophisticated and cost-effective practices and techniques for performance measurement and analysis. Most programming problems have several parallel solutions, and therefore parallel software design cannot easily be reduced to recipes. At best, the software designer has an idea of the organisation, and would like to decide whether or not to use it as the basis of the parallel system. A solution is commonly proposed based only on the information available at this stage and the intuition of the designer. However, as the cost of the parallel design is high, complementing the information available with quantifiable performance information would be an important advantage.

Building a parallel application in several ways normally tends to result in parallel programs that yield incorrect results, or execute slower than their sequential counterpart. Furthermore, the cost of effort from one project to the next would tend to be the same, since all of them have the same starting point, described above. Moreover, such an approach would tend to defer performance considerations until later phases of software development which means to use the "fix-it-later" approach: once a parallel application has been built (perhaps in several ways), if performance requirements are not met, the software still has to be "tuned" to correct it, or additional hardware has to be used.

The "fix-it-later" approach is precisely what we seek to avoid, in particular for parallel systems. If severe performance problems are discovered once the parallel system has been built, extensive changes to the whole software and system architecture may be required to deal with them. Furthermore, as these changes are made late in the development process, they increase the already high costs of parallel programming.

As an alternative, the present thesis proposes to design for performance from the beginning, by selecting a parallel architecture using simulations. These simulations estimate the performance for the particular parallel software architecture. Early performance estimation, based on parallel software architecture and simulations, allows the selection of the appropriate architecture before detailed implementation, using a quantitative criteria.

Hence, the Architectural Performance Modelling Method is proposed as a systematic guidance to Parallel Software Design, based on the layered description of software architectures and on the Architectural Patterns for Parallel Programming. It is used to obtain models that provide early performance estimates of the behaviour of a parallel software system. This information is valuable not only for a present parallel application, but for other later parallel applications developed from an architectural pattern, and using a given parallel platform and programming language.

The Architectural Performance Modelling Method supports Parallel Software Design since a simulation model can be reused as necessary to simulate the behaviour of later sequential processing component, decreasing the cost of having to re-code the simulation model. Also, as parallel coordinations are based on the Architectural Patterns for Parallel Programming, their implementation within the Architectural Performance Modelling Method can be reused in later problems with similar characteristics of algorithm order and/or data access, thus decreasing parallel design and implementation costs.

Therefore, in contrast with just building a parallel application in several ways, the cost of using the Architectural Performance Modelling Method is worth the effort for a parallel development, since it:

- provides information about the potential performance of a prospective parallel application without recurring to the "fix-it-late" approach; and

- tends to decrease for future parallel applications, by reusing already implemented code.

9.3 Contributions Restatement

The main goal of the present thesis is the development of a method based on early performance estimation to identify the best performing architectural pattern, covering the following contributions:

1. The development of the Architectural Performance Modelling Method, which allows parallel program developers to consider performance issues early during design, by estimating the performance of a parallel program based on information from a particular architectural pattern (Chapter 4). This method is based on the selection of one or several architectural patterns (Chapter 5) and on the development and execution of Architectural Performance Models, as implementations that combine a Coordination Simulation and Component Simulations (Chapters 6 and 7). Using this method, it is possible to identify the best performing architectural pattern by estimating the performance of the parallel software system during early design phases.

2. The selection process of one or several architectural patterns from the Architectural Patterns for Parallel Programming, which describe the coordination level of parallel software programs (Chapter 5).

3. The construction of a Component Simulation that represents the processing time behaviour of the processing components of a parallel software program (Chapter 6). As an implementation for simulation, the Component Simulation uses the Active Object pattern and elements of Queuing Theory.

9.4 Future Work

This work has aimed to introduce performance considerations during early software design for parallel programming, using a method to select an architectural pattern by producing performance estimates of a parallel system. Nevertheless, it raises further issues and identifies avenues for further research topics, such as:

- *Study and evaluation of the performance behaviour for the coordination organisations described by architectural patterns for different platforms, problems and amounts of data.* The study and evaluation of the performance behaviour for coordination organisations can be continued, considering variations of platform and amounts of data. The intention is to further study the relations for various platforms, problems and different amounts of data, searching for a more general method that can be used for performance estimation of particular real case problems.

- *Study the Architectural Description of Software for evaluating other quality attributes.* The Architectural Description of Software can potentially be also used to evaluate other quality attributes, like extensibility and maintainability. Furthermore, as the description represents the structure of the complete system, it may be possible to use it for measuring other quality attributes, as an initial evaluation criteria.

- *Development of a Pattern Language for Parallel Programming.* A long term goal is to contribute to the development of a Pattern Language for Parallel Programming, by gathering further design experience and techniques for parallel software design and implementation with other authors' work. The Architectural Patterns for Parallel Programming are only an initial attempt to describe successful solutions to common architectural parallel software problems. Even though there is still a long way to go to reach that goal, architectural patterns have been considered as a step forward towards the development of a handbook of design experience and techniques for parallel software development. A Pattern Language of Parallel Programming is necessary to document design and implementation experience, and to deliver systems that have good performance characteristics. In general, documenting design and implementation experience is the necessary first step toward designing required properties in software systems.

Appendix A

Codes for the Case Studies

This appendix presents the codes of the examples developed for evaluating the Architectural Performance Modelling Method (see Section 8.3). Here, we present the codes used to solve the Matrix Multiplication problem (see Section 8.3.1), the Prime Number Sieve problem (see Section 8.3.2), and the Heat Equation problem (see Section 8.3.3). Such codes represent the Coordination Simulation model (see Section 6.1) of the Communicating Sequential Elements pattern (CSE, see Section 5.2.10), the Manager-Workers pattern (MW, see Section 5.2.11), and the Pipes and Filters pattern (PF, see Section 5.2.8). All these frameworks are developed using the Java programming language (Smith, 2000; Hartley, 1998), executing using a JPVM environment (Ferrari, 1997; Geist *et al.*, 1994) on a cluster platform of sixteen computers.

Notice that even though the codes representing each architectural pattern are mostly similar for the three examples, the difference among them relies on the amount and type of data to be operated, the considerations taken to adequate the processing to the proposed architectural pattern, and the amount of communication and synchronisation among components depending on the solution proposed. Such a difference is noticeable mainly during execution.

Each represents a skeleton of code in Java, representing the structural communication relations among parallel components, and executed using the given data and available hardware an software resources only to show the communication and synchronisation interactions among sequential software components.

A.1 The Communicating Sequential Elements Code

The main idea of the CSE pattern is that all data is partitioned and assigned to a group of communicating sequential elements.

A.1.1 Partitioning

The CSE pattern describes a cooperation between identical sequential elements, which communicate partial results by exchanging values with their neighbours. For our actual purposes, the basic communicating element focuses on partitioning the data structure and on representing its elements, and not on the processing activity to be carried out. The code for class Heat is developed in Java, and shown in Figure A.1 (Ferrari, 1997).

```
import jpvm.*;

class Heat{
    . . .
    static int       nprocs  = DEFAULT_NUM_PROCS;
    static int       procdim;
    static jpvmTaskId  tids[];
    static jpvmTaskId  childTids[];
    static int       my_id = -1, my_x = -1;
    static int       left_id, right_id;
    static int       N;
    static int       Np;
    static double    X[];
    static double    B[];
    static double    tmpBorder;
    static int       iteration = 0;
    static double    start_time, end_time;
    . . .
}
```

Figure A.1 Relevant attributes of the class Heat for representing the CSE pattern.

The most relevant attributes of class Heat used to organise and perform the partitioning activities are described as follows:

- nprocs. An int value, whose purpose is to define the number of processes to be created into the JPVM environment.
- procdim. An int value that specifies the number of processes per processor.
- tids and childTids. Two arrays of jpvmTaskId values, which are used to store the task identifiers of all workers.
- my_id and my_x. Two int values which specify the location of the local value in the array of processes.
- left_id and right_id. Two int values holding the numbers of the process neighbours on each side.
- N. An int value defining the size of the total segment of points.
- Np. An int value defining the size of the sub-segment of points.
- X. A one-dimensional array of double values, holding the present and next values of the points within the local sub-segment.
- B. A one-dimensional array of double values, holding the past values of the points

within the local sub-segment.

- `tmpBorder`. A `double` value, which temporary holds the value to be sent to or received from the neighbouring sub-segments.
- `iteration`. An array of `int` value, which keeps record of the number of iterations so far.
- `start_time` and `end_time`. Two `double` values, which hold the timing information of the program's execution.

A.1.2 Communication

Communication is defined using JPVM methods for sending and receiving data to and from the neighbouring elements. Two pieces of code of the class `Heat` shown in Figure A.2, carry out these communication activities, based on the JPVM environment (Ferrari, 1997).

```
import jpvm.*;

class Heat{
    ...
    static void send_border(double x)throws jpvmException{
        ...
        jpvmBuffer buf;
        if(left_id!=NOBODY) {
            ...
            /* Send out eastern border */
            tmpBorder = x;
            buf = new jpvmBuffer();
            buf.pack(tmpBorder,1,1);
            jpvm.pvm_send(buf,tids[left_id],RED_RIGHT_TAG);
        }
        ...
    }
    static void recv_border(double x)throws jpvmException{
        ...
        jpvmMessage m;
        if(left_id!=NOBODY) {
            ...
            m = jpvm.pvm_recv(tids[left_id],RED_LEFT_TAG);
            m.buffer.unpack(tmpBorder,1,1);
            x = tmpBorder;
        }
        else {
        if(iteration<=1)
         x = 0.0;
        }
        ...
    }
    ...
}
```

Figure A.2 Communication methods for the CSE pattern.

274

The methods that implement the communication between sequential elements (see Section 5.2.10) as described by the CSE architectural pattern are described as follows:

- `void send_border()`. This method is used to send the value x to the two neighbouring elements. Notice that the code used for the left neighbour has to be repeated for the right neighbour, considering the adequate values for x. The method makes use of `jpvm.pvm_send()`, to actually send the value.

- `void recv_border()`. This method is used to receive data from the two neighbouring elements, and store it in the value x. Notice again that the code used for the left neighbour has to be repeated for the right neighbour, considering the adequate values for x. The method makes use of `jpvm.pvm_recv()`, to actually receive the value.

A.1.3 Agglomeration and Mapping

Finally, for the Coordination Simulation execution, tasks are created and connected as determined by the data structure representing the complete one-dimensional structure. Each communicating element considers two neighbours with which exchange partial results. The Coordination Simulation is executed on the given platform, representing how the data is divided among the communicating elements, how the communicating elements exchange data, and how they iteratively carry out the whole computation. The parts of the Java code in the `main()` function of the parallel application, which creates and spawns the elements within the JPVM environment (Ferrari, 1997), is presented in Figure A.3.

A.2 The Manager-Workers Code

The MW pattern is based on two types of participants: a manager and a set of workers. The manager preserves the order of data. On the other hand, each worker is capable of performing the same independent computation on different pieces of data. It repeatedly seeks a task to perform, performs it, and repeats; when no tasks remain, the program is finished.

A.2.1 Partitioning

The MW pattern describes a cooperation between a manager and a set of identical workers, which communicate partial results. The basic manager implementation focuses on partitioning the data structure and on representing its workers. Nevertheless, the manager

```
import jpvm.*;

class Heat{
    ...
    public static void main(String args[]) {
        try {
            jpvm = new jpvmEnvironment();
            ...
            tids = new jpvmTaskId[nprocs];
            childTids = new jpvmTaskId[nprocs-1];
            tids[0] = my_tid;
            my_id = my_x = 0;

            /* Spawn workers */
            if(nprocs>1) {
                jpvm.pvm_spawn("Heat",nprocs-1,tids);
                tids[nprocs-1] = tids[0];
                for(i=0;i<(nprocs-1);i++)childTids[i] = tids[i];
                tids[0] = my_tid;
                ...
            }
            ...
        }
        catch (jpvmException jpe) {
            error("jpvm Exception - "+jpe.toString());
        }
        catch (Exception e) {
            error("Exception - "+e.toString());
        }
    }
    ...
}
```

Figure A.3 Main elements of the `main` function for the CSE pattern.

does not perform any processing activity. The code for class `mat_mult` developed in Java (Ferrari, 1997) is shown in Figure A.4.

```
import jpvm.*;

class mat_mult {
    ...
    static int numTasks = 0;
    static int matDim = 0;
    static int taskMeshDim= 0;
    static int localPartitionDim= 0;
    static int localPartitionSize= 0;
    static int taskMeshRow= 0;
    static int taskMeshCol= 0;
    ...
    static jpvmTaskId myTaskId = null;
    static jpvmTaskId masterTaskId  = null;
    static jpvmEnvironment jpvm      = null;
    static jpvmTaskId tids[];
    static float C[], A[], B[], tempA[];
    ...
}
```

Figure A.4 Relevant attributes of the class `mat_mult` for representing the MW pattern.

The most relevant attributes of class `mat_mult` used to organise and perform the partitioning activities are described as follows:

- nTasks. An `int` value, defining the number of processes to be created into the JPVM enrironment.
- matDim. An `int` value defining the size of the square matrices to be multiplied.
- taskMeshDim. An `int` value that specifies the size of the square array of processes.
- localPartitionDim. An `int` value defining the size of the sub-matrices.
- localPartitionSize. An `int` value defining the number of values to multiply by each process.
- taskMeshRow and taskMeshCol. Two `int` values which specify the location of the local process in the array of processes.
- myTaskId and masterTaskId. Two `jpvmTaskId` values, which are used to store the task identifiers of workers and the manager.
- tids. An array of `jpvmTaskId` values, that the manager uses to keep track of its workers.
- C, A, B, and tempA. Four two-dimensional arrays of `float` values, keeping the matrices to be multiplied, as well as intermediate results.

A.2.2 Communication

Workers communicate with the manager, requesting data to operate on. Hence, workers are defined so they receive data from the manager, operate on it, and return a partial result. The code for the method `Pipe()` of the class `mat_mult` allows these communications between manager and workers. The code developed in Java (Ferrari, 1997) is shown in Figure A.5).

```
import jpvm.*;

class mat_mult {
    ...
    public static void Pipe(int iter) throws jpvmException {
        if (taskMeshCol == (taskMeshRow+iter)%taskMeshDim) {
            jpvmBuffer buf = new jpvmBuffer();
            buf.pack(A,localPartitionSize,1);
            for (i=0;i<taskMeshDim;i++)
                if (localTaskIndex != taskMeshRow*taskMeshDim+i) {
                jpvm.pvm_send(buf,
                tids[taskMeshRow*taskMeshDim+i],PipeTag);
                }
        }
        else {
            jpvmMessage m = jpvm.pvm_recv(PipeTag);
            m.buffer.unpack(tempA,localPartitionSize,1);
        }
    }
}
```

Figure A.5 Communication method Pipe() for the MW pattern.

The methods `Pipe()` implements the communication exchange between manager and worker as described by the MW architectural pattern. This method verifies if a worker has data to operate on. If this is the case, then it returns an array (which represents the eventual product) using the method `jpvm.pvm_send()` of the JPVM environment (Ferrari, 1997) to send the result to the manager. On the other hand, if the worker is not busy, then it is able to receive more work, using the method `jpvm.pvm_recv()`.

A.2.3 Agglomeration and Mapping

Finally, for the Coordination Simulation execution, manager and workers are instantiated, and connected as determined by the MW pattern. Each worker considers the manager to read in and write out partial results, referencing it. The Coordination Simulation is executed on the given platform, representing how the data is divided among the workers, how the workers operate, and how they write back results. The Java code for the `main()` function (Ferrari, 1997) is presented in Figure A.6.

```
import jpvm.*;

class mat_mult {
    ...
    public static void main(String args[]) {
        ...
        try {
        jpvm = new jpvmEnvironment();
        myTaskId = jpvm.pvm_mytid();
        masterTaskId = jpvm.pvm_parent();
        if(masterTaskId==jpvm.PvmNoParent) {
            ...
            tids = new jpvmTaskId[numTasks];
            if(numTasks>1)jpvm.pvm_spawn("mat_mult",numTasks-1,tids);
            tids[numTasks-1] = tids[0];
            tids[0] = myTaskId;
            localTaskIndex = 0;
            ...
        }
        else {
          for(localTaskIndex=0;localTaskIndex<numTasks;localTaskIndex++)
            if (myTaskId.equals(tids[localTaskIndex]))break;
                matDim = m.buffer.upkint();
        }
        /* Include here the code for the matrix multiplication */
        ...
        jpvm.pvm_exit();
        }
        catch (jpvmException jpe) {
            error("jpvm Exception - "+jpe.toString(),true);
        }
    }
}
```

Figure A.6 Main elements of the `main` function for the MW pattern

A.3 The Pipes and Filters Code

The PF pattern proposes a solution in which different operations are simultaneously performed on different ordered pieces of data that "flow" through the operations.

A.3.1 Partitioning

The PF pattern describes a computation decomposed into a sequence of steps which can
be simultaneously executed until completion. Data flows through each step, being incrementally operated. The code for class prime is developed in Java (Ferrari, 1997), as
shown in Figure A.7.

```
import jpvm.*;

class prime{
    ...
    static int nprocs   = DEFAULT_NUM_PROCS;
    static int procdim;
    static int N;
    int answer[];
    jpvmTaskId sieve_tid;
    jpvmTaskId parent_tid;
    jpvmTaskId next_tid = 0;
    int prime, candidate;
    int length = 0;
    ...
}
```

Figure A.7 Relevant attributes of the class primes for representing the PF pattern.

The most relevant attributes of class primes used to organise and perform the partitioning activities are described as follows:

- nprocs. An int value, whose purpose is to define the number of processors to be
  used into the JPVM enrironment.
- procdim. An int value that specifies the number of processes per processor.
- N. An int value defining the number of primes to be obtained.
- answer. An array of int values, which represents the set of prime numbers.
- sieve_tid. A jpvmTaskId value, which serves to identify the local filter within
  the sieve.
- parent_tid. A jpvmTaskId value, which identifies who is the previous filter
  within the sieve.
- next_tid. A jpvmTaskId value, which is assigned to the next filter within the
  sieve, if it has to be created to obtain another prime number.
- prime. An int value, used to store the local prime number in the actual filter.

- `candidate`. An `int` value, used to store the number to be tested if it is a prime number in the present filter.
- `length`. An `int` value, used as a counter to keep track about how many prime numbers have been obtained.

A.3.2 Communication

Communications allow data flow though the structure, coordinating the execution. Hence, communications are defined so they receive data from a filter and send it to the next one, taking care only on the direction of the flow. At the same time, they perform the synchronisation activities, so filters are able to process. The code for the class `Pipe` was developed in Java (Ferrari, 1997) as shown in Figure A.8.

```
import jpvm.*;

class prime{
    ...
    /* Now test each new incoming candidate */
    while (candidate < N){
        /* Receive the next number */
        jpvmMessage m = jpvm.pvm_recv (parent_tid, NUMBERTAG);
        m.buffer.unpack(candidate, 1, 1);
        if (candidate < N){
            /* Perform here the primes test */
            ...
            if (! next_tid)
            /* Create a new sieve */
            jpvm.pvm_spawn("prime","", next_tid);
            /* Send the candidate to the next sieve */
            jpvmBuffer buf = new jpvmBuffer();
            buf.pack(sieve_tid);
            buf.pack(candidate);
            jpvm.pvm_send (buf, NUMBERTAG);
        }
    }
    ...
}
```

Figure A.8 Communications for the PF pattern

Each time a new prime number is found, it is set into a filter. Each filter receives the `parent_tid`, and a new `candidate` number to be tested, using the method `jpvm.pvm_recv()`. If a new prime is found, a new filter is created for it, sending at the same time the actual tid (`sieve_tid`) and the next candidate to be tested. using the method `jpvm.pvm_send()` of the JPVM environment (Ferrari, 1997).

A.3.3 Agglomeration and Mapping

For the Coordination Simulation execution, a PF structure is composed of filters connected as determined by the PF pattern. Each filter references to a previous and a next filters. The Coordination Simulation is executed on the given platform, representing how the data flows through the filters. The main Java code for the `main()` function (Ferrari,1997) is presented in Figure A.9.

```
import jpvm.*;

class prime{
    ...
    public static void main (String args[]){
        try {
            jpvm = new jpvmEnvironment();
            ...
            /* Enroll in JPVM */
            sieve_tid = jpvm.pvm_mytid();
            /* Spawn off the first worker process */
            jpvm.pvm_spawn ("prime", 1, sieve_tid);
            /* Send out the numbers that are to be sieved. */
            /* When == N, then the sieve should stop.  */
            for (number = 2; number <= N; number++){
                    jpvmBuffer buf = new jpvmBuffer();
                    buf.pack(sieve_tid);
                    buf.pack(candidate);
                    jpvm.pvm_send (buf, NUMBERTAG);
            }
            ...
            /* Tell JPVM that we are about to stop */
            jpvm.pvm_exit();
        }
        catch (jpvmException jpe) {
            error("jpvm Exception - "+jpe.toString());
        }
        catch (Exception e) {
            error("Exception - "+e.toString());
        }
    }
    ...
}
```

Figure A.9 Main elements of the main function for the PF pattern.

Bibliography

Aarsten, A., Brugali, D., and Menga G. (1996), *Patterns for Cooperation.* Pattern Languages of Programming Conference. Allerton Park, Illinois, USA. September 1996.

Aarsten, A., Elia, G., and Menga, G. (1995), *G++: A Pattern Language for the Object Oriented Design of Concurrent and Distributed Information Systems, with Applications to Computer Integrated Manufacturing.* In *Patterns Languages of Programming.* Addison-Wesley.

Abowd, G., Bass, L., Clements, P., Kazman, R., Northrop, L., and Zaremski, A. (1997), *Recommended Best Industrial Practice for Software Architecture Evaluation.* Technical Report CMU/SEI-96-TR-025 ESC-TR-96-025.

Agha, G. (1990), *Concurrent Object-Oriented Programming.* Communications of the ACM. Vol. 33, No. 9.

Agha, G., Mason, I. A., Smith, S.F., and Talcott, C.L.(1993a), *A Foundation for Actor Computation.* Journal of Functional Programming, Vol. 1, No. 1. Cambridge University Press.

Agha, G., Wegner, P., and Yonezawa, A., eds. (1993b), *Research Directions in Concurrent Object-Oriented Programming.* The MIT Press, Cambridge, Massachusets.

Agha, G., Frolund, S., Kim, W. Y., Panwar, R., Patterson, A., and Sturman, D. (1993c), *Abstraction and Modularity Mechanisms for Concurrent Computing.* In Agha, G., Wegner, P., and Yonezawa, A., eds. *Research Directions in Concurrent Object-Oriented Programming.* The MIT Press.

Agrawal, R.and Shafer, J. C. (1996), *Parallel Mining of Association Rules: Design, Implementation and Experience.* IBM Research Report RJ 10004. IBM Research Division, Almaden Research Center. San Jose, CA.

Ajmone, M., Balbo, G. and Conte, G. (1986), *Performance Models of Multiprocessor Performance.* The MIT Press

Akenhust, D., and Waters, G. (1999a), *UML Specification of Distributed System Environments.* Computing Laboratory, University of Kent at Canterbury, Technical Report 18-99, May 1999.

Akenhust, D., and Waters, G. (1999b), *UML Deficiencies from the Perspective of Automatic Performance Model Generation.* Proceedings of the Workshop on Rigorous Modelling and Analysis with the UML: Challenges and Limitations. OOPSLA'99, November 1999.

Akenhust, D., Waters, G., Utton, P., and Martin, G. (1999), *Predictive Performance Analysis for Distributed Systems - PERMABASE position.* Proceedings of the One Day Workshop on Software Performance Prediction Extracted from Designs. Heriott-Watt University, Edinburgh, November 1999.

Alexander, C., Ishikawa, S., Silverstein, M., Jacobson, M., Fiksdahl-King, I., and Angel, S. (1977), *A Pattern Language.* Oxford University Press, New York.

Alexander, C. (1979), *The Timeless Way of Building.* Oxford University Press, New York.

Andolfi, F., Aquilani, F., Balsamo, S., and Inverardi, P. (2000), *Deriving Performance Models of Software Architectures from Message Sequence Charts.* In WOSP 2000.

Andrews, G.R. (1991), *Concurrent Programming. Principles and Practice.* The Benjamin/Cummings Publishing Company, Inc.

Andrews, G.R. (2000), *Foundations of Multithreaded, Parallel, and Distributed Programming.* Addison-Wesley Longman, Inc.

Aquilani, F., Balsamo, S., and Inverardi, P. (2000), *Performance Analysis at the Software Architecture design level.* Technical Report TR-SAL-32, Saladin project.

Arief, L.B. (2001), *A Framework for Supporting Automatic Simulation Generation from Design.* PhD Thesis, Department of Computer Science, University of Newcastle Upon Tyne, July 2001.

Arief, L.B. and Speirs N.A. (1999a), *Automatic Generation of Distributed System Simulations from UML.* Proceedings of the 13th European Simulation Multiconference, Warsaw, Poland, June 1999.

Arief, L.B. and Speirs N.A. (1999b), *Using SimML to bridge the Transformation from UML to Simulation.* Proceedings of the One Day Workshop on Software Performance and Prediction Extracted from Design, Heriott-Watt University, Edinburgh, Scotland, November 1999.

Arief, L.B. and Speirs N.A. (2000), *A UML Tool for an Automatic Generation of Simula-*

tion Programs. In WOSP 2000.

Ayles, T., Field, A.J., and Magee, J.N. (2003), *Adding Performance Evaluation to the LTSA Tool.* 13th International Conference on Modelling Techniques and Tools for Computer Performance Evaluation, Performance TOOLS 2003. Urbana, Illinois. September 2003.

Balsamo, S., Inverardi, P., and Mangano, C. (1998), *An Approach to Performance Evaluation of Software Architectures.* Proceedings of Workshop on Software and Performance, WOSP'98. Santa Fe, New Mexico, October 1998.

Barbacci, M. M., Longstaff, T. H., Klein M. H., and Weinstock, C. B. (1995), *Quality Attributes.* Technical Report CMU/SEI-95-TR-021 ESC-TR-95-021.

Barbacci, M. M., Klein M. H., and Weinstock, C. B. (1997), *Principles for Evaluating the Quality Attributes of a Software Architecture.* Technical Report CMU/SEI-96-TR-036 ESC-TR-96-136.

Bass, L., Clements, P., and Kazman, R. (1998), *Software Architecture in Practice.* Addison-Wesley, Reading Massachusets.

Bellay, B., Gall, H., Hasler, V., Klosch, R., Trausmuth, G., Beckman, H., and Eixelsberger, W. (1997), *Software Architecture through Architectural Properties.* Technical Report TUV-1841-97-03. Distributed Systems Department, Information Systems Institute, Technical University of Vienna.

Bennett, D. (1997), *Designing Hard Software. The Essential Tasks.* Manning Publication Co., Greenwich, Connecticut.

Berczuk, S. (1994), *Finding solutions through pattern languages.* IEEE Computer, Vol. 27, No. 12.

Bernardi, S., Donatelli, S., and Merseguer, J. (2002), *From UML Sequence Diagrams and Statecharts to Analysable Petri Net Models.* In WOSP 2002.

Bernardo, M. (2000), *Theory and Application of Extended Markovian Process Algebra.* PhD thesis, University of Bologna, Italy.

Bernardo, M., Ciancarini, P., and Donatiello, L. (2000), *AEMPA: A Process Algebraic Description Language for the Performance Analysis of Software Architectures.* In WOSP 2000.

Bolch, G., Greiner, S., de Meer, H., and Trivedi, K.S. (1998), *Queueing Networks and Markov Chains. Modeling and Performance Evaluation with Computer Science Applications.* John Wiley & Sons, Inc.

Bond, J. (1987), *Parallel-processing concepts finally come together in real systems.* Computer Design, Penn Well publications. June 1, 1987.

Booch, G., Rumbaugh, J., and Jacobson, I. (1999), *The Unified Modeling Language User Guide.* Addison-Wesley.

Bosch, J. (2000), *Design & Use of Software Architecture. Adopting and Evolving a Product-line Approach.* ACM Press.

Botti, O., and Capra, L. (1996), *Performance indices to characterise concurrent applications: experimenting GSPN evaluation techniques in plant automation.* Proceedings of the First IFIP TC10 International Workshop on Parallel and Distributed Software Engineering. March, 1996.

Brand, S. (1994), *How Buildings Learn. What happens after they're built.* Phoenix Illustrated, Orion Books Ltd.

Brinch Hansen, P. (1977), *The Architecture of Concurrent Programs.* Series in Automatic Computetion. Prentice-Hall, Inc. Englewood Cliffs, New Jersey.

Brinch-Hansen, P. (1978), *Distributed Processes: A Concurrent Programming Concept.* Communications of the ACM, Vol. 21, No. 11. November, 1978.

Brooks, F. (1975) *The Mythical Man-Month.* Addison-Wesley, Reading Massachusetts.

Broy, M., Deimel, A., Henn, J., Koskimies, K., Plásil, F., Pomberger, G., Pree, W., Stal, M., and Szyperski, C. (1998), *What characterizes a (software) component?* Software — Concepts & Tools, Srpinger-Verlag, Vol. 19, pp 49-56.

Budgen, D. (1994), *Software Design.* Addison-Wesley.

Burke, M., Cytron, R., Ferrante, J., Hsieh, W., Sarkar, V., and Shields, D. (1988), *Automatic Discovery of parallelism: a tool and an experiement.* Proceedings of the ACM/SIGPLAN conference on Parallel programming: experience with applications, languages and systems. New Haven, Connecticut, USA.

Burns, A., and Wellings, A. (1997), *Concurrency in Ada.* Cambridge University Press, November, 1997.

Buschmann, F., Meunier, R., Rohnert, H., Sommerland, P., and Stal, M. (1996), *Pattern-Oriented Software Architecture. A System of Patterns*. John Wiley & Sons, Ltd. Chichester, United Kingdom.

Campbell, D. K. G. (1996), *Towards the Classification of Algorithmic Skeletons*. Department of Computer Science, University of York.

Carriero, N., and Gelernter, D. (1988), *How to Write Parallel Programs. A Guide to the Perplexed*. Yale University, Department of Computer Science, New Heaven, Connecticut.

Chandy, K. M., and Taylor, S. (1992), *An Introduction to Parallel Programming*. Jones and Bartlett Publishers, Inc., Boston.

Chandy, K.M. (1994), *Concurrent Program Archetypes*. Computer Science, California Institute of Technology. Keynote of the International Parallel Processing Symposium.

Chien, A. A. (1993), *Supporting Modularity in Highly-Parallel Programs*. In Agha, G., Wegner, P., and Yonezawa, A. (editors), *Research Directions in Concurrent Object-Oriented Programming*. The MIT press.

Cole, M. (1989), *Algorithmic Skeletons: Structured Management of Parallel Computation*. MIT Press.

Coplien, J. O. (1994), *Generative pattern languages; An emerging direction of software design*. Proceedings of the 5th Annual Borland International Conference, Orlando, FL. June 1994.

Coplien, J.O., and Schmidt, D. C., eds. (1995), *Pattern Languages of Program Design*. Addison Wesley, Reading, Massachusets.

Coplien, J.O. (1997), *Idioms, Patterns, and Other Architectural Literature*. IEEE Software Special Issue on Objects, Patterns, and Architectures. January 1997.

Cortellesa, V., and Mirandola (2000), *Deriving a Queueing Network based Performance Model from UML diagrams*. In WOSP 2000.

Cortellesa, V., and Mirandola (2002), *Prima-UML: a Performance Validation Incremental Methodology on Early UML diagrams*. In WOSP 2002.

Crane, S., Magee, J., and Pryce, N. (1995) *Design Patterns for Binding in Distributed Systems*. OOPSLA'95, Workshop on Design Patterns for Concurrent, Parallel and Distributed Object-Oriented Systems. October 1995.

Culler, D., Singh, J. P., and Gupta, A. (1997), *Parallel Computer Architecture. A Hardware/Software Approach.* Morgan Kaufmann Publishers.

Darlington, J. and To, H. W. (1993), *Building Parallel Applications without Programming.* Department of Computing, Imperial College. United Kingdom. In *Abstract Machine Models*, Leeds.

Darlington, J., Field, A.J., Harrison, P.G., Kelly, P.H.J., Sharp, D.W.N., Wu, Q., and While, R.L. (1993), *Parallel Programming Using Skeleton Functions.* In *Parallel Architectures & Languages Europe*, Springer-Verlag.

Deldarie, H., Davy, J. R., and Dew, P. M. (1995), *The Performance of Parallel Algorithmic Skeletons.* Report 95/6, University of Leeds, School of Computer Studies.

De Miguel, M., Lambolais, T., Hannouz, M., Betgè-Brezetz, S., and Piekarec, S. (2000), *UML Extensions for the Specification and Evaluation of Latency constraints in Architectural Models.* In WOSP 2000.

Dijkstra, E.W. (1968), *Co-operating Sequential Processes.* F. Genyus. Ed. Programming Languages. Academic Press, New York, 1968.

Dobson, S., and Wadsworth, C.P., *Towards a theory of shared data in distributed systems.* Software Engineering for Parallel and Distributed Systems. Proceedings of the First IFIP TC10 International Workshop on Parallel and Distributed Software Engineering, March 1996. Chapman & Hall.

El-Sayed, H., Cameron, D., and Woodside, M. (1998), *Automated Performance Modeling from Scenarios and SDL Designs of Distributed Systems.* Proceedings of the International Symposium on Software Engineering for Parallel and Distributed Systems. Kyoto, Japan, April 1998.

Ferrari, A.J. (1997), *JPVM: Network Parallel Computing in Java.* Technical Report CS-97-29. Department of Computer Science, University of Virginia.

Finkelstein, A., Easterbrook, S., Kramer, J., and Nuseibeh, B. (1993), *Multi-view Requirements Engineering.* In DRA Colloquium on Analysis of Requirements for Software Intensive Systems. Defense Research Agency.

Flynn, M. (1966), *Very high-speed computing systems.* Proceedings of the IEEE.

Foster, I. (1994), *Designing and Building Parallel Programs, Concepts and Tools for Parallel Software Engineering.* Addison-Wesley Publishing Co. Reading, Massachusets.

Freeman, E., Hupfer, S., and Arnold, K. (1999), *JavaSpaces Principles, Patterns, and Practice.* Addison Wesley Publishing Company.

Freeman, T.L. and Phillips, C. (1992), *Parallel Numerical Algorithms.* Prentice-Hall International Series in Computer Science.

Frolund, S. (1996), *Coordinating Distributed Objects, An Actor-based Approach to Synchronization.* The MIT Press. Cambridge, Massachusets.

Gabriel, R. P. (1996), *Patterns of Software: Tales from the Software Community.* Oxford University Press.

Gacek, C., Abd-Allah, A., Clark, B., and Boehm, B. (1994), *Focused Workshop on Software Architectures: Issue Paper.* USC Center for Software Engineering.

Gamma, E., Helm, R., Johnson, R., and Vlissides, J. (1994), *Design Patterns: Elements of Reusable Object-Oriented Systems.* Addison-Wesley. Reading, Massachusets.

Garcia-Nocetti, D. F., Solano-Gonzalez, J., Valdivieso-Casique, M. F., Ortiz-Ramirez, R., and Moreno-Hernandez, E. (1997) *Parallel Processing in Real-Time Ultrasonic Imaging.* 4th IFAC Workshop on Algorithms and Architectures for Real-Time Control, AARTC'97. Vilmoura, Portugal.

Geist, A., Beguelin, A., Dongarra, J., Jiang, W., Mancheck, R., and Sunderam, V. (1994), *PVM: Parallel Virtual Machine. A User's Guide and Tutorial for Networked Parallel Computing.* The MIT Press. Cambridge, Massachusets.

Gemund, A.J.C. van (2003), *Symbolic Performance Modeling of Parallel Systems.* IEEE Transactions on Parallel and Distributed Systems. Vol. 14, No. 2. February 2003.

Ghezzi, C., Jazayeri, M., and Mandrioli, D. (1991), *Fundamentals of Software Engineering (Chapter 6).* Prentice-Hall International.

Glass, R.L. (1999), *The Realities of Software Technology Payoffs.* Communications of the ACM, Vol. 42, No. 2.

Goldsworthy, D. R., and Loader, R. J. (1988), *An Object Oriented Approach to the Modelling of Parallel Systems.* Department of Computer Science, Reading University.

Gomaa, H., and Menascè, D.A. (2000), *Design and Performance Modeling of Component Interconnection Patterns for Distributed Software Architectures.* In WOSP 2000.

Gomaa, H., and Menascè, D.A. (2001), *Performance Engineering of Component-based Distributed Software Systems.* In Performance Engineering - State of the Art and Current Trends, LNCS 2047, Springer-Verlag.

Gu, G., and Petriu, D.C. (2002), *XSLT transformation from UML models to LQN performance models.* In WOSP 2002.

Harrison, T. and Schmidt, D. (1997), *Thread-Specific Storage. A Behavioral Pattern for Efficiently Accessing per-Thread State.* Second annual European Pattern Languages of Programming Conference. Kloster Irsee, Germany. July 1997.

Hartley, S. (1998), *Concurrent Programming: The Java Programming Language.* Oxford University Press, Inc.

Henning, A., and Eckardt, H. (2001), *Challenges for Simulation of Systems in Software Performance Engineering.* Proceedings of the 15th European Simulation Multiconference, ESM'01, Prague, Czech Republic, June 2001.

Henning, A., Hentschel, A., and Tyack, J. (2003a), *Performance Prototyping - Generating and Simulating a Distributed IT-System from UML models.* Proceeding of the 17th European Simulation Multiconference, ESM'03, Nottingham, UK, June 2003.

Henning, A., Revill, D., and Ponitsch, M. (2003b), *From UML to Performance Measures - Simulative Performance Predictions of IT-System using the Jboss application server with OMNET++.* Proceeding of the 17th European Simulation Multiconference, ESM'03, Nottingham, UK, June 2003.

Hermanns, H., Herzog, U., and Hillston, J. (1995), *Stochastic Process - A Formal Approach to Performance Modelling.* PERFORMACE TOOLS'95, MMB'95. Heidelberg, Germany, September, 1995.

High Performance Computing and Networking (HPCN) (1998), *Film, entertainment and video page.* ESPRIT project. http://www.hpcn-ttn.org/themegroupsswitch.html.

Hillier, W. (1996), *Space is the Machine.* Cambridge University Press, Cambridge.

Hoare, C.A.R. (1974), *Monitors: An Operating System Structuring Concept.* Communications of the ACM, Vol. 17, No. 10. October, 1974.

Hoare, C.A.R. (1978), *Communicating Sequential Processes.* Communications of the ACM, Vol. 21, No. 8. August, 1978.

Hoare, C.A.R. (1985) *Communicating Sequential Processes.* Prentice-Hall.

Hoeben, F. (2000), *Using UML Models for Performance Calculation.* In WOSP 2000.

Hrischuk, C., Rolia, J., and Woodside, M. (1995), *Automated Generation of Software Performance Model using an Object-Oriented Prototype.* International Workshop on Modeling and Simulation, Analysis and Simulation of Computer and Telecommunication Systems, MASCOT'95.

Huber, F., Molterer, S., Raush, A., Schätz, B., Sihling, M., and Slotosch, O. (1998), *Tool supported Specification and Simulation of Distributed Systems.* Proceedings of the International Symposium on Software Engineering for Parallel and Distributed Systems. IEEE Computer Society.

Hyde, D.C. (1994), *Deadlock and Deadlock-free Routing.* In Laboratories for Parallel Computing, Nevison, C.H., Hyde, D.C., Schneider, G.M., and Tymann, P.T. Jones and Bartlett Publishers.

IEEE (1995), *The Artistry of Software Architecture.* IEEE Software magazine, november 1995.

IEEE (1998), *IEEE Recommended Practice for Software Design Descriptions.* IEEE Std. 1016-1998, IEEE.

Inverardi, P., and Wolf, A.L. (1995), *Formal Specification and Analysis of Software Architectures Using the Chemical Abstract Machine Model.* IEEE Transactions on Software Engineering, Vol. 21, No. 4.

Jacobson, I., Booch, G., and Rumbaugh, J. (1999), *The Unified Software Development Process.* Addison-Wesley.

Jacobson, I., Booch, G., and Rumbaugh, J. (1999), *The Unified Software Development Process.* Addison-Wesley.

Jain, P. and Schmidt, D. (1996), *Service Configurator. A Pattern for DynamicConfiguration and Reconfiguration of Communication Services.* Third Annual Pattern Languages of Programming Conference, Allerton Park, Illinois. September 1996.

Jarvinen, H.M., and Kurki-Sunio, R. (1991), *DisCo Specification Language: Marriage of Action and Objects.* Proceedings of the 11th International Conference on Distributed Computing Systems, Arlington, Texas, May 1992. IEEE Computer Society Press.

Jezequel, J. M., and Pacherie, J. L. (1997), *The "Ubiquitous Agent" Design Pattern.* IRISA Campus de Beaulieu. 3rd Pattern Languages of Programming Conference, Allerton Park, Illinois, February 1997.

The JOLT project (1999), *Active Object.* A research cooperation between Siemens Corporate Technology and the Washington University. http://www.cs.wustl.edu/~schmidt/patterns/patterns.html

Jonkers, H., Janssen, W., Verschut, A., and Wierstra, E. (1998), *A Unified Framework for Design and Performance Analysis of Distributed Systems.* Proceedings of the 3rd Annual IEEE International Computer Performance and Dependability Symposium, IPDS'98. Durham, North Carolina, September 1998.

Kähkipuro, P. (1999), *UML based Performance Modeling Framework of Object-Oriented Distributed Systems.* Proceedings of the One Day Workshop on Software Performance Prediction Extracted from Designs, Heriott-Watt University, Edinburgh, November 1999.

Kähkipuro, P. (2001), *UML-based Performance Modelling Framework for Component-based Distributed Systems.* In Performance Engineering, R.R. Dumke, C. Rautenstrauch, A. Schmietendorf, and A. Sholz (editors), LNCS 2047, Springer-Verlag.

Kemppainen, J., Levanto, M., Valmari, A., and Clegg, M. (1992), *"ARA" Puts Advanced Reachability Analysis Techniques Together.* In Proceedings of the 5th Nordic Workshop on Programming Environment Research, Tampere, Finland, January 1992.

Kendall, E. A., Malkoun, M. T., and Jiang, C. H. (1996), *The Layered Agent Pattern Language.* Third Annual Pattern Languages of Programming Conference, Allerton Park, Illinois. September 1996.

Kerth, N. L. (1998), *Customer Requirements for Video Store Rental.* Elite Systems, Portland, Oregon.

King, P., and Pooley, R. (1999), *Derivation of Petri Net Performance Models from UML Specifications of Communication Software.* Proceedings of the 15th UK Performance Engineering Workshop, University of Bristol, July 1999.

King, P., and Pooley, R. (2000), *Derivation of Petri Net Performance Models from UML Specifications of Communication Software*. In Computer Performance Evaluation Tools, B.R. Haverkort, H.C. Hohnenkamp, and C.U. Smith (editors), LNCS 1786, Springer-Verlag.

Keliman, S., Shah, D., and Smaalders, B. (1996), *Programming with Threads*. SunSoft Press, Prentice-Hall.

Kleinrock, L. (1975), *Queueing Systems, Vol. 1: Theory*. John Wiley & Sons.

Kopetz, H. (1997), *Real-time Systems: Design Principles for Distributed Embedded Applications*. Kluwer. Boston, Massachusetts.

Krutchen, P. (1995), *Architectural Blueprints — The "4+1" View Model of Software Architecture*. In The Artistry of Software Architecture. IEEE Software magazine, november 1995.

Kuck, D.J., Davidson, E.S., Lawrie, D.H., Sameh, A.H., and Zhu, C.Q. (1998), *The Cedar System and an Initial Performance Study*. 25 Years ISCA: Retrospectives and Reprints, 1998.

Lavender, R. G., and Schmidt, D. C. (1996), *Active Object, an Object Behavioral Pattern for Concurrent Programming*. ISODE Consortium Inc. and Department of Computer Science, Washington University. In J. Vlissides, J. Coplien and N. Kerth (eds.), *Pattern Languages of Program Design 2*. Addison-Wesley. Reading, Massachusets.

Law, A. M. and Kelton, W. D. (1991), *Simulation Modeling & Analysis*. Second edition. McGraw-Hill International Editions.

Lazowska, E. D., Zahorjan, J., Graham, G. S., Sevcik, K. C. (1984), *Quantitative System Performance. Computer Systems Analysis using Queueing Network Models*. Prentice-Hall, Inc.

Lewis, B. and Berg, D.J. (2000), *Multithreaded Programming with Java Technology*. Sun Microsystems, Inc.

Lindermann, C., Thümmler, A., Klemm, A., Lohmann, M., and Waldhorst, O.P. (2002), *Performance Analysis of Time-Enhanced UML diagrams based on Stochastic Processes*. In WOSP 2002.

Luckham, D.C. (1996), *Rapide: A Language Tool for Simulation of Distributed Systems by Partial Ordering of Events*. Partial Order Methods Workshop IV, DIMACS, University of Princeton, July 1996.

Lynch, N. (1996), *Distributed Algorithms.* Morgan Kaufmann Publishers, 1996.

Maffeis, S. (1996), *Object Group, An Object Behavioral Pattern for Fault-Tolerance and Group Communication in Distributed Systems.* Department of Computer Science, Cornell University. Proceedings of the USENIX Conference on Object-Oriented Technologies. Toronto, Canada.

Magee, J., and Kramer, J. (1995), *Modeling Distributed Software Architectures.* Proceedings of the First International Workshop on Architecture of Software Systems. Carnegie Mellon University.

Marr, M. I., and Cole, M. (1995), *Hierarchical Skeletons and ad hoc Parallelism.* Department of Computer Science, University of Edimburg. ParCo'95.

Marsan, M.A., Balbo, G., Conte, S., Donatelli, S., and Franceschinis, G. (1995), *Modeling with Generalized Stochastic Petri Nets.* John Wiley & Sons.

Massingill, B.L., and Chandy, K.M. (1997), *Parallel Program Archetypes.* Technical Report CS-TR-96-28. Computer Science, California Institute of Technology.

Menascè, D.A. (1997), *A Framework for Software Performance Engineering of Client/ Server Systems.* Proceedings of the 1997 Computer Measurement Group Conference. Orlando, Florida.

Menascè, D.A., and Gomaa, H. (1998), *On a Language based Method for Software Performance Engineering of Client/Server Systems.* Proceedings of the Wokshop on Software and Performance, WOSP'98. Santa Fe, New Mexico, October 1998.

McKenney, P.E. (1996), *Selecting Locking Primitives for Parallel Programs.* In *Patterns Languages of Programming 2.* Addison-Wesley.

Montgomery, D.C. (1991), *Design and Analysis of Experiments.* John Wile & Sons, Inc.

Nevison, C. H., Hyde, D. C., Schneider, G. M., and Tymann, P. T. (1994), *Laboratories for Parallel Computing.* Jones and Bartlett Publishers. Boston, Massachusets.

Object Management Group (1998), *CORBA Messaging Specification.* OMG TC Document orbos/98-05-05, May 1998.

Object Management Group (2001), *UML Profile for Schedulability, Performance and Time.* OMG Document ad/2001-06-14, http://www.omg.org/cgi-bin/

doc?ad/2001-06-14

Ortega-Arjona, J.L. (1998), *Abstract of the PhD research Architectural Patterns for Parallel Systems*. Doctoral Sympoium. Proceedings of the 20th International Conference on Software Engineering, ICSE'98, "Forging New Links", Volume II. IEEE Computer Society.

Ortega-Arjona, J.L., and Roberts, G. (1998a), *Architectural Patterns for Parallel Programming*. Proceedings of the 3rd European Conference on Pattern Languages of Programming and Computing, EuroPLoP'98. J. Coldewey and P. Dyson (editors). UVK Universitatsverlag Konstanz GmbH.

Ortega-Arjona, J.L., and Roberts, G. (1998b), *The Concept of Software Structure and its relations with Software Architecture and Software Patterns*. Proceedings of the Object-Oriented Software Architecture Workshop, OOSA'98, in the 12th European Conference of Object-Oriented Programming, ECOOP'98. S. Demeyer and J. Bosch (editors). Lecture Notes in Computer Science, Vol. 1543/1998, Springer-Verlag Heidelberg.

Ortega-Arjona, J.L., and Roberts, G. (1999a), *The Layers of Change in Software Architecture*. Position paper in the 1st Working IFIP Conference on Software Architecture, WICSA1.

Ortega-Arjona, J.L., and Roberts, G. (1999b), *Architectural Development Pattern*. Proceedings of the 4th European Conference on Pattern Languages of Programming and Computing, EuroPLoP'99. M. Devos and P. Dyson (editors). UVK Universitatsverlag Konstanz GmbH.

Ortega-Arjona, J.L., and Roberts, G. (1999c), *Architectural Performance Models. Estimating the Contribution of Software Structure to the Performance of a Parallel Software Architecture*. Proceedings of the Second Nordic Workshop on Software Architecture, NOSA'99. Research Report 13/99. Dept. of Computer Science and Engineering, University of Karlskrona/Ronneby.

Ortega-Arjona, J.L. (2000), *The Communicating Sequential Elements Pattern. An Architectural Pattern for Domain Parallelism*. Proceedings of the 7th Conference on Pattern Languages of Programming, PLoP 2000. Technical Report wucs-00-29, Washington University.

Ortega-Arjona, J.L., and Roberts, G. (2001), *Pattern-based Simulation. Simulating the Actor Model using the Active Object Behavioral Pattern.* Computación y Sistemas. Iberoamerican Journal of Computing. Vol. 5, Num. 1. July-September, 2001. Centro de Investigaciones en Computación, Instituto Politécnico Nacional. ISSN 1405-5546.

Ortega-Arjona, J.L. (2003), *The Shared Resource Pattern. An Activity Parallelism Architectural Pattern for Parallel Programming.* Proceedings of the 10th Conference on Pattern Languages of Programming, PLoP 2003.

Ortega-Arjona, J.L. (2004), *The Manager-Workers Pattern. An Activity Parallelism Architectural Pattern for Parallel Programming.* Proceedings of the 9th European Conference on Pattern Languages of Programming and Computing, EuroPLoP 2004.

Pancake, C. M. (1996), *Is Parallelism for You?* Oregon State University. Originally published in Computational Science and Engineering, Vol. 3, No. 2.

Pancake, C. M., and Bergmark, D. (1990), *Do Parallel Languages Respond to the Needs of Scientific Programmers?* Computer Magazine, IEEE Computer Society.

Parnas, D.L. (1972), *On the Criteria to be used in Decomposing Systems into Modules.* Communications of the ACM, Vol. 15, No. 12, december 1972.

Papathomas, M. (1989), *Concurrency Issues in Object-Oriented Programming Languages.* In D.C. Tsichritzis, ed., *Object Oriented Development*, Chapter 12. Centre Universitaire d'Informatique, University of Geneva.

Perihelion Software (1991), *The Helios Parallel Operating System.* Prentice-Hall.

Perrot, R.H. (1992), *Parallel Language Development in Europe: An Overview.* Concurrency, Practice and Experience, Vol. 4(8). John Wiley & Sons, Ltd.

Perry, D. E., and Wolf, A. L. (1992), *Foundations for the Study of Software Architecture.* ACM SIGSOFT, Software Engineering Notes, Vol. 17 No. 4.

Peterson, J.L. and Silberschatz, A. (1985), *Operating Systems Concepts.* 2nd edition. Addison -Wesley, New York.

Petri, K. A. (1962), *Kommunikation mit automaten.* PhD Thesis. Institut fur Instrumentelle Mathematik, Bonn, 1962.

Petriu, D. (2000), *Deriving Performance Models from UML Models by Graph Transformations.* Tutorial in WOSP 2000.

Petriu, D.C., and Shen, H. (2002), *Applying the UML performance profile: graph grammar-based derivation of LQN models from UML specifications.* In Computer Performance Evaluation Tools, T. Field, P.G. Harrison, J. Bradley, and U. Harder (editors), LNCS 2324, Springer-Verlag.

Petriu, D., and Wang, X. (1999), *From UML descriptions of High-Level Software Architectures to LQN Performance Models.* In Proceedings of AGTIVE'99. Springer-Verlag LNCS 1779.

Petriu, D., and Woodside, M. (2002), *Software Performance Models from System Scenarios in Use Case Maps.* In Proceedings of Performance TOOLS 2002, April, 2002.

Pfleeger, S.L. (1998), *Software Engineering. Theory and Practice.* Prentice-Hall.

Pfister, G. P. (1995), *In search of Clusters, The coming battle in lowly parallel computing.* Prentice Hall, Inc. Upper Saddle River, New Jersey.

Philippsen, M. (1995), *Imperative Concurrent Object-Oriented Languages.* Technical report TR-95-050. International Computer Science Institute. Berkeley University.

Pooley, R., and King, P. (1999), *The Unified Modeling Language and Performance Engineering.* Proceedings of IEE Software, Vol. 146, No. 1, February 1999.

Pooley, R. (1999), *Using UML to derive Stochastic Process Algebra Models.* Proceedings of the 15th UK Performance Engineering Workshop.

Pooley, R. (2000), *Software Engineering and Performance: A Road-map.* ACM Proceedings of The Future of Software Engineering.

Pountain, D. and May, D. (1987), *A Tutorial Introduction to Occam Programming.* INMOS, BSP Professional Books, Oxford.

Pressman, R.S. (1997), *Software Engineering. A Practitioner's Approach.* McGraw-Hill.

Rabinovich, A. (1992), *Checking Equivalences between Concurrent Systems of Finite Agents.* In Proceedings of the 19th International Colloquium on Automata, Languages and Programming, Wien, Austria, July 1992. Lecture Notes in Computer Science 623, W. Kuich, editor.

Rechtin, E. and Maier, M (1997), *The Art of Systems Architecting.* CRC Press.

Rifkin, A. (1993), *Teaching Archetypal Design with an Electronic Textbook.* Technical Report CS-TR-93-13. Department of Computer Science, California Institute of Technology.

Rifkin, A. and Massingill, B.L. (1996), *Performance Analysis for Mesh and Mesh-Spectral Archetype Applications.* Technical Report CS-TR-96-27. Department of Computer Science, California Institute of Technology.

Rolia, J.A., and Sevcik, K.C. (1995), *The Method of Layers.* IEEE Transactions on Software Engineering, Vol. 21, No. 8.

Sane, A., and Campbell, R. (1995), *Composite Messages: A Structural Pattern for Communication Between Components.* OOPSLA'95, Workshop on Design Patterns for Concurrent, Parallel and Distributed Object-Oriented Systems. October 1995.

Sanz, R., and Zalewski, J. (2003), *Pattern-based Control Systems Engineering. Using Design Patterns to Document, Transfer, and Exploit Design Knowledge.* IEEE Control Systems Magazine. June 2003.

Schmidt, D. (1995), *Accepted Patterns Papers for the OOPSLA'95 Workshop on Design Patterns for Concurrent, Parallel and Distributed Object-Oriented Systems.* http://www.cs.wustl.edu/~schmidt/OOPSLA-95/html/papers.html.

Schmidt, D.and Harrison, T. (1996), *Double-Checked Locking. An Object Behavioral Pattern for Initializing and Accessing Thread-safe Objects Efficiently.* Third annual Pattern Languages of Programming Conference. Allerton Park, Illinois. September 1996.

Schmidt, D. (1998a), *Design Patterns for Concurrent, Parallel and Distributed Systems.* http://www.cs.wustl.edu/~schmidt/patterns-ace.html.

Schmidt, D. (1998b) *Other Pattern URL's. Information on Concurrent, Parallel and Distributed Patterns.* http://www.cs.wustl.edu/~schmidt/patterns-info.html.

Schmidt, D., Stal, M., Rohert, H., and Buschmann, F. (2000), *Pattern-Oriented Software Architecture, Volumen 2. Patterns for Concurrent and Networked Objects.* Wiley Series in Software Design Patterns. John Wiley & Sons, Ltd.

Schopf, J. M. (1997), *Structural Prediction Models for High-Performance Distributed Applications.* Computer Science and Engineering Department, University of California, San Diego. Presented in the Cluster Computing Conference, 1997.

Schopf, J.M. and Berman, F. (1997), *Performance Prediction Using Intervals.* Technical Report CS97-541. Computer Science and Engineering Department, University of California, San Diego.

Schopf, J.M. and Berman, F. (1998), *Performance Prediction in Production Environments*. Computer Science and Engineering Department, University of California, San Diego. Presented in IPPS/SPDP'98.

Selic, B., Gullekson, G., and Ward, P.T. (1994), *Real Time Object-Oriented Modeling*. John Wiley and Sons, Inc.

Shaw, M. (1995), *Patterns for Software Architectures*. Carnegie Mellon University. In J. Coplien and D. Schmidt (eds.), *Pattern Languages of Program Design*. Addison-Wesley. Reading, Massachusets.

Shaw, M., and Garlan, D. (1996), *Software Architecture: Perspectives on an Emerging Discipline*. Prentice Hall Publishing.

Skillicorn, D. B., and Talia, D. (1996), *Models and Languages for Parallel Computation*. Computing and Information Science, Queen's University and Universita della Calabria. October 1996.

Smith, C.U. (1990), *Performance Engineering of Software Systems*. Addison-Wesley.

Smith, C. U. and Williams, L. G. (1993), *Software Performance Engineering: A Case Study Including Performance Comparison with Design Alternatives*. IEEE Transactions on Software Engineering, Vol. 19, No. 7.

Smith, C.U., and Williams, L.G. (1997), *Performance Engineering Evaluation of Object-Oriented Systems with SPEED*. Computer Performance Evaluation: Modelling Techniques and Tools, LNCS 1245 (R. Marie et al., editors), Springer-Verlag

Smith, M. (2000), *Java: An Object-Oriented Language*. McGraw-Hill International Ltd.

Sommerville, I. (1989), *Software Engineering*. Third edition. Addison-Wesley Publishing Company.

Stankovic, J.A., Spuri, M., Di Natale, M., and Buttazzo, G.C. (1995), *Implications of Classical Scheduling Results for Real-time Systems*. IEEE Computer. June 1995.

Stone, H. S. (editor), Chen, T. C., Flynn, M. J., Fuller, S. H., Lane, W. G., Loomis, H. H., McKeeman, W. M., Magleby, K. B., Matick, R. E., and Whitney, T. M. (1975), *Introduction to Computer Architecture*. Science Research Associates, Inc.

Stroustrup, B. (1991), *The C++ Programming Language*. Second edition. Addison-Wesley Publishing Co.

Tichy, W. F. (1998), *Should Computer Scientists Experiment More?* IEEE Computer, May 1998.

Utton, P., Martin, G., Akenhust, D., and Waters, G. (1999), *Performance Analysis of Object-Oriented Designs for Distributed Systems.* Computing Laboratory, University of Kent at Canterbury, Technical Report 17-99, March 1999.

Valmari, A. (1992), *Alleviating State Explosion during Verification and Behavioural Equivalence.* Department of Computer Science, University of Helsinki, Finland. Research Report A-1992, August 1992.

Vermeulen, A., Beged-Dov, G.,and Thompson, P. (1995), *The Pipeline Design Pattern.* OOPSLA'95, Workshop on Design Patterns for Concurrent, Parallel and Distributed Object-Oriented Systems. October 1995.

Vlissides, J. M., Kerth, N. L., and Coplien, J. O., eds. (1996), *Pattern Languages of Program Design 2.* Addison-Wesley. Reading, Massachusets.

Von Neumann, J. (1958), *The Computer Brain.* Yale University Press.

Waters, G., Linington, P., Akenhust, D., Utton, P., and Martin, G. (2001), *Permabase: Predicting the Performance of Distributed Systems at the design Stage.* IEE Proceedings-Software, Vol. 148, No. 4, August 2001.

Watt, A. (1993) *3D Computer Graphics.* Second Edition, Addison-Wesley.

Weiss, B. (1999) *Introductory Statistics.* Addison-Wesley.

Wegner, P. (1987), *Dimensions of Object-Based Language Design.* Proceedings of the OOPSLA'87 conference. October 4-8, 1987.

Williams, L.G., and Smith, C.U. (1998), *Performance Evaluation of Software Architectures.* Proceedings of the Wokshop on Software and Performance, WOSP'98. Santa Fe, New Mexico, October 1998.

Winblad, A. L., Edwards, S. D., and King, D. R. (1990), *Software Orientado a Objetos.* Addison-Wesley Iberoamericana/Diaz de Santos, 1993. Spanish version of the book titled *Object-Oriented Software*, published by Addison-Wesley Publishing Company, Inc., Reading, Massachusetts.

Winder, R., Roberts, G., and Poole, J. (1995), *The UC++ Project.* http://

`www.dcs.kcl.ac.uk/UC++/`.

Winder, R., Roberts, G., McEwan, A., Poole, J. and Dzwig, P. (1996), *UC++*. Chapter 16 in Wilson G., and Lu., P., *Parallel Programming Using C++*. The MIT Press. Massachussets Intitute of Technology, Cambridge Massachussets.

Woodside, C., Neilson, J., Petriu, S., and Majumdar (1995), *The Stochastic Rendevouz Network Model for Performance of Synchronous Client/Server-like Distributed Software*. IEEE Transactions on Computer, Vol. 44. No. 1, January 1995.

WOSP (2000), ACM Proceedings of the Workshop on Software and Performance, WOSP 2000. Ottawa, Canada.

WOSP (2002), ACM Proceedings of the 3rd International Workshop on Software and Performance, WOSP 2002. Rome, Italy, July 2002.

Xiuping, W., McMullan, D., and Woodside, M. (2003), *Component Based Performance Prediction*. Proceedings of the 6th Workshop on Component-based Software Engineering Automated Reasoning and Prediction, CBSE6. In the International Conference of Software Engineering ICSE 2003. Portland Oregon, May 2003.

Zelkowitz, M. V., and Wallace, D. R. (1998), *Experimental Models for Validating Technology*. IEEE Computer, May 1998.